Smile Pricing Explained

Financial Engineering Explained

About the series

Financial Engineering Explained is a series of concise, practical guides to modern finance, focusing on key, technical areas of risk management and asset pricing. Written for practitioners, researchers and students, the series discusses a range of topics in a non-mathematical but highly intuitive way. Each self-contained volume is dedicated to a specific topic and offers a thorough introduction with all the necessary depth, but without too much technical ballast. Where applicable, theory is illustrated with real world examples, with special attention to the numerical implementation.

Series Editor:
Wim Schoutens, Department of Mathematics, Catholic University of Leuven.

Series Advisory Board:
Peter Carr, Executive Director, NYU Mathematical Finance; Global Head of Market Modeling, Morgan Stanley.
Ernst Eberlein, Department of Mathematical Stochastics, University of Freiburg.
Matthias Scherer, Chair of Mathematical Finance, Technische Universität München.

Titles in the series:
Smile Pricing Explained, Peter Austing
Equity Derivatives Explained, Mohamed Bouzoubaa
The Greeks and Hedging Explained, Peter Leoni

Forthcoming titles:
Interest Rates Explained Volume 1, Jörg Kienitz
Interest Rates Explained Volume 2, Jörg Kienitz
Dependence Modeling Explained, Matthias Scherer and Jan-Frederik Mai

Submissions: Wim Schoutens – wim@schoutens.be

Financial Engineering Explained series
Series Standing Order ISBN: 978–1137–32733–8

You can receive future titles in this series as they are published by placing a standing order. Please contact your bookseller or, in case of difficulty, write to us at the address below with your name and address, the title of the series and the ISBN quoted above.

Customer Services Department, Macmillan Distribution Ltd, Houndmills, Basingstoke, Hampshire RG21 6XS, England

---

Smile Pricing Explained

Peter Austing

Imperial College, London

palgrave
macmillan

First published 2014 by
PALGRAVE MACMILLAN

Palgrave Macmillan in the UK is an imprint of Macmillan Publishers Limited,
registered in England, company number 785998, of Houndmills, Basingstoke,
Hampshire RG21 6XS.

Palgrave Macmillan in the US is a division of St Martin's Press LLC,
175 Fifth Avenue, New York, NY 10010.

Palgrave Macmillan is the global academic imprint of the above companies
and has companies and representatives throughout the world.

Palgrave® and Macmillan® are registered trademarks in the United States,
the United Kingdom, Europe and other countries.

ISBN: 978–1–137–33571–5

This book is printed on paper suitable for recycling and made from fully
managed and sustained forest sources. Logging, pulping and manufacturing
processes are expected to conform to the environmental regulations of the
country of origin.

A catalogue record for this book is available from the British Library.

A catalog record for this book is available from the Library of Congress.

To Bertie

Contents

List of Symbols   xi

Acknowledgements   xiii

Preface   xiv

1 Introduction to Derivatives   1
   1.1 Hedging with Forward Contracts   1
   1.2 Speculation with Forward Contracts   2
   1.3 Arbitrage   2
   1.4 Vanilla Options   3
   1.5 Interest Rates   5
   1.6 Valuing a Forward Contract   6
   1.7 Key Points   9
   1.8 Further Reading   9

2 Stochastic Calculus   10
   2.1 Brownian Motion   10
   2.2 Stochastic Model for Stock Price Evolution   13
   2.3 Ito's Lemma   14
   2.4 The Product Rule   15
   2.5 Log-Normal Stock Price Evolution   16
   2.6 The Markov Property   17
   2.7 Term Structure   18
   2.8 Ito's Lemma in More than One Dimension   19
   2.9 Key Points   20
   2.10 Further Reading   20

3 Martingale Pricing   21
   3.1 Setting the Scene   21
   3.2 Tradeable Assets   22
   3.3 Zero Coupon Bond   22
   3.4 Rolling Money Market Account   22
   3.5 Choosing a Numeraire   23
   3.6 Changing the Measure   23
   3.7 Girsanov's Theorem   24
   3.8 Martingales   27
   3.9 Continuous Martingales   28
   3.10 Black–Scholes Formula for a Call Option   28

3.11 At-the-Money Options   32
3.12 The Black–Scholes Equation   32
3.13 An Elegant Derivation of the Black–Scholes Formula   34
3.14 Key Points   38
3.15 Further Reading   39

4   Dynamic Hedging and Replication   40
4.1   Dynamic Hedging in the Absence of Interest Rates   40
4.2   Dynamic Hedging with Interest Rates   42
4.3   Delta Hedging   43
4.4   The Greeks   43
4.5   Gamma, Vega and Time Decay   44
4.6   Vega and Volatility Trading   45
4.7   Key Points   46
4.8   Further Reading   46

5   Exotic Options in Black–Scholes   47
5.1   European Options   47
5.2   Asian Options   48
5.3   Continuous Barrier Options   50
        5.3.1   The Reflection Principle   51
        5.3.2   The Reflection Principle with Log-Normal Dynamic   53
        5.3.3   Valuing Barrier Options in Black–Scholes   54
        5.3.4   Discretely Monitored Barrier Options   56
5.4   Key Points   56
5.5   Further Reading   57

6   Smile Models   58
6.1   The Volatility Smile   58
6.2   Smile Implied Probability Distribution   62
6.3   The Forward Kolmogorov Equation   65
6.4   Local Volatility   66
6.5   Key Points   69
6.6   Further Reading   70

7   Stochastic Volatility   71
7.1   Properties of Stochastic Volatility Models   72
7.2   The Heston Model   73
        7.2.1   What Makes the Heston Model Special   73
        7.2.2   Solving for Vanilla Prices   76
        7.2.3   The Feller Boundary Condition   80
7.3   The SABR Model   82
7.4   The Ornstein–Uhlenbeck Process   86
7.5   Mixture Models   88
7.6   Regime Switching Model   89
7.7   Calibrating Stochastic Volatility Models   92
7.8   Key Points   95
7.9   Further Reading   95

8	Numerical Techniques	96
	8.1 Monte Carlo	97
	8.1.1 Monte Carlo in One Dimension	97
	8.1.2 Monte Carlo in More than One Dimension	100
	8.1.3 Variance Reduction in Monte Carlo	102
	8.1.4 Limitations of Monte Carlo	104
	8.2 The PDE Approach	105
	8.2.1 Stable and Unstable Schemes	108
	8.2.2 Choice of Scheme	113
	8.2.3 Other Ways of Improving Accuracy	114
	8.2.4 More Complex Contracts in PDE	114
	8.2.5 Solving Higher Dimension PDEs	116
	8.3 Key Points	119
	8.4 Further Reading	120
9	Local Stochastic Volatility	121
	9.1 The Fundamental Theorem of On-smile Pricing	122
	9.2 Arbitrage in Implied Volatility Surfaces	123
	9.3 Two Extremes of Smile Dynamic	126
	9.3.1 Sticky Strike Dynamic	126
	9.3.2 Sticky Delta Dynamic	127
	9.4 Local Stochastic Volatility	128
	9.5 Simplifying Models	131
	9.5.1 Spot–Volatility Correlation	131
	9.5.2 Term Structure Vega for a Barrier Option	134
	9.5.3 Simplifying Stochastic Volatility Parameters	137
	9.5.4 Risk Managing with Local Stochastic Volatility Models	138
	9.6 Practical Calibration	140
	9.7 Impact of Mixing on Contract Values	141
	9.8 Key Points	147
	9.9 Further Reading	148
10	Volatility Products	149
	10.1 Overview	149
	10.2 Variance Swaps	149
	10.2.1 The Variance Swap Contract	149
	10.2.2 Idealised Variance Swap Trade	150
	10.2.3 Valuing the Idealised Trade	151
	10.2.4 Beauty in Variance Swaps	153
	10.2.5 Delta and Gamma of a Variance Swap	155
	10.2.6 Practical Considerations	157
	10.3 Volatility Swaps	158
	10.3.1 Volatility Swap in Stochastic Volatility Models and LSV	159
	10.3.2 Volatility Swap Versus Variance Swap	161
	10.3.3 Valuing a Volatility Swap	162
	10.3.4 Stochastic versus Local Volatility	163

10.4	Forward Volatility Agreements	164
	10.4.1 Practicalities	168
10.5	Key Points	170
10.6	Further Reading	171
11	**Multi-Asset**	**172**
11.1	Overview	172
11.2	Local Volatility with Constant Correlation	172
11.3	Copulas	173
11.4	Correlation Smile	175
11.5	Marking Correlation Smile	175
	11.5.1 Common Correlation Products	176
	11.5.2 The Triangle Rule	179
11.6	Modelling	181
	11.6.1 Local Correlation	182
	11.6.2 Practicalities	183
	11.6.3 Local Stochastic Correlation	184
11.7	Valuing European Contracts	187
	11.7.1 Special Properties of Best-of Options	187
	11.7.2 Valuing a Best-of Option in Black–Scholes	188
	11.7.3 Construction of a Joint PDF	190
	11.7.4 Using the Density Function for Pricing	191
11.8	Numeraire Symmetry	193
11.9	Baskets as Correlation Instruments	194
11.10	Summary	196
11.11	Key Points	197
11.12	Further Reading	197
	Afterword	198
	Appendix: Measure Theory and Girsanov's Theorem	200
	References	207
	Further Reading	213
	Index	216

List of Symbols

Symbol	Description	Page
A_t	Value of tradeable asset at time t	22
B	Shorthand for bond price B_t at time t,	33
	Barrier level	143
$B(S)$	Bump function	65
B_t	Value of a bond at time t,	22
	Notation for Brownian motion in alternative measure	25
$C(\{S_t\})$	Contract payout given spot path $\{S_t\}$	21
C	Cholesky decomposition of correlation matrix	101
Δ	Sensitivity of a contract to change in spot level	43
$\delta(x)$	Dirac delta function	64
d_1, d_2	Standard parameters used in Black–Scholes formula	31
$d\mathbb{P}$	Infinitesimal probability measure	25
$\frac{d\mathbb{Q}}{d\mathbb{P}}$	Radon–Nikodým derivative	25
dW	Shorthand for Brownian increment dW_t	33
dW_t	Brownian increment at time t	10
η	Vol-of-vol or vol-of-var	74
F	Shorthand for the forward level at valuation time to an expiry time T	30
F_i	Forward level at discrete time t_i,	50
	Forward levels for multiple assets distinguished using integer indices $F_1, F_2, \cdots$	188
$F_i(S)$	Smile implied cumulative probability distribution for asset i	174
F_t	Shorthand for the forward to expiry time T as measured at time t	83
$\mathcal{F}_t$	Filtration at time t	17, 204
Γ	Second order sensitivity of contract price to spot level	44
K	Strike	2
L	Barrier level,	53
	Matrix discretisation of differential operator	109
$\mathcal{L}$	Differential operator	106
λ	Mean reversion rate	74
m_T	Minimum value taken by a Brownian motion in time interval $[0, T]$	51
M_T	Maximum value taken by a Brownian motion in time interval $[0, T]$	144

μ	Drift of a stochastic process,	14
	Mean return	149
N	Notional amount,	2
	Number in a sequence, e.g. Monte Carlo paths	99
$N(0,1)$	Standard normal distribution	11
$N(x)$	Cumulative normal function	31
$N_2(x_1, x_2; \rho)$	Bivariate cumulative normal function with correlation ρ	174
Ω	Set of all possible outcomes of a random process	200
$\mathbb{P}$	Probability measure	25
PV	Present value of a contract	30
ρ	Sensitivity of contract price to interest rate,	44
	Correlation,	19
	Correlation matrix	101
r	Continuously compounding interest rate	6
$r(t)$	Continuously compounding interest rate applying instantaneously at time t	6
r_{dom}	Continuously compounding interest rate of the natural pricing currency (domestic currency) for an asset	7, 31
r_{yield}	Continuously compounding yield rate of an asset	7, 31
σ	Constant volatility,	14
	Terminal volatility,	18
	Shorthand for stochastic instantaneous volatility σ_t applying at time t	72
σ_{ATM}	At-the-money volatility	93
$\sigma_{imp}(K, T)$	Implied volatility at strike K and expiry time T	58
$\sigma_{local}(S, t)$	Local volatility at spot S and time t	66
$\sigma_{realised}$	Volatility realised in a time interval $[0, T]$	72
σ_t	Instantaneous volatility applying at time t	18
$\sigma(t)$	Alternative representation of instantaneous volatility σ_t	31
S	Shorthand for spot price applying at time t	33
S_i	Spot level at discrete time t_i,	50
	Spot levels for multiple assets distinguished using integer indices $S_1, S_2, \cdots$	172
S_t	Spot level at time t	2
S_T	Spot level at contract expiry time T	2
Θ	Sensitivity of contract price to passage of time	44
t	Time, measured in years from now	2
T	Time to contract expiry in years from now	2
V	Realised variance	149
$vega$	Sensitivity of contract price to volatility	44
W	Shorthand for Brownian motion W_t at time t	33
W_t	Brownian motion at time t	10
W_i	Multiple Brownian motions distinguished using integer indices $W_1, W_2, \cdots$	19
Z	Standard normal random variable	17
Z_T	Radon–Nikodým derivative applying in time interval $[0, T]$	25, 205

Acknowledgements

I am indebted to the many friends and colleagues from whom I have learned this trade, and who have generously offered their insight and support including Quentin Adam, Mariam Aitichou, Jennifer Austing, Richard Austing, Guillaume Bascoul, Marko Bastianic, Marouane Benchekroun, Oleg Butkovsky, Iain Clark, Jeremy Cohen, John Darlington, Houman Falakshahi, Gareth Farnan, Markus Fritz, Ian Hamilton, Johnson Han, Duncan Harrison, Robert Hayes, Peter Jäckel, Amy Kam, Piotr Karasinski, Vladislav Krasin, Mark Lenssen, Minying Lin, Alex Lipton, Vladimir Lucic, Arthur Mountain, Jean-Pierre O'Brien, Neil Oliver, Vladimir Piterbarg, Juliette Pubellier, Tino Senge, David Shelton, Peter Spoida, Richard Summerbell, Lin Sun, Neil Waldie, Zoe Wang, Claudia Yastremiz and Mathieu Zaradzki.

Preface

In modern derivatives pricing, Black–Scholes theory is only a starting point. Asset volatilities are not constant, but change with market conditions. Large price moves tend to be associated with periods of high market turbulence and this leads to a smile shaped curve of the volatility implied from vanilla option prices.

Smile pricing is a core area of practice and research in modern quantitative finance. There are a number of models that seek to explain the volatility smile. Two famous examples are Dupire's local volatility model, and the Heston stochastic volatility model. While they agree on vanilla option prices, their asset dynamics are very different, leading to large disagreement in exotic option prices.

This book aims to provide a clear but thorough explanation of the concepts of smile modelling that are at the forefront of modern derivatives pricing theory. The key models used in practice are covered, together with numerical techniques and calibration.

I have kept the needs of students and time-pressed practitioners very much in mind while writing. Topics are presented succinctly, with unnecessary complexity carefully avoided. Intuition is provided before mathematics so that readers may enjoy the book without having to follow every mathematical detail. Extended calculations are rarely necessary, but where they are (as in the solution of the Heston model for example) guidance is provided for those who wish to understand the result without ploughing through the maths.

Smile Pricing Explained is a self-contained textbook and desktop reference. In addition it tells a story, of which each chapter is an integral part. We start, naturally enough, right at the beginning, by using the principle of no arbitrage to value simple forward contracts. Then models are built up, starting with Black–Scholes and adding complexity and numerical techniques until we can create a full local stochastic volatility model. It is only having developed all this technology that we are able to step back and understand just what it is that makes a derivative pricing model good.

Peter Austing
Imperial College

www.smilepricingexplained.com

1 Introduction to Derivatives

1.1 Hedging with Forward Contracts

A derivative is any financial product that is derived from a simpler underlying asset. The simplest derivative is a forward contract. For example, it could be a forward contract on wheat. A grower in England plants a field of wheat, and goes to significant expense in buying seed and fertiliser and maintaining the crop. This makes sense because of the current value of wheat. However, unfortunately, an excellent growing season in France means that there is a glut of wheat on the market just at the time he has harvested and needs to sell, and the price he can achieve is much lower than expected. This could be disastrous.

To avoid this situation, the grower could enter into a forward contract with his client, a cereal producer. At the time of sowing, the grower agrees with the cereal company to sell ten tonnes of wheat at a price K pounds per tonne, to be delivered within a given short interval in, say, six months' time. The grower is happy because he knows what price he will achieve for the wheat, and can budget appropriately. If the market view on the future price of wheat is too low, the grower can look at the forward price of other crops, and plant something else. If at the delivery time the value of wheat has gone up, he will regret missing out, but on the other hand if the price has dropped he will have avoided ruin.

Meanwhile, the cereal company is happy because it knows in advance it can obtain enough wheat at a reasonable price, even if bad weather conditions lead to low crop yields and high prices at harvest time.

The grower and cereal producer are both acting in the market to hedge their risk. This is the main benefit of using derivatives, and in this way derivatives help to make markets more stable and more efficient. If used wisely, they can prevent bankruptcies and job losses in times of sudden market stress.

This example can also illustrate some of the risks in using derivatives. What if, due to a bad growing season, the grower is unable to deliver ten tonnes of wheat? Then, since he has entered into a firm obligation to deliver the crop, he would have to go into the market and purchase enough to make up his delivery. Assuming other participants in the market had also experienced poor conditions, this could be ruinously expensive. So in reality, the grower ought only to enter into the contract for a quantity of wheat he is absolutely certain he can deliver, even in the worst possible case.

1.2 Speculation with Forward Contracts

A second, entirely different, participant in the market is a wealthy individual who does not own, nor have any capacity to grow, wheat. However, she has the strong view that, due to political problems in an important wheat growing country, the price of wheat will increase. She wishes to profit from the increase in price without any outlay now. So she enters into a forward contract to buy N tonnes of wheat at a price K at a future time T (say one year's time). If the price has risen, she will immediately sell the wheat and make a profit

$$N(S_T - K) \tag{1.1}$$

where S_T is the price of wheat at the expiry time T of the contract. Needless to say, if the price has fallen, she makes a loss.

In reality, the speculator does not want to be bothered with receiving and then delivering N tonnes of wheat, and so she will close out the contract before the delivery date. That is, she will either sell the contract, or enter into an opposite contract. Alternatively, she may have originally entered into a cash settled contract with a third party. This third party will handle the buying and selling of contracts, and at the expiry simply pay the cash profit (or demand payment of the loss). Banks perform this kind of service in huge volumes, not necessarily for wheat contracts, but certainly for contracts in shares (equities), foreign currencies (FX), and precious metals, oil or energy (commodities).

In the jargon of derivatives, S_t is the *spot price* or simply *spot* at time t, namely the value of the asset in the open market at time t. The quantity N is known as the *notional* amount, since from the point of view of a speculator entering into a cash settled transaction, the cash flow of NK agreed for the commodity never actually takes place. The agreed price in the contract, K, is known as the *strike* price, since it is the price at which the deal is struck.

1.3 Arbitrage

The third type of participant in the market aims to make money by arbitrage. An arbitrage opportunity arises when it is possible to make money *without any risk*. In the simplest example, let's suppose an investor notices that it is possible to buy wheat contracts on one exchange for 59 US dollars and to sell on another for 62 dollars. Then he can make an instant profit by simultaneously buying on one and selling on the other.

If arbitrage exists in a market, then very quickly prices will be forced up in the underpriced asset as buyers charge in, and prices will be forced down on the overpriced asset as more and more people sell on that exchange. This does not mean that in an efficient market arbitrage never exists. Usually though, it only exists for a fleeting moment, until it is eliminated by the most sophisticated investors.

The concept of arbitrage is fundamental in pricing derivatives contracts. A quant[1] working for a bank will often be asked to price a new style of exotic derivative. If the price she comes up with can be demonstrated to be arbitrageable against other liquid assets in the market, then the bank will certainly lose money. Let's suppose that this particular bank has an electronic dealing system in, say, foreign exchange derivatives. When outsiders spot the arbitrage, they will continually buy the liquid assets and sell the new exotic derivative, or vice versa, mercilessly making money at the expense of the bank (and no doubt the unfortunate quant).

When we price a derivative, the price must be arbitrage free. We shall see that in many cases, the arbitrage-free price is unique, and so finding it gives the true value of the derivative.

1.4 Vanilla Options

So far, we have looked at the simplest derivative, a forward contract. This is an agreement made now to buy a quantity of some asset at a future date (the expiry date). The deal is struck at the strike price K, and at the expiry time T the payout is

$$N(S_T - K) \tag{1.2}$$

where N is the notional (the quantity of asset), S_T is the spot price (value of the underlying asset) at expiry. At any time, this contract has a certain value for a given strike. This value can be positive or negative depending on whether the strike is above or below the market view of the forward value of the asset. Often, the strike will be chosen so that the value is zero when the contract is entered into, and no exchange of money is required between the buyer and seller at the start.

An investor who believes that the asset price will rise may enter into a forward contract to buy at strike K, but what if the asset price actually falls sharply? Her losses could be enormous. So let's consider a contract that gives her the *option, but not the obligation,* to buy N units of the asset at strike price K. If, at the expiry time T, the spot price is larger than K then the investor would *exercise* the option. She could then immediately sell at the prevailing price S_T and make profit $N(S_T - K)$. On the other hand, if the spot price ends up smaller than the strike, she would certainly not exercise the option. So the payout at expiry is

$$N\max(S_T - K, 0) \tag{1.3}$$

which we write as

$$N(S_T - K)_+. \tag{1.4}$$

---

[1] A *quant* (shortened from quantitative analyst) is the name given to a mathematician working for a bank or hedge fund who comes up with the pricing methods for derivatives.

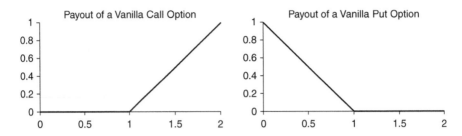

Figure 1.1 Payouts of vanilla call and put options.

This contract is called a vanilla call option. In finance, call means *buy* and this is an option to buy the asset. The opposite of call is to put, namely to sell. The term vanilla indicates that these are the most basic option contracts. Supposing the investor entered into a contract giving the option to sell the asset at strike price K, that is the investor bought a vanilla put option, the payout would be

$$N(K - S_T)_+. \tag{1.5}$$

The call and put payouts as a function of the spot price at expiry are plotted in Figure 1.1. In these diagrams, the notional is 1 and the strike price 1. As you can see, if you buy a call option, you have limited loss, but unlimited potential gain if spot ends up very high. On the other hand, if you sell a call option, you have unlimited potential liability.

It is now time to whet your appetite for some of the beautiful facts we will soon be encountering. If you are new to this subject, you might well argue that it is impossible to attach a fair value to the contracts that we have been discussing. Imagine we are a bank selling a forward contract, and we cannot find any other counterparty with whom to do the opposite trade to eliminate the risk. Even if we could know in advance the probability distribution of the spot at expiry, the best we could work out would be the probability distribution of money made or lost. As your argument would go, there is surely no way the bank could prevent itself from being annihilated by a massive unfavourable movement in the market. *You would be absolutely wrong.*

In fact, there is a simple strategy that the bank can follow when selling a forward contract to ensure they have exactly enough money to pay the client at the end. The value of the forward contract is the cost of following this strategy, and will be completely independent of the random process that the spot follows.

In the case of vanilla options, we do need to know something about the random spot process: its *volatility*. Armed with this knowledge, we will be able to trade in the underlying asset through the life of the option in just such a way as to have exactly enough to pay the client at the end, *and we will know in advance how much it will cost us to do this trading.* This statement is stunning. If we know how volatile a stock price is, we can tell a trader just how to trade in that stock over the coming year to replicate a particular payout agreed with a client and, incredibly, we can calculate in advance how much that trading strategy will cost the bank, even though the asset spot price could eventually end up anywhere.[2]

We will learn that trading vanilla options amounts to trading volatility, and this will give us a handle on pricing exotic options with more general underlying dynamics in which the volatility may not be constant. At the same time, we will learn that there are still challenges in pricing some types of contract that may have simple payout but happen to probe the aspects of asset dynamics that are not easily understood. In short, we will arrive at the forefront of modern derivatives pricing.

1.5 Interest Rates

We cannot proceed without a discussion of interest rates. We assume that at any time, a trader can go into the market and find a counterparty with whom to either borrow or lend money for any fixed period at a fixed interest rate. The interest rate achieved when lending will depend on the counterparty's credit rating. We would require a much higher interest rate to lend to a company having, in our opinion, a high probability of going bust and defaulting. The rate that we are interested in is the *risk free rate*. This is the hypothetical rate for a counterparty that has zero risk of defaulting.

The risk free rate is often described as the rate at which we could lend to the central bank for the currency in question. This is considered close to being risk free because the central bank can always print more money if necessary. However, in practice, central banks do not provide such a service. You cannot go to the central bank and demand to lend to it for a given fixed period of your choosing. In any case, there always remains risk that a central bank will default for political reasons.

However, there are many interest rate instruments trading interbank in the market, and these can be used to determine the simple interest rate for a fixed term of borrowing. The instruments that are often considered to give the closest thing to a risk free rate are called *overnight indexed swaps* (OIS). An OIS is agreed for a fixed period of time, say two years, and involves a notional amount of money that does not actually change hands. The institution on one side of the deal pays a fixed interest rate (agreed at the beginning) over the two years. This is called the swap rate. In return, the counterparty pays interest every day at the rate that prevails in the market on that day. In the case of US dollars, this daily floating rate will be the federal funds rate, which is the average rate at which banks with excess reserves lend overnight to banks with shortfall of reserves. The swap itself is considered low risk because the notional amount does not change hands. The daily rate is also considered low risk because it is unlikely that an institution will default overnight. Therefore the simple two year rate that one can extract from the swap rate is considered low risk.

The calculations required to convert between the rates that apply for the various instruments one can see in the market are simple but tedious. Fortunately, they will not concern us. What is important is that it is possible to look at instruments trading in the market and determine a good proxy to the risk free rate. In this book, we will always quote the continuously compounding interest rate. Imagine investing one unit

---

[2] This is the famous theory of Black and Scholes (1973). In addition to constant volatility, it assumes that there is no spread between the buying and selling price of the underlying stock, and that one can buy and sell the stock continuously.

of currency at a fixed interest rate r that compounds continuously. This means that rather than compounding once per year, or once per month, or even once per second, it compounds once every ϵ years where $\epsilon \to 0$. Then after time T years, our one unit of currency will be worth[3]

$$\lim_{\epsilon \to 0} (1 + r\epsilon)^{T/\epsilon} = e^{rT}. \tag{1.6}$$

This is everything we need. If we want to know how much it will cost in interest to borrow N pounds for T years, the answer is

$$N(e^{rT} - 1). \tag{1.7}$$

Of course, the interest rate at which you can borrow for one month will not necessarily match the rate at which you can borrow for one year. So in reality, the continuously compounding interest rate is a function of time. Therefore, we define $r(t)$ to be the rate at which you can borrow at time t for duration dt. Then it is straightforward to extend (1.6) to see that after time T, one unit of currency invested will return

$$e^{\int_0^T r(t)dt}. \tag{1.8}$$

More often than not, our formulas will only depend on the integral of the continuous rate, and so we will denote the quantity $\frac{1}{T}\int_0^T r(t)dt$ by r_T or simply r. The fact that rates depend on time is described as the interest rates having *term structure*, and the interest rate curve, which we have chosen to represent by $r(t)$, is often called the *yield curve*.

Needless to say, interest rates change, and there is a big market, the *fixed income market*, in interest rate derivatives. However, throughout this book we are going to assume that interest rates are deterministic, that is that the yield curve $r(t)$ has no random component. This is usually a good assumption for pricing derivatives on equities, commodities and FX as long as the maturities do not exceed around two years.

1.6 Valuing a Forward Contract

We are ready to value the forward contract, and we are going to consider a forward contract on foreign exchange. Specifically, the contract is to deliver N euros in exchange for the agreed price of NK pounds sterling, at a time T years from now. The notional quantity of the contract is N euros, and the strike price is K, which has units of pounds per euro.

---

[3] The limit formula (1.6) giving the exponential function is well known, and readers who are not familiar with it may simply take it as read.

In this example, our asset is a quantity of euros. The asset provides a *yield*, which is the euro interest rate. If we were valuing a forward contract on a stock, the yield would be the dividend rate. In order to maintain a consistent notation throughout, we will denote the euro interest rate by r_{yield}. We refer to the natural pricing currency of an asset as the *domestic* currency, and therefore we will denote the sterling interest rate by r_{dom}.

At expiry, the contract valued in pounds will be worth

$$N(S_T - K) \tag{1.9}$$

and our task is to set up a portfolio that will be worth exactly this amount at the expiry time T so that we can pay the client. As we know in advance how many euros we are going to have to deliver, the trick is to buy them now. Let's suppose r_{yield} and r_{dom} are the risk free interest rates for the two currencies for a fixed lending or borrowing period to time T. If we put $Ne^{-r_{yield}T}$ euros on deposit now, then we will have exactly N euros at expiry. The cost of this in pounds is

$$Ne^{-r_{yield}T}S \tag{1.10}$$

where S is the current spot price (the current exchange rate pounds per euro).

So far, we have valued the cash payment of euros that we will have to make at time T. In addition, we will receive a payment of NK pounds at that time. How much is this future payment worth now? If we wish to realise its value now, we could borrow

$$Ne^{-r_{dom}T}K \tag{1.11}$$

pounds. At the expiry time T, after adding interest, the amount we need to pay back would be NK, which is precisely what we will receive from our forward contract. Therefore the value now of this future cash flow is given by (1.11).

Putting (1.10) and (1.11) together gives us the value of the forward contract

$$N(e^{-r_{yield}T}S - e^{-r_{dom}T}K). \tag{1.12}$$

To summarise, we worked out how much cash we would have to pay now to guarantee having enough asset to meet our obligation at expiry, and we worked out how much cash we could receive now (by borrowing) with the knowledge that we will receive cash at expiry to pay off the debt.

Another way of looking at this is that we can *replicate* the payout. Imagine we are a bank, and sold the forward contract to a client for a premium given by (1.12). Then we can immediately borrow $Ne^{-r_{dom}T}K$ cash, and use this plus the premium we were paid to invest in the asset (in this case euros). At expiry, we will have exactly enough asset to pay the client, and receive exactly enough cash to pay off our debt. This means we are perfectly *hedged*. There is no way we can lose money due to adverse moves in the market. If we charge a small spread on top of the fair value (1.12), then we are guaranteed to make this as profit, and we can realise this profit immediately by following the replication strategy.

The strategy of replication for derivatives pricing is closely related to the more fundamental necessity of avoiding arbitrage. Arbitrage occurs when it is possible to make money with zero risk. Suppose we sold the forward contract for less than its fair value (1.12). Then the counterparty would be able to buy this contract, and at the same time set up an opposite replicating portfolio (borrow euros and lend pounds). There will be a bit of cash left over since they bought the forward below the cost of its replicating portfolio. At expiry they will have enough cash to buy the euros at the strike price, and these will pay off their euro debt. And then that bit of cash that was left over at the start will be pure profit, and what is more, it is profit made right away when the trades were done. This is a disaster. If we are a bank, then the counterparty may well set up the replicating portfolios with us. This means we will have given away free money to the counterparty.

If, on the other hand, we had valued the forward contract higher than (1.12), then counterparties would not buy it (they could replicate it themselves cheaper, or buy from another bank who could do the replication). However, they would be delighted to sell to us and make money straight away with no risk by setting up the original replicating portfolio we discussed.

So we have seen that there is a unique fair value for the forward contract. If we sell or buy the contract at this level, we can set up a replicating portfolio that will exactly allow us to meet our obligations, and the overall cost to us will be zero. Valuing the contract at any other level will allow immediate arbitrage. The practice of setting up portfolios that neutralise risk to the bank is called *hedging*.

Note that the value of a forward contract is absolutely independent of expectations of the asset's future growth. The principle of *no arbitrage* shows that these are already built into the current spot price. If the market has strong reasons for believing that euros will be much more valuable relative to pounds in one year's time, then market participants will buy forward contracts. This might open up an arbitrage through the replicating portfolio. Those seeking to take advantage of the arbitrage by setting up the replicating portfolio will 'buy spot' (that is, buy euros), and this will force the spot price up until the arbitrage is closed.[4]

We have used foreign exchange to illustrate forward pricing because it is simple to understand how the yield curve of the asset (in this case euros) comes into play. However, the same arguments work for all assets. Stocks and shares (equities) have a yield curve determined by the market expectations of their dividends. There is a large market in lending and borrowing equities, and the 'interest' charged will be equivalent to the lenders' expectation of their loss of dividends. Rather than being paid in cash, an agreement could be made that this would be paid in shares and then we are back to a situation exactly equivalent to foreign exchange. Alternatively, in commodities, let's think of a forward contract on gold. There is a cost associated with storing gold in a warehouse, which will have a negative effect on the gold yield curve. On the other hand, gold could be lent and one would expect compensation for this. The point is

---

[4] Alternatively, market participants might re-evaluate the rates at which they are prepared to borrow or lend the asset, and so it might be the yield curve that changes.

that every asset has an implied yield curve that can be used in the calculation of the forward price. For a commodity like wheat, it will be costly to store it in a warehouse, and the wheat might deteriorate, so it is quite possible that the effective interest rate will be negative. This is sometimes referred to as cost of carry.

1.7 Key Points

- A derivative is a financial product that is derived from a simpler underlying asset.
- If a market has arbitrage, then it is possible to make money with zero risk. Efficient markets avoid arbitrage.
- Derivatives can be valued by making sure there is no arbitrage.
- The value of a forward contract does not depend on the true growth rate of the asset, but instead on the interest rate and yield.

1.8 Further Reading

Classic and highly regarded texts for learning about derivative pricing include Hull (2010) and Wilmott (2006, 2007). Those who are mathematically minded will find Joshi (2003) particularly rewarding.

2 Stochastic Calculus

2.1 Brownian Motion

If you were to visit the trading floor of an investment bank, and look over the shoulder of any of the scores of traders working there, you would see plenty of graphs plotting asset price movements. These might be for stock prices, foreign exchange rates or commodity prices depending on the trader, but they all look qualitatively the same. The price of an asset follows a random jagged path as its value fluctuates up and down throughout the day. If you were to compare the graph of price movements over one day to the graph over one year, you would not notice any qualitative difference. We say that asset prices follow a *stochastic process*, and our task is to model this as effectively as possible.

We need a way to model a variable that can take a random value at any time t. Its path should be continuous, but may be very jagged. Our tool to achieve this is going to be *Brownian motion*. We denote a Brownian motion by W_t, and it starts at zero at time $t = 0$, $W_0 = 0$. In order to precisely specify the random path followed by W_t for $t > 0$, we split the time axis into infinitesimal pieces of length dt. In any infinitesimal time interval dt, the change in W_t will be a random variable that we denote dW_t. In other words, we write the value of the Brownian motion W_t as the sum of all its infinitesimal changes

$$W_t = \int_{t'=0}^{t} dW_{t'}. \qquad (2.1)$$

All that remains is to specify the probability distribution from which the dW_t are drawn. Firstly, we insist that dW_t be independent of $W_{t'}$ for $t' \leq t$. If we translate this into asset prices, this is saying that we cannot look at the historical path followed by the price and use this to predict how it will change. If that were possible, then the price would not be fair, and market participants would buy or sell until it became fair.

A moment or two's thought shows that the dW_t should be normally distributed. To see this, further subdivide the interval dt into n subintervals. Since dW_t is the sum of n independent random variables with n arbitrarily large, dW_t must be normally distributed.[5] Specifically, we choose the dW_t to be independent normally distributed

---

[5] The central limit theorem says that the sum of n independent identically distributed random variables is normally distributed when $n \to \infty$.

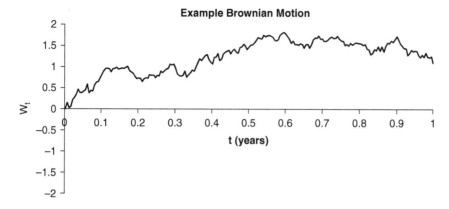

Figure 2.1   An example Brownian motion path.

random variables with mean 0 and variance dt,

$$dW_t \sim \sqrt{dt}N(0,1). \tag{2.2}$$

It is straightforward to perform the stochastic integral in equation (2.1) to find the distribution of the random variable W_t (the value of the Brownian motion at time t). The right hand side represents the sum of independent normal variables, each having variance dt. So W_t is also a normal variable whose variance is the sum $\int_0^t dt' = t$,

$$W_t \sim \sqrt{t}N(0,1). \tag{2.3}$$

Brownian motion has some very interesting properties.

1   Continuity

A Brownian motion W_t is continuous since its change in a small time interval dt is dW_t whose mean is zero and variance dt is infinitesimal.

2   Infinite jaggedness

In any time interval, the expected total up and down movements of W_t are infinite. To see this, let's add them up and calculate the expectation

$$l = E\left[\int_0^T |dW_t|\right] \tag{2.4}$$

$$= \int_0^T E[|dW_t|] \tag{2.5}$$

which, as dW_t is a normal variable with variance dt, is straightforward to evaluate

$$l = \int_0^T \sqrt{dt}(\pi/2)^{-\frac{1}{2}} \tag{2.6}$$

$$= \frac{1}{\sqrt{dt}} \int_0^T (\pi/2)^{-\frac{1}{2}}\, dt \tag{2.7}$$

$$= \frac{1}{\sqrt{dt}} T(\pi/2)^{-\frac{1}{2}} \tag{2.8}$$

$$= \infty \tag{2.9}$$

since dt is infinitesimal.

3 Deterministic sum square returns

Left to last is the most important and fascinating property of Brownian motion; the property that allows *everything* to work. When applied inside an integral, the square of the random variable dW_t is deterministic and given by

$$(dW_t)^2 = dt. \tag{2.10}$$

Certainly, if we compute the expectation of $(dW_t)^2$ we get

$$E[(dW_t)^2] = dt \tag{2.11}$$

since, by definition, dW_t is a normal variable with mean zero and variance dt. On the other hand, the variance of $(dW_t)^2$ is

$$\mathrm{Var}[(dW_t)^2] = E[(dW_t)^4] - E[dW_t^2]^2 \tag{2.12}$$
$$= 3(dt)^2 - (dt)^2 = 2(dt)^2 \tag{2.13}$$

as a simple calculation shows, using the fact that $dW_t = \sqrt{dt}N(0,1)$.
To understand this, we need to remember that dW_t and dt only have meaning inside an integral. So let's sum up the squared returns by computing the integral

$$I = \int_0^T (dW_t)^2. \tag{2.14}$$

This has expectation

$$E[I] = \int_0^T E[(dW_t)^2] \tag{2.15}$$

$$= \int_0^T dt \tag{2.16}$$

$$= T, \tag{2.17}$$

and variance

$$\mathrm{Var}[I] = \mathrm{Var} \int_0^T (dW_t)^2 \tag{2.18}$$

$$= \int_0^T \mathrm{Var}[(dW_t)^2] \tag{2.19}$$

$$= 2 \int_0^T (dt)^2 \tag{2.20}$$

$$= 2\,dt \int_0^T dt \tag{2.21}$$

$$= 2\,dt\,T \tag{2.22}$$

$$= 0. \tag{2.23}$$

So I is deterministic, and since we could have chosen any arbitrary interval over which to do the integral, this establishes the relation (2.10).

Property 3 truly is remarkable. How can the square of a random variable be deterministic? The answer is that it is an *infinitesimal* random variable and ordinary intuition does not apply. We will use this property again and again throughout the book. For example, it is this property that allows the trader to know the cost of hedging in advance in Black–Scholes theory.

It is important to emphasise that the formula $(dW_t)^2 = dt$ is true inside an integral and not in a more general algebraic sense. For example, the quantity $(dW_t)^2/dt$ is the square of a standard normal variable, and certainly not deterministically equal to 1 as naive division by dt would suggest. In this book, we take the approach that $(dW_t)^2$ only makes sense inside an integral, and so can be replaced by dt without further clarification.

2.2 Stochastic Model for Stock Price Evolution

Although the title of this section refers to stock prices, the model we are about to write down is used universally in quantitative finance for stocks, foreign exchange and commodities. So let us now call it the model for spot evolution where spot means the price of any of those.

It is clear that asset prices cannot follow Brownian motion directly, since the value can never be negative. Instead, we model changes in the spot price using the *stochastic differential equation,*

$$dS_t = S_t(\mu dt + \sigma dW_t). \tag{2.24}$$

Here S_t is the value of the asset at time t, and dS_t is the change in the value during infinitesimal time interval dt. The important point is that the change dS_t is proportional to the current price S_t. So the Brownian motion dW_t causes percentage changes in the asset price rather than absolute changes. As we shall shortly see, this keeps S_t positive.

The parameter σ is called the volatility. Since it multiplies the Brownian motion, it acts like a standard deviation. Large σ means the price is very volatile, while small σ indicates only a small amount of randomness. The time t is usually measured in years, and the volatility is an annualised number that can be thought of as the 'standard deviation per year'. Finally, μ is known as the drift since it allows us to give the asset price an overall upward drift if μ is positive, or downward if negative. Again, its units are annual.

We do not yet have the tools to solve the stochastic differential equation (SDE) (2.24) to find the probability distribution of spot S_t at a given time T. This will follow shortly with the Ito calculus. But let's at least calculate the mean of the distribution. By taking the expectation of (2.24) we obtain

$$dE[S_t] = E[S_t]\mu dt + \sigma E[S_t dW_t]. \tag{2.25}$$

Our starting point for Brownian motion was that dW_t is independent of all information known at time t, and in particular it is independent of S_t so that $E[S_t dW_t] = E[S_t]E[dW_t]$, which is zero since $E[dW_t] = 0$. This is an absolutely classic trick of stochastic calculus. It leaves us with the simple ordinary differential equation

$$dE[S_t] = E[S_t]\mu dt, \tag{2.26}$$

with solution

$$E[S_T] = S_0 e^{\mu T}. \tag{2.27}$$

On average, the spot grows exponentially at rate μ.

2.3 Ito's Lemma

We would like to know how to do stochastic calculus. That is, we would like to learn how to integrate and differentiate functions of Brownian motions. For example, the fundamental stock price model (2.24) is given by the stochastic differential equation

$$dS_t = S_t(\mu dt + \sigma dW_t). \tag{2.28}$$

If σ and μ are constant we would like to know how to solve this to find a solution for S_T, the spot at time T. This solution would tell us the probability distribution of S_T.

As with ordinary calculus, the only way to integrate a stochastic differential equation is to guess a function which it is the derivative of. Hence, there is little more to stochastic calculus than knowing how to differentiate functions of stochastic variables. Ito's lemma tells us how to do this.

We define an *Ito process* by

$$dX_t = a(t, X_t)dt + b(t, X_t)dW_t, \tag{2.29}$$

and take a twice continuously differentiable function $f(t, X_t)$. Then Ito's lemma states

$$df(t, X_t) = \frac{\partial f}{\partial t}dt + \frac{\partial f}{\partial X_t}dX_t + \frac{1}{2}\frac{\partial^2 f}{\partial X_t^2}(dX_t)^2. \tag{2.30}$$

Ito's lemma, (2.30), tells us the change in f during an infinitesimal time interval dt. The difference between (2.30) and the chain rule in ordinary (non-stochastic) calculus is the presence of the final $(dX_t)^2$ term.

The proof is straightforward. We first Taylor expand f, and then remember that the expression df only makes sense inside an integral. Then any terms that integrate to zero are dropped. In particular, we drop the terms $dt\,dW_t$, $(dt)^2$, and higher order. If dX_t were not stochastic, we could also drop the $(dX_t)^2$ term. But as we saw earlier, the fundamental property of Brownian motion is the relation

$$(dW_t)^2 = dt \tag{2.31}$$

so that expanding $(dX_t)^2$ gives

$$(dX_t)^2 = b(t, X_t)^2 dt. \tag{2.32}$$

Since $(dX_t)^2$ is of order dt, it does not integrate to zero and so must remain in equation (2.30).

Ito's lemma is often expanded out using (2.29) and (2.32):

$$df(t, X_t) = \frac{\partial f}{\partial t}dt + \frac{\partial f}{\partial X_t}(a(t, X_t)dt + b(t, X_t)dW_t) + \frac{1}{2}\frac{\partial^2 f}{\partial X_t^2}b(t, X_t)^2 dt. \tag{2.33}$$

2.4 The Product Rule

We can easily extend Ito's lemma to find the product rule for stochastic differentiation. We want to find a formula for $d(fg)$. So we take the Taylor expansion for the function of two variables $h(f,g) = fg$ and drop those terms that vanish under an integral sign

$$d(fg) = dh \tag{2.34}$$

$$= \frac{\partial h}{\partial f} df + \frac{\partial h}{\partial g} dg + \frac{1}{2}\left[\frac{\partial^2 h}{\partial f^2}(df)^2 + 2\frac{\partial^2 h}{\partial f \partial g} df\, dg + \frac{\partial^2 h}{\partial g^2}(dg)^2\right] + \cdots \tag{2.35}$$

$$= f\, dg + g\, df + df\, dg. \tag{2.36}$$

2.5 Log-Normal Stock Price Evolution

Now that we know how to do calculus with stochastic processes, we can solve the stochastic model for stock price evolution given by equation (2.24)

$$dS_t = S_t(\mu\, dt + \sigma\, dW_t). \tag{2.37}$$

Let's begin with the drift μ and volatility σ being constant. As we have already recalled, the only way to do integration is to guess the form of the solution first. So let us use Ito's lemma to study the random variable that is the log of the spot process,[6]

$$X_t = \log S_t. \tag{2.38}$$

The function f on which we need to apply Ito is $f(S_t) = \log S_t$. There is no explicit time dependence, so the first term of (2.30) vanishes, leaving

$$dX_t = \frac{\partial \log S_t}{\partial S_t} dS_t + \frac{1}{2}\frac{\partial^2 \log S_t}{\partial S_t^2}(dS_t)^2 \tag{2.39}$$

$$= \frac{1}{S_t} S_t(\mu\, dt + \sigma\, dW_t) + \frac{1}{2}\frac{-1}{S_t^2}[S_t(\mu\, dt + \sigma\, dW_t)]^2 \tag{2.40}$$

$$= (\mu\, dt + \sigma\, dW_t) + \frac{1}{2}\frac{-1}{S_t^2}[S_t(\mu\, dt + \sigma\, dW_t)]^2 \tag{2.41}$$

$$= \mu\, dt + \sigma\, dW_t - \tfrac{1}{2}\sigma^2\, dt \tag{2.42}$$

$$= (\mu - \tfrac{1}{2}\sigma^2)dt + \sigma\, dW_t. \tag{2.43}$$

We can now integrate to find X_T,

$$X_T = X_0 + (\mu - \tfrac{1}{2}\sigma^2)T + \sigma\, W_T \tag{2.44}$$

---

[6] We always use log to mean the logarithm to base e.

and we recall that W_T is a normal variable with variance T, so

$$X_T = X_0 + (\mu - \tfrac{1}{2}\sigma^2)T + \sigma\sqrt{T}Z \qquad (2.45)$$

where Z is a random normal variable, $Z = N(0,1)$. Finally then, we have the *log-normal* probability distribution for the spot at time T

$$S_T = S_0 e^{(\mu - \frac{1}{2}\sigma^2)T + \sigma\sqrt{T}Z}, \quad Z = N(0,1), \qquad (2.46)$$

where $S_0 = e^{X_0}$. We showed earlier that $E[S_T] = S_0 \exp(\mu T)$. Readers are encouraged to check this again starting from (2.46) by integrating against the probability density of the normal distribution. The appearance of the term $-\tfrac{1}{2}\sigma^2 T$ in (2.46) exactly cancels the contribution from the random normal variable Z when one calculates the expectation.

2.6 The Markov Property

When we first motivated Brownian motion, we insisted that the random Brownian increment dW_t should be independent of the current state of the Brownian motion and its past history. That is, dW_t is independent of $\{W_s : s \leq t\}$. As a result, any future value of a Brownian motion W_u (with $u > t$) is a random variable that is dependent on the current value W_t, but independent of the historical path that lead to W_t.

This is the Markov property, and it can be summarised as *given the present, the future does not depend on the past*. It is often helpful to introduce notation for the *filtration* $\mathcal{F}_t$, which is the set of all events whose outcome is known at time t. In that case, the Markov property for W_t can be written

$$P(W_u \in A|\mathcal{F}_t) = P(W_u \in A|W_t) \qquad (2.47)$$

for $u > t$.

As the log-normal spot process is built from Brownian motion, it also has the Markov property. All knowledge that could be used to predict future spot prices is encoded in the current spot price.

The Markov property makes it easy to write down the probability distribution of spot at multiple dates. For example, if we are interested in two dates T_1 and T_2 with $T_2 > T_1$ then we have

$$S_{T_1} = S_0 e^{(\mu - \frac{1}{2}\sigma^2)T_1 + \sigma\sqrt{T_1}Z_1} \qquad (2.48)$$

$$S_{T_2} = S_{T_1} e^{(\mu - \frac{1}{2}\sigma^2)(T_2 - T_1) + \sigma\sqrt{T_2 - T_1}Z_2} \qquad (2.49)$$

where Z_1 and Z_2 are *independent* normal variables.

2.7 Term Structure

If we make the drift μ and volatility σ time dependent in equation (2.24) this is called adding term structure to the model. Then (2.43) becomes

$$dX_t = (\mu_t - \tfrac{1}{2}\sigma_t^2)dt + \sigma_t dW_t, \tag{2.50}$$

and we can integrate to obtain

$$X_T = X_0 + \int_0^T (\mu_t - \tfrac{1}{2}\sigma_t^2)dt + \int_0^T \sigma_t dW_t. \tag{2.51}$$

The stochastic term can be simplified by remembering that the dW_t are independent normal variables, each having variance dt. So the integral is the sum of independent normal variables, and is normal with variance $\int \sigma_t^2 dt$. Thus (2.46) becomes

$$S_T = S_0 \exp\left(\int_0^T (\mu_t - \tfrac{1}{2}\sigma_t^2)dt + \left\{ \int_0^T \sigma_t^2 dt \right\}^{\frac{1}{2}} Z \right), \quad Z = N(0,1). \tag{2.52}$$

This is a useful simplification. When a contract depends only on the spot level at the expiry T and not the full path of spot levels, we can often work with a single *terminal volatility* σ defined by

$$\sigma = \sqrt{\frac{1}{T} \int_0^T \sigma_t^2 dt} \tag{2.53}$$

and terminal drift defined by

$$\mu = \frac{1}{T} \int_0^T \mu_t dt. \tag{2.54}$$

If we do so, then we arrive back at the expression (2.46), which originally assumed constant drift and volatility. For this reason, even when there is a term structure, we are often able to work directly with the terminal volatility treated as constant.[7]

Term structure is important in option pricing models and reflects the fact that the market may have different views on the volatility at different future dates.

---

[7] This applies when the derivative payout only depends on the spot at one future date.

2.8 Ito's Lemma in More than One Dimension

Later, we will want to consider models having more than one Brownian motion. For example, we may allow the volatility itself to be stochastic and driven by a second Brownian motion, or we may consider models driving multiple assets. Here, for simplicity of notation, we will consider two Brownian motions $dW_{t,1}$ and $dW_{t,2}$, and from now on, we will drop the t subscripts, and write simply dW_1, dW_2.

As we have emphasised, the property (2.10), $(dW_t)^2 = dt$, is fundamental in the single-dimensional case, and allows us to write down Ito's lemma, which tells us how to do calculus. Therefore our aim is to extend this to two or more dimensions.

The definition of a Brownian increment is given in equation (2.2). It says that in time interval dt a Brownian motion changes by a random variable $\sqrt{dt}Z$, where Z is a standard normal variable $Z = N(0,1)$. Then in our two-dimensional case, we have

$$dW_1 = \sqrt{dt}Z_1, \quad Z_1 = N(0,1) \tag{2.55}$$

$$dW_2 = \sqrt{dt}Z_2, \quad Z_2 = N(0,1). \tag{2.56}$$

In most cases, the Brownian motions will be correlated with one another. Imagine, for example, that W_1 is driving the price of IBM stocks, while W_2 is driving the price of Microsoft stocks. Then we might expect that they are positively correlated, and that if W_1 increases in a given time interval, W_2 is likely to also increase.

Put this way, it is clear that correlating the two Brownian increments in (2.55) and (2.56) is a simple matter of assuming that the normal variables Z_1 and Z_2 are correlated, with correlation ρ say. This is equivalent to saying $E[Z_1 Z_2] = \rho$, and of course we insist that the correlation is sensible, $-1 < \rho < 1$.

We have seen that $(dW_1)^2 = dt$ and $(dW_2)^2 = dt$, but what can we say about $dW_1 dW_2$? The trick in the single-dimensional case was to look at the expectation and variance, and to note that the variance is of order $(dt)^2$, and therefore vanishes under an integral sign. As this is the only place it makes sense, it can be treated as zero.

Beginning with the expectation, we have

$$E[dW_1 \, dW_2] = E[\sqrt{dt}Z_1 \sqrt{dt}Z_2] \tag{2.57}$$

$$= \rho dt, \tag{2.58}$$

using the definition of correlation for random normal variables.

Next, the variance is

$$\text{Var}[dW_1 \, dW_2] = E[(dW_1 \, dW_2)^2] - E[dW_1 \, dW_2]^2 \tag{2.59}$$

and the first term can be dealt with by using our favourite result $(dW_1)^2 = (dW_2)^2 = dt$, while we have just calculated the second term. Putting them together gives

$$\text{Var}[dW_1 \, dW_2] = (dt)^2 - \rho^2 (dt)^2 = (1 - \rho^2)(dt)^2. \tag{2.60}$$

As, being of order $(dt)^2$, it vanishes under an integral sign, we can say that

$$\mathrm{Var}[dW_1\, dW_2] = 0, \tag{2.61}$$

and the product of the two Brownian increments is deterministic, and given by

$$dW_1\, dW_2 = \rho\, dt. \tag{2.62}$$

To obtain Ito's lemma in two or more dimensions, we use the same trick as in the single-dimensional case. Suppose we have a function $f(t, X_t, Y_t)$, where X_t and Y_t are Ito processes (that is, of the form (2.29)). Then we Taylor expand, and drop all terms of order $(dX)^3$ and higher since they are zero by the above argument. The result is

$$df(t, X_t, Y_t) = \frac{\partial f}{\partial t} dt + \frac{\partial f}{\partial X_t} dX_t + \frac{\partial f}{\partial Y_t} dY_t$$

$$+ \frac{1}{2}\frac{\partial^2 f}{\partial X_t^2}(dX_t)^2 + \frac{\partial^2 f}{\partial X_t \partial Y_t} dX_t dY_t + \frac{1}{2}\frac{\partial^2 f}{\partial Y_t^2}(dY_t)^2. \tag{2.63}$$

2.9 Key Points

- We model the random path of asset prices using Brownian motion.
- The most important property of Brownian motion is the relation $(dW_t)^2 = dt$, which says that the square returns are deterministic.
- Ito's lemma tells us how to differentiate functions of stochastic processes and therefore how to do stochastic calculus. It adds an additional term to the standard (non-stochastic) differentiation formula.
- The most common process driven by a Brownian motion that is used to model asset prices is the log-normal process.
- The log-normal process has a volatility and a drift.

2.10 Further Reading

The mathematics of diffusion was pioneered by Bachelier (1900), and it is a source of some pride to financial mathematicians that this was in application to stock price evolution. A classic text on stochastic calculus and Brownian motion is Karatzas and Shreve (1991).

3 Martingale Pricing

We have seen that the fair value of a derivative contract must have the property that it is impossible to construct an arbitrage. In other words, if we are willing to buy and sell at that price, it must be impossible for a counterparty to make money with zero risk by setting up a portfolio containing that contract.

Martingale pricing is an elegant way of finding an arbitrage-free price for any contract. Therefore the contents of this chapter form the basis for all derivatives pricing.

The idea is to begin with a known *real world* stochastic process for the stock price. We then construct a new process, by following a simple rule, known as a *risk-neutral* process. Then the value of any contract will be calculated from a simple formula known as the Martingale pricing formula. This involves calculating the expected value of the contract payout assuming the stock follows the risk-neutral (rather than real world) process.

3.1 Setting the Scene

For simplicity, let's work with a real world process for a stock price S_t with constant drift and volatility

$$\frac{dS_t}{S_t} = \mu \, dt + \sigma \, dW_t. \tag{3.1}$$

Let's assume that the stock is valued in US dollars and the continuously compounding dollar interest rate is r_{dom}, a constant. Let's also assume that the stock pays dividends at a constant percentage rate r_{yield}.

By way of a little further explanation, a stock dividend can be treated just like an interest payment on a currency holding. Even though the dividends are paid at discrete times, we can model them with a continuously compounding dividend rate r_{yield}. An alternative way of thinking of this is that $S_t \, r_{yield} \, dt$ is the cost of borrowing one unit of the stock for infinitesimal time dt. Clearly if you borrow a stock, then the lender will miss out on the dividend payments, so the cost of borrowing must exactly compensate for these, and add up to the dividend payments. In fact, there is an active lending market in stocks, and also commodities like gold. This means that even gold has an interest rate that we should use for the parameter r_{yield}.

Finally, let's have in mind that we are going to price a contract that has payout $C(\{S_t\})$. This could be a forward contract, $C = S_T - K$, having expiry time T and strike K. It could be a call option, paying $(S_T - K)_+$. Or it could be a more complicated contract depending on the values of S_t at a number of times $\{t_i\}$.

3.2 Tradeable Assets

At this stage, we need the notion of a *tradeable asset*. If we own a stock, then we will receive dividends at the rate $r_{yield}S_t$. This means we cannot consider the value of the stock by its price S_t alone. If we sell it, we will lose the right to the dividends. So selling it now at a given price S is less favourable than selling it in one year's time at S since we would miss out on the dividend payments. We can circumvent this difficulty with a simple strategy. We set up a new asset that is actually a portfolio of the stock. At time zero (now) it contains one unit of stock. Then, whenever we receive a dividend, we immediately use it to buy new stock. This new asset is *tradeable* since its value does not depend on any obligations (to pay interest) or benefits (to receive dividends). In terms of the stock price S_t the value of this new tradeable asset that we have constructed is

$$A_t = e^{r_{yield}t} S_t. \tag{3.2}$$

For the same reason, we cannot use money (for example pounds sterling or US dollars) to measure the value of assets when constructing arbitrage arguments. Inflation causes money to lose value. On the other hand, if we have money, we can invest it in a bank account and receive interest. If we invest it in a government bond, then we can receive risk free interest.

For this reason, when constructing arbitrage arguments, we use portfolios of tradeable assets rather than money.

3.3 Zero Coupon Bond

The tradeable asset that will become, perhaps, our favourite is a zero coupon bond. Given an expiry time T, it pays one unit of currency (say one dollar) at time T. We can construct a simple replication argument to work out its value now. Let's suppose the continuously compounding interest rate is r_{dom}. Then, if we have sold a zero coupon bond, we can make sure we have enough money at expiry T to pay our client by investing $e^{-r_{dom}T}$ dollars in a bank account now. Then the value of the bond at time t must be exactly

$$B_0 = e^{-r_{dom}(T-t)}. \tag{3.3}$$

If we charge less than this, the client could make money with no risk by borrowing from a bank at the risk free rate r_{dom} and using the money borrowed to buy the bond. On the other hand, if we would charge more than this, we would be making money with no risk.

3.4 Rolling Money Market Account

Another useful tradeable asset is the *rolling money market account*. The choice of a particular expiry for a zero coupon bond can be a little restrictive. Instead, we could construct an asset by investing one unit of currency at the risk free rate. Then at time t this asset is worth

$$B_t = e^{r_{dom}t}.$$ (3.4)

The rolling money market account is closely related to a zero coupon bond, but can be more convenient because it has no expiry time.

3.5 Choosing a Numeraire

The first step in Martingale pricing is to choose a *numeraire*. This will be the tradeable asset that we use to measure the value of other assets in our portfolio. We can use any tradeable asset as the numeraire, but the most common choice is to use a zero coupon bond that pays in the same currency as the stock on which we want to price an option. It is usually convenient to choose a zero coupon bond with the same expiry as the option we are pricing.

Let's assume the option we want to price expires at time T. Then, for now, let us use a zero coupon bond that expires at T as our numeraire.

3.6 Changing the Measure

As we have already hinted, we do not care too much about every detail of the real world stochastic process (3.1) followed by the stock. We are concerned with arbitrage. In particular, we want to know whether it is possible to make money with zero risk, or in other words, with probability 1. To show that an arbitrage is not possible, we only need to find one possible path that the stock can take in which we do not make money.

For this reason, the only thing that is important about the real world stochastic process (3.1) is the set of *possible* paths. We are entirely indifferent to how *probable* each path is.

Therefore, we will allow ourselves to change the stochastic process (3.1), under the condition that the new stochastic process has exactly the same set of possible paths as the original. That is, we will allow ourselves to change the *probability measure*.

What are our options? If you were given a graphical plot of one possible path allowed by the driving process (3.1), there is absolutely no way that you could work out what the drift is. Each change in S_t is random, and although you might judge that on average the path is drifting at a certain rate, you have no way of knowing whether this is because it actually has this drift, or because the spot moved randomly in one of the more extreme of its possible paths.

Then, we can change the drift μ of the real world process (3.1) in any way that may be convenient to us. This will not change the set of possible paths, and so any arbitrage argument that we construct will be unaffected.

The volatility σ in (3.1) is a different matter. Let's again take a graphical plot of a single path obtained from the real world stochastic process. We can choose any arbitrarily small time interval in that path and then, since we have been given the spot value S_t at every point in that interval, perform the integral

$$\int_{\tau}^{\tau+\Delta\tau} \left(\frac{dS_t}{S_t}\right)^2. \tag{3.5}$$

If we were really doing this experiment, we would split the time interval $[\tau, \tau + \Delta\tau]$ into N segments, and calculate the ratio $\Delta S/S$ for each of these segments, square them and add them up.

Alternatively, we can perform this stochastic integral by substituting the process (3.1). We obtain

$$\int_{\tau}^{\tau+\Delta\tau} \left(\frac{dS_t}{S_t}\right)^2 = \int_{\tau}^{\tau+\Delta\tau} (\mu dt + \sigma dW_t)^2 \tag{3.6}$$

$$= \int_{\tau}^{\tau+\Delta\tau} \sigma^2 dt \tag{3.7}$$

$$= \sigma^2 T, \tag{3.8}$$

where we have used the properties $(dt)^2 = dt\, dW_t = 0$ and $(dW_t)^2 = dt$. The remarkable property $(dW_t)^2 = dt$ (equation (2.10)) has forced what we naively thought would be a random property of the path to be a predetermined number.

We have shown that, if we are given any path from the real world stochastic process, we can calculate its volatility σ. This means that if we change σ then we change the set of possible paths. So we must never do this when constructing arbitrage arguments. We say that two probability measures that have an identical set of possible paths are *equivalent measures*.

In conclusion, we may change the drift in any convenient way without affecting any arbitrage argument, but we must not change the volatility. This result is formalised in Girsanov's theorem.

3.7 Girsanov's Theorem

In this section we provide an introduction to Girsanov's theorem that will be enough for our purpose in this book. A formal presentation of the measure theory we use is offered to interested readers in the appendix.

Girsanov's theorem tells us we can perform a measure change that has the impact of changing the drift of a stochastic process. Furthermore, it tells us just how to reweight probabilities in order to achieve this.

We begin with a Brownian motion W_t, and have in mind a particular time interval $[0, T]$ that is of interest to us. We then pick a constant or time-dependent parameter v, and construct a random variable called the *Radon–Nikodým derivative*

$$Z_T = \exp\left\{-\int_0^T v\, dW_t - \frac{1}{2}\int_0^T v^2\, dt\right\}. \tag{3.9}$$

We can think of Z_T as a function of the Brownian path $\{W_t, t \in [0, T]\}$. The path is random, but once it is known we can use it to calculate Z_T.

We represent the probability of any particular path $\{W_t\}$ by the infinitesimal quantity $d\mathbb{P}$. The probabilities of all possible paths add up to 1, so that $\int d\mathbb{P} = 1$. As the expectation of a random variable X is equal to the sum of the possible values multiplied by the infinitesimal probabilities, we can express it via $E[X] = \int X \, d\mathbb{P}$.

Girsanov's theorem states that if we reweight the probability of the path $\{W_t, t \in [0, T]\}$ by Z_T, then we obtain a new probability measure $\mathbb{Q}$, which is equivalent to $\mathbb{P}$. In the new measure, the probability of a particular path $\{W_t\}$ is

$$dQ = Z_T \, d\mathbb{P}. \tag{3.10}$$

As we have changed the probabilities of paths, W_t is no longer a Brownian motion under the new measure. Girsanov's theorem tells us that with respect to $\mathbb{Q}$, the process $dB_t = dW_t + v \, dt$ is a Brownian motion. We can write $dW_t = -v \, dt + dB_t$, and so the process W_t that was a Brownian motion under $\mathbb{P}$ has acquired a drift of $-v$ under the new measure $\mathbb{Q}$.

Often, we can simply use Girsanov's theorem to tell us that there is a measure change with the effect of altering the drift of a process, and never need to write down the Radon–Nikodým derivative. In other cases, it can be useful to calculate the expectation of a random variable under the new measure as an expectation under the original measure. This is achieved very simply via

$$E_{\mathbb{Q}}[X] = E_{\mathbb{P}}[Z_T X], \tag{3.11}$$

where $E_{\mathbb{P}}$ and $E_{\mathbb{Q}}$ are expectations under the original and new measures respectively. The Radon–Nikodým derivative Z_T is often denoted $d\mathbb{Q}/d\mathbb{P}$. In that case, the change of measure formula (3.10) becomes

$$dQ = \frac{d\mathbb{Q}}{d\mathbb{P}} \, d\mathbb{P} \tag{3.12}$$

in analogy with the chain rule.

To understand why Girsanov's theorem is true, we can use the following informal argument. Firstly, we note that Z_T is positive, which is certainly necessary for it to be a candidate for reweighting probabilities. Furthermore, Z_T is a standard log-normal variable (as in Section 2.5) so has expectation 1. We can use this to check that probabilities add up to 1 in our new measure,

$$\int dQ = \int Z_T \, d\mathbb{P} \tag{3.13}$$

$$= E_{\mathbb{P}}[Z_T] \tag{3.14}$$

$$= 1. \tag{3.15}$$

Clearly events with probability zero under $\mathbb{P}$ also have probability zero under $\mathbb{Q}$ and vice versa, and therefore $\mathbb{P}$ and $\mathbb{Q}$ are equivalent probability measures. It remains to check the properties of the process B_t under $\mathbb{Q}$. We begin by calculating its drift.

Using the standard multiplicative property of the exponential function, we can decompose the Radon–Nikodým derivative into three parts

$$Z_T \equiv Z_{t_-} e^{-v\,dW_t - \frac{1}{2}v^2\,dt} Z_{t_+,T} \qquad (3.16)$$

Here t_- and t_+ are times infinitesimally below and above t, and $Z_{t_+,T}$ is the natural extension of the Radon–Nikodým derivative (3.9) with integrals starting from t_+ rather than 0.

As they are constructed from Brownian increments dW_s with $s \neq t$, both random variables Z_{t_-} and $Z_{t_+,T}$ are independent of dW_t, and each have expectation 1. Then we can calculate the drift of B_t under $\mathbb{Q}$ as

$$E_{\mathbb{Q}}[dB_t] = E_{\mathbb{P}}\left[Z_{t_-} e^{-v\,dW_t - \frac{1}{2}v^2\,dt} Z_{t_+,T}\, dB_t \right] \qquad (3.17)$$

$$= E_{\mathbb{P}}\left[Z_{t_-} \right] E_{\mathbb{P}}\left[e^{-v\,dW_t - \frac{1}{2}v^2\,dt}\, dB_t \right] E_{\mathbb{P}}\left[Z_{t_+,T} \right] \qquad (3.18)$$

$$= E_{\mathbb{P}}\left[e^{-v\,dW_t - \frac{1}{2}v^2\,dt} (dW_t + v\,dt) \right]. \qquad (3.19)$$

To calculate the final expectation we expand the exponential function and, as always, use the relations $(dW_t)^2 = dt$, $dt\,dW_t = 0$, and so on,

$$E_{\mathbb{Q}}[dB_t] = E_{\mathbb{P}}\left[\{1 - v\,dW_t + \mathcal{O}(dt)\}(dW_t + v\,dt) \right] \qquad (3.20)$$

$$= E_{\mathbb{P}}\left[dW_t + v\,dt - v\,(dW_t)^2 \right] \qquad (3.21)$$

$$= E_{\mathbb{P}}\left[dW_t \right] + v\,dt - v\,dt \qquad (3.22)$$

$$= 0. \qquad (3.23)$$

Having established that dB_t has zero drift under $\mathbb{Q}$, we can consider the square $(dB_t)^2$. This is much easier to handle since under $\mathbb{P}$ we have $(dB_t)^2 \equiv (dW_t + v\,dt)^2 = dt$. Then

$$E_{\mathbb{Q}}\left[(dB_t)^2 \right] = E_{\mathbb{P}}\left[Z_T\, dt \right] = dt \qquad (3.24)$$

and

$$\mathrm{Var}_{\mathbb{Q}}\left[(dB_t)^2 \right] = E_{\mathbb{P}}\left[Z_T\,(dB_t)^4 \right] - \left(E_{\mathbb{P}}\left[Z_T\,(dB_t)^2 \right] \right)^2 = 0. \qquad (3.25)$$

Under the measure $\mathbb{Q}$, the process B_t has drift 0, and satisfies $(dB_t)^2 = dt$. This is enough to determine that it is a Brownian motion.[8] To see why, we recall that a Brownian motion is a process with normally distributed increments, and consider

$$\delta B_t = B_{t+\delta t} - B_t = \int_t^{t+\delta t} dB_t. \qquad (3.26)$$

---

[8] Formally, this characterisation of Brownian motion is provided by a theorem due to Lévy.

This is an infinite sum of independent identically distributed random variables. The central limit theorem tells us it is normally distributed, and we are done.

3.8 Martingales

A Martingale M_t is a time-dependent random process with the property that, given everything we know at time s, its expected value at a future time $t > s$, is equal to its value at s,

$$E[M_t|\mathcal{F}_s] = M_s, \quad t > s. \tag{3.27}$$

Here, as in Section 2.6, we have denoted the information available at time s by the filtration $\mathcal{F}_s$. If we think of s as being the time now, and $\mathcal{F}_s$ as what we know now, then the expected future value of a Martingale is equal to its value now.

Of course, this property depends on the stochastic process driving M_t, or in the language of the previous section, it depends on the probability measure. So, since we will be changing the measure, we will often make it explicit that M_t is Martingale with respect to a particular measure.

Why are Martingales useful? Well, let's suppose that M_t is the value of a portfolio of tradeable assets measured with respect to some numeraire. For example, suppose

$$M_t = A_t/B_t \tag{3.28}$$

where A_t is the tradeable asset constructed from the stock price (3.2), and the numeraire B_t is the rolling money market account (3.4). If M_t is a Martingale, then for a given expiry time T we have

$$E[M_T|\mathcal{F}_0] = M_0. \tag{3.29}$$

If there is one or more paths for which $M_T > M_0$, then there *must* also be one or more paths with $M_T < M_0$, otherwise the Martingale condition (3.29) could not be true. Therefore, this particular portfolio does not represent an arbitrage opportunity because its value as measured by the numeraire can go both up and down.

Taking this argument one step further, let's suppose we have found a probability measure for which all tradeable assets are Martingale with respect to the numeraire B_t. Then a linear combination of the assets must also be Martingale, and so it is impossible to set up a portfolio of the assets that contains an arbitrage opportunity.

Our aim is to find an arbitrage-free price for a derivative contract. To begin with, we find a measure so that the tradeable asset $A_t = e^{r_{yield}t}S_t$ is Martingale with respect to the numeraire. Let's say the price of the derivative at time t is $C(S_t, t)$. For concreteness, suppose the payout of the option is $C(S_T, T) = (S_T - K)_+$, a call option. Then as long as we can find a function $C(S_t, t)$ that has the correct payout at expiry T, and which is Martingale with respect to the numeraire, then we will know we have found a price such that it is impossible to set up a portfolio of the option, stock and bonds to create an arbitrage.

If this is possible, then the Martingale condition gives us a simple formula for $C(S_0, 0)$ which is the value of the contract now

$$\frac{C(S_0, 0)}{B_0} = E\left[\frac{C(S_T, T)}{B_T}\right].$$

(3.30)

This is known as the Martingale pricing equation.

3.9 Continuous Martingales

So far, we have concentrated on avoiding arbitrage at a particular expiry time T. But the reality is that we need to avoid arbitrage at all times up to T when the option expires. If we insist that the Martingale condition holds for all times t

$$E[M_t|\mathcal{F}_0] = M_0, \quad \text{for } t > 0,$$

(3.31)

then by differentiating, we can rewrite the Martingale condition as

$$E[dM_t] = 0.$$

(3.32)

As shorthand, we have now dropped the filtration from the formula.

If M_t is an Ito process

$$dM_t = a(M_t, t)dt + b(M_t, t)dW_t$$

(3.33)

then we have[9]

$$E[dM_t] = E[a(M_t, t)]dt$$

(3.34)

and we can ensure M_t is Martingale by imposing zero drift, $a = 0$. This is a very important result. A stochastic process is Martingale if it has zero drift.

In the next two sections, we will work through this process in order to find the Black–Scholes formula for a call option, and then the Black–Scholes pricing equation for more general options.

3.10 Black–Scholes Formula for a Call Option

Let's assume that spot follows the real world process

$$\frac{dS_t}{S_t} = \mu\, dt + \sigma\, dW_t.$$

(3.35)

---

[9] For a reminder of why the stochastic term drops out of the expectation, please refer back to Section 2.2.

We form a tradeable asset A from the stock S which has value

$$A_t = e^{r_{yield}t} S_t. \tag{3.36}$$

As a numeraire, we choose the rolling money market account. At time t it has value

$$B_t = e^{r_{dom}t}. \tag{3.37}$$

Our first task is to find a probability measure that is equivalent to the real world measure and in which A_t/B_t is a Martingale. That is, we need the drift of A_t/B_t to be zero. So let's apply the Ito product rule from Section 2.4

$$d(A_t/B_t) = d(e^{(r_{yield}-r_{dom})t} S_t) \tag{3.38}$$

$$= d(e^{(r_{yield}-r_{dom})t}) S_t + e^{(r_{yield}-r_{dom})t} dS_t + d(e^{(r_{yield}-r_{dom})t}) dS_t \tag{3.39}$$

$$= e^{(r_{yield}-r_{dom})t} S_t [(r_{yield} - r_{dom} + \mu)dt + \sigma dW_t]. \tag{3.40}$$

We are allowed to change the drift μ of the real world process to a new value μ'. If we choose

$$\mu' = r_{dom} - r_{yield}, \tag{3.41}$$

then the total drift in equation (3.40) goes away and A_t/B_t is Martingale with respect to the corresponding new probability measure.

Then our *risk-neutral* process for S_t is

$$\frac{dS_t}{S_t} = (r_{dom} - r_{yield})dt + \sigma dW_t. \tag{3.42}$$

Under the probability measure defined by this risk-neutral process, the tradeable asset A_t is a Martingale with respect to the numeraire B_t.

Using the results of the previous chapter, we can solve for the probability distribution of spot at a given expiry time T, and obtain the log-normal behaviour

$$S_T = S_0 \exp\left[(r_{dom} - r_{yield} - \tfrac{1}{2}\sigma^2)T + \sigma\sqrt{T}Z\right], \quad Z = N(0,1). \tag{3.43}$$

The hard part is over. Since we have found a probability measure in which our tradeable assets A_t and B_t are Martingale with respect to the numeraire B_t, then as long as any price we propose for a derivative contract is also Martingale, it must be free of arbitrage. We can impose this if we choose the value now to be given by the Martingale pricing equation (3.30)

$$\frac{C(S_0, 0)}{B_0} = E\left[\frac{C(S_T, T)}{B_T}\right]. \tag{3.44}$$

Since B is not stochastic, this can be rewritten

$$C(S_0,0) = \frac{B_0}{B_T} E[C(S_T,T)] \tag{3.45}$$

$$= e^{-r_{dom}T} E[C(S_T,T)]. \tag{3.46}$$

We have discovered that if we use the probability measure that is risk-neutral with respect to the money market account, we can calculate the value of a derivative contract by calculating the expected value of its payout and multiplying by $e^{-r_{dom}T}$. Since it is very common to use the zero coupon bond or money market account as numeraire, many quants and traders begin from the outset with the above risk-neutral process for spot, and think of the premium as the expected value of the payout at expiry discounted back to the valuation time to take account of the time value of money. The factor $e^{-r_{dom}T}$ is known as the *discount factor*.

Before valuing a call option, let's price a forward contract and compare the price to the value we found in Section 1.6. At expiry time T, the payout is $S_T - K$, where K is the strike. Then using the formula (3.45) we find the value at time 0 (present value, or PV) is

$$PV = e^{-r_{dom}T} E[S_T - K] \tag{3.47}$$

$$= e^{-r_{dom}T} E[S_T] - e^{-r_{dom}T} K \tag{3.48}$$

$$= e^{-r_{yield}T} S_0 - e^{-r_{dom}T} K. \tag{3.49}$$

This should be compared with (1.12), which was the value of a forward contract to buy euros valued in sterling.

Many quants and traders automatically think of a derivative value as the discounted expectation of the payout in the risk-neutral probability measure. It is then nice to rewrite the value of the forward contract as

$$PV = e^{-r_{dom}T}[F - K] \tag{3.50}$$

where F is the forward level, usually known simply as the *forward* and is given by

$$F = e^{(r_{dom}-r_{yield})T} S_0. \tag{3.51}$$

Note that the forward is the expected value of spot at expiry in the risk-neutral measure, which is the money market account in the natural payment currency of the forward contract (dollars in this case).

We now want to price a call option that expires at time T. We know that, in our risk-neutral measure, S_T is log-normally distributed. So it is just a matter of integrating the payout against the probability distribution. The payout is

$$(S_T - K)_+ \tag{3.52}$$

and so the value is

$$PV = e^{-r_{dom}T} E[(S_T - K)_+] \qquad (3.53)$$

$$= \int_{-\infty}^{\infty} \frac{e^{-\frac{1}{2}z^2}}{\sqrt{2\pi}} (S_T(z) - K)_+ \, dz \qquad (3.54)$$

where $S_T(z)$ is given by formula (3.43). It is straightforward to perform the integral and obtain

$$PV = e^{-r_{dom}T} [FN(d_1) - KN(d_2)] \qquad (3.55)$$

where F is the forward, the two parameters d_1 and d_2 are given by

$$d_1 = \frac{\log(F/K) + \frac{1}{2}\sigma^2 T}{\sigma\sqrt{T}} \qquad (3.56)$$

$$d_2 = \frac{\log(F/K) - \frac{1}{2}\sigma^2 T}{\sigma\sqrt{T}}, \qquad (3.57)$$

and $N(x)$ is the cumulative normal function

$$N(x) = \int_{-\infty}^{x} \frac{e^{-\frac{1}{2}z^2}}{\sqrt{2\pi}} \, dz. \qquad (3.58)$$

We have assumed up to now that the interest rates and volatility are constant. If they vary with time, that is if they have term structure, then we can extend the formula in a simple manner. Looking back to equation (2.52), which gives the distribution of spot at time T when there is term structure, we can simply make the replacements

$$r_{dom} = \frac{1}{T} \int_0^T r_{dom}(t) \, dt \qquad (3.59)$$

$$r_{yield} = \frac{1}{T} \int_0^T r_{yield}(t) \, dt \qquad (3.60)$$

$$\sigma^2 = \frac{1}{T} \int_0^T \sigma(t)^2 \, dt. \qquad (3.61)$$

3.11 At-the-Money Options

If the strike K is equal to the forward level F, then we say the option is *at-the-money*.[10] This is the most popular choice for the strike when an option is first traded. As the forward level is the risk-neutral expectation of the spot level at expiry date, setting the strike to this level means the market view is that there is roughly even chance of the contract ending up worth something, or valueless. The terms *in-the-money* and *out-of-the-money* are used to indicate that a contract is respectively likely to pay out, or unlikely to pay out. If an option is initially traded at-the-money, it will move in- or out-of-the-money depending on the underlying spot movements as time goes on towards the expiry date.

If we do a Taylor expansion of the Black–Scholes formula (3.55) in the special case of $K = F$ so that the option is at-the-money, we obtain

$$PV = e^{-r_{dom}T} F \left[N(\tfrac{1}{2}\sigma\sqrt{T}) - N(-\tfrac{1}{2}\sigma\sqrt{T}) \right] \qquad (3.62)$$

$$= \frac{1}{\sqrt{2\pi}} e^{-r_{dom}T} F\sigma\sqrt{T} + \mathcal{O}([\sigma\sqrt{T}]^3) \qquad (3.63)$$

$$\equiv \frac{1}{\sqrt{2\pi}} e^{-r_{yield}T} S_0\sigma\sqrt{T} + \mathcal{O}([\sigma\sqrt{T}]^3) \qquad (3.64)$$

where we replaced the forward F by its definition (3.51).

The factor of S_0 appearing in equation (3.64) merely represents conversion to the units that the price is expressed in. If, for example, it is a derivative contract on IBM shares, we could divide by S_0 to obtain the price in units of IBM shares rather than US dollars. The PV expressed this way is known as the *percentage notional* price. If we assume the yield is small, and replace π with its numerical value, this gives

$$PV_\% \approx 0.4\sigma\sqrt{T} + \mathcal{O}([\sigma\sqrt{T}]^3). \qquad (3.65)$$

As the term of order σ^2 is missing from the Taylor expansion, the value of an at-the-money option is linear in volatility to a very good approximation.

This fact is key in option trading. Vanilla traders consider buying an option as taking on a position in volatility. It will be invaluable to us later, but for now it helps us to easily understand the typical cost of a vanilla option. Say we buy a one-year option on a million dollars worth of shares, and the volatility is 10%. Then the price will be around 4% of the notional, or 4,000 dollars.

3.12 The Black–Scholes Equation

In the previous sections, we have learned how to assign a value to a derivative contract in a manner that ensures it is not possible to create an arbitrage by trading in the

---

[10] Some markets use alternative definitions for trading an at-the-money option. These include setting strike equal to the spot rather than forward level, or choosing a strike so that the combination of a call plus a put option has zero delta.

contract and underlying asset. We used this method to find the value of a call option in a market in which the volatility is constant or has term structure.

We are now ready to tackle the pricing of a general derivative contract. We shall soon see that the value of a derivative satisfies a partial differential equation, and in a world in which volatility is constant, or at worst time dependent, this is known as the Black–Scholes equation.

As usual, we use the domestic money market account $B(t) = e^{r_{dom}t}$ as numeraire. It is common to simplify notation by dropping t subscripts so that S_t becomes S, W_t becomes W and so on. We shall regularly do this from now on without further warning. Then equation (3.42) tells us that our risk-neutral process for S_t is given by

$$\frac{dS}{S} = (r_{dom} - r_{yield})dt + \sigma\, dW. \tag{3.66}$$

If $C(t, S)$ is the value of our derivative contract at time t and spot level S, then we would like the ratio $C(t, S)/B(t)$ to be a Martingale. If we can find a function C that achieves this, then it will be impossible to create an arbitrage from the tradeable assets.

To test whether C/B is Martingale, we should find its stochastic process and check whether it has zero drift. So our task is to apply Ito's lemma to C/B.

We begin by applying the Ito product rule from Section 2.4

$$d(C/B) = dC/B + C\,d(1/B) + dC\,d(1/B). \tag{3.67}$$

Since $B \equiv e^{-r_{dom}t}$ is not stochastic, $d(1/B)$ is of order dt (there are no dW terms). Then $dC\,d(1/B)$ is of order $dt\,dW \equiv 0$, and we have

$$d(C/B) = dC/B + C\,d(1/B). \tag{3.68}$$

We can expand dC by using Ito's lemma, and also replace $B = e^{r_{dom}t}$ to obtain

$$d(C/B) = \left(\frac{\partial C}{\partial t}dt + \frac{\partial C}{\partial S}dS + \frac{1}{2}\frac{\partial^2 C}{\partial S^2}(dS)^2\right) \Big/ B + C\,d(e^{-r_{dom}t}). \tag{3.69}$$

It is easy to differentiate $e^{-r_{dom}t}$

$$d(C/B) = \left(\frac{\partial C}{\partial t}dt + \frac{\partial C}{\partial S}dS + \frac{1}{2}\frac{\partial^2 C}{\partial S^2}(dS)^2\right) \Big/ B - C r_{dom} e^{-r_{dom}t}\,dt \tag{3.70}$$

and finally we can replace $dS = S[(r_{dom} - r_{yield})\,dt + \sigma\,dW]$ and $(dS)^2 = S^2\sigma^2 dt$ to give

$$d(C/B) = \left(\frac{\partial C}{\partial t}dt + \frac{\partial C}{\partial S}S[(r_{dom} - r_{yield})\,dt + \sigma\,dW] + \frac{1}{2}\frac{\partial^2 C}{\partial S^2}S^2\sigma^2 dt\right) \Big/ B$$
$$- r_{dom}C/B\,dt. \tag{3.71}$$

If $d(C/B)$ has zero drift then it is a Martingale and there can be no arbitrage. For the drift to be zero, all the dt terms should add to zero and this gives us our pricing equation

$$\frac{\partial C}{\partial t} + \frac{\partial C}{\partial S} S(r_{dom} - r_{yield}) + \frac{1}{2} \frac{\partial^2 C}{\partial S^2} S^2 \sigma^2 - r_{dom} C = 0. \qquad (3.72)$$

The partial differential equation (PDE) (3.72) is known as the Black–Scholes equation. If we are given the payout of the option at expiry time T, this acts as a boundary condition for the PDE. We can then solve the PDE backwards in time to find the value at any earlier time t.

In practice, there are three main approaches to solving the PDE in order to value a derivative contract. With luck, we might find an analytic solution, or approximate solution. Failing that, we might solve the PDE numerically by discretising the solution on a grid. Alternatively, we often simulate the risk-neutral random process by generating a large number of random spot values. We can then calculate the expected value of the payout over all these random paths. This is known as a Monte Carlo simulation.

All in good time. For now let us be content with the knowledge that we can, in principle, value any derivative contract in the Black–Scholes world by solving the Black–Scholes equation. We have found one particular analytic solution, that for a vanilla option payout, and we shall return to find solutions for other more exotic contracts later.

3.13   An Elegant Derivation of the Black–Scholes Formula

There is an elegant derivation of the Black–Scholes formula (3.55) that gives a good illustration of the technique of changing measure. We begin by using the dollar money market account as numeraire. Then equation (3.42) provides our risk-neutral process for the spot rate S_t

$$\frac{dS_t}{S_t} = (r_{dom} - r_{yield}) dt + \sigma\, dW_t. \qquad (3.73)$$

As in equation (3.43), we can rewrite this as a process for the log-spot, and then solve to obtain

$$S_T = S_0 \exp\left[(r_{dom} - r_{yield} - \tfrac{1}{2}\sigma^2)T + \sigma\sqrt{T}Z\right], \quad Z = N(0,1) \qquad (3.74)$$

$$\equiv F \exp\left(-\tfrac{1}{2}\sigma^2 T + \sigma\sqrt{T}Z\right). \qquad (3.75)$$

Our aim is to price the call option payout $(S_T - K)_+$ by calculating its expectation under the risk-neutral measure. The trick is to split the payout into two component parts

$$(S_T - K)_+ = S_T 1_{S_T > K} - K 1_{S_T > K} \qquad (3.76)$$

and to price them individually.

We begin with the second payout $K1_{S_T>K}$. It pays a fixed amount K if spot ends up greater than K, and zero otherwise. Such payouts are called cash digital options. Its value is equal to the dollar discount factor multiplied by the expected payout

$$V_2 = e^{-r_{dom}T}E[K1_{S_T>K}] \tag{3.77}$$

$$= e^{-r_{dom}T}KP(S_T > K) \tag{3.78}$$

since the expected value of a step function is just the cumulative probability. As S_T is log-normal, it is simple to rewrite the formula as a standard normal probability by manipulating equation (3.74), and we obtain

$$V_2 = e^{-r_{dom}T}KN(d_2) \tag{3.79}$$

$$d_2 = \frac{\log(F/K) - \frac{1}{2}\sigma^2 T}{\sigma\sqrt{T}}. \tag{3.80}$$

Next we consider the payout $S_T1_{S_T>K}$. This is also a digital option, but paying one unit of the asset (whose value is S_T) at expiry if $S_T > K$. This provides a hint that we could use the asset itself as numeraire rather than the dollar money market account.

As we saw in Section 3.2, for an asset to be suitable as a numeraire, it must be tradeable. That is, it must not pay out any interest or dividends. Therefore we will actually use an artificial asset created from beginning with one unit of the asset, and reinvesting all dividends by buying more asset. Then at time t our tradeable asset A_t consists of $\exp(r_{yield}t)$ units of the asset.

This asset account is no different to the money market account we constructed for dollars. There is a perfect symmetry between working with a dollar numeraire and treating the asset as risky, or working with the asset as numeraire and treating dollars as risky. Indeed, if the asset were pounds sterling, then it would seem just as natural to use it as numeraire as to use dollars, and even more so for an investor in London.

As we are working with the asset as numeraire, we need a stochastic process analogous to S_t that will tell us what the value of one dollar is in units of the asset. This is simply the inverse process $U_t = 1/S_t$.

Starting from equation (3.73), which is the risk-neutral process for S_t with respect to the dollar numeraire, we can apply Ito's lemma to find the process for U_t

$$\frac{dU_t}{U_t} = (r_{yield} - r_{dom} + \sigma^2)dt - \sigma dW_t. \tag{3.81}$$

This tells us the process that is risk-neutral with respect to the dollar numeraire. But we are using the asset as numeraire, and therefore need to change the probability measure to get a process that is risk-neutral with respect to the new numeraire.

The proper way to do this would be to follow Section 3.10 and set up a tradeable asset, which would be the dollar money market account, and then to insist that the value of this (in units of the asset) divided by the numeraire be Martingale. To achieve this we change the measure, which is the same as changing the drift.

In practice, though, there is no need because the problem is exactly symmetric with the original case in which we used dollars as numeraire. Then by looking at equation

(3.73) and swapping r_{dom} with r_{yield} we can write down the answer

$$\frac{dU_t}{U_t} = (r_{yield} - r_{dom})dt - \sigma \, dW_t. \tag{3.82}$$

We should note that the negative sign in front of the dW_t term does not matter: we could rewrite $-dW_t = dW_t'$ and dW_t' is a Brownian motion.

Using $S_t = 1/U_t$ we can now use Ito again to convert back to the process for S_t that is risk-neutral with respect to the asset measure. The calculation is identical to the one we used to get from the S_t process to the U_t process with respect to the dollar measure (getting equation (3.81) from (3.73)) and so we can write down the answer:

$$\frac{dS_t}{S_t} = (r_{dom} - r_{yield} + \sigma^2)dt + \sigma \, dW_t. \tag{3.83}$$

In this way, we can see that the impact of moving from the dollar measure to the asset measure is to add an extra σ^2 term to the drift of the process.

In order to price the payout, we use the Martingale pricing equation (3.30). In that formula, we denoted the value of the numeraire by B since we had in mind using the dollar bond. Here, the numeraire is the asset account, and has value at time t (in dollars)

$$A_t = e^{r_{yield}t} S_t. \tag{3.84}$$

Then the price in dollars is

$$P_1 = A_0 \, E_{\text{Asset}} \left[\frac{S_T 1_{S_T > K}}{A_T} \right] \tag{3.85}$$

$$= S_0 \, E_{\text{Asset}} \left[\frac{S_T 1_{S_T > K}}{e^{r_{yield}T} S_T} \right] \tag{3.86}$$

$$= S_0 e^{-r_{yield}T} E_{\text{Asset}} \left[1_{S_T > K} \right]. \tag{3.87}$$

Looking back to our formula (3.51) for the forward level, we can rewrite this to replace spot S_0 with forward F_T

$$V_1 = e^{-r_{dom}T} F_T E_{\text{Asset}} \left[1_{S_T > K} \right]. \tag{3.88}$$

This formula is quite fascinating. We still have a dollar discount factor, but the spot conversion of the payout at expiry has come into the valuation formula as the forward level. It remains to compute the expectation of the digital payout $1_{S_T > K}$ under the asset measure. The result is identical to that for the other component V_2 except that now we have that extra σ^2 term in the drift. Then we can write down the answer

$$V_1 = e^{-r_{dom}T} F_T N(d_1) \tag{3.89}$$

$$d_1 = \frac{\log(F/K) + \frac{1}{2}\sigma^2 T}{\sigma\sqrt{T}}, \tag{3.90}$$

with the difference between d_1 and d_2 being an additional $\sigma^2 T$ term in the numerator resulting from that difference in drift caused by the measure change.

Putting the two components together, we obtain the price of the call option

$$V = V_1 - V_2 = e^{-r_{dom}T} [F_T N(d_1) - K N(d_2)]. \tag{3.91}$$

Once one gets used to the concept of measure change, the steps involved in this section become so familiar that they can simply be written down. The only part that appears to need any calculation is the measure change introducing a σ^2 term into the drift. However, this step is also simple if one works in log space. In that case, following Section 2.5, the risk-neutral process for S_t under the dollar numeraire is

$$d\log S_t = \left(r_{dom} - r_{yield} - \frac{1}{2}\sigma^2\right) dt + \sigma\, dW_t. \tag{3.92}$$

If we look at the process for $\log(1/S_t)$, this is simply $-\log S_t$, and so we can write down

$$d(-\log S_t) = -\left(r_{dom} - r_{yield} - \frac{1}{2}\sigma^2\right) dt - \sigma\, dW_t \tag{3.93}$$

$$= \left(r_{yield} - r_{dom} - \frac{1}{2}\sigma^2\right) dt + \sigma^2 dt + \sigma\, dW_t' \tag{3.94}$$

where $dW_t' = -dW_t$. There we see that the impact of using the asset measure rather than the dollar measure is exactly a σ^2 term in the drift. The perfect symmetry between treating dollars as the numeraire and the asset as risky, or alternatively treating the asset as numeraire and the dollar account as risky, allows us to move effortlessly between the processes under the two risk-neutral measures using that trick.

Foreign exchange analysts are particularly adept with this technique since for them an asset is just another currency, and they have no particular preference for using one currency as numeraire over another. If challenged to derive the Black–Scholes formula (or perhaps, more likely, to recall which is which of d_1 and d_2 when using the formula), an experienced FX quant is likely to begin by writing down the risk-neutral process for spot in log space (equation (3.92)), then to write down the log-normal solutions under the two measures

$$S_T^{\text{dollar}} = F \exp\left(-\tfrac{1}{2}\sigma^2 T + \sigma\sqrt{T}Z\right), \quad Z = N(0,1) \tag{3.95}$$

$$S_T^{\text{asset}} = F \exp\left(+\tfrac{1}{2}\sigma^2 T + \sigma\sqrt{T}Z'\right), \quad Z' = N(0,1) \tag{3.96}$$

and finally to simply write down the solution (equation (3.91)) with the intermediate step of expressing the probabilities in terms of standard normal variables being considered straightforward.

Later, in Section 11.7.2, when we study multi-asset derivatives, we will use this technique to 'write down' the Black–Scholes formula for a particularly important contract, the best-of option. This is truly something to look forward to.

3.14 Key Points

- Martingale pricing is an elegant way of finding an arbitrage-free price for any contract.
- We use a tradeable asset (rather than money) as the numeraire to measure the value of a portfolio when checking for arbitrage.
- When checking for arbitrage, we are indifferent to the true probability of events. All that is important are the sets of certain events and impossible events.
- Therefore we can change the probability measure as long as we preserve the events that have probability zero and one.
- Girsanov's theorem tells us that we can use a measure change to change the drift but not the volatility of a stochastic process (Ito process).
- A Martingale is a random variable whose expected future value is equal to its value now.
- If we can change to a probability measure in which all asset prices are Martingales when measured in the numeraire, then we can be sure there is no arbitrage. This is the risk-neutral measure.
- The value of a derivative contract is arbitrage free if it is a Martingale when measured in units of the numeraire in the risk-neutral measure.
- Practically speaking this means we can value a derivative by calculating the expected value of its payout in the risk-neutral measure and discounting using the numeraire.
- The Black–Scholes formula for valuing a vanilla call or put option can be derived in this way.
- More complicated derivative contracts can be valued by solving a PDE backwards in time from the contract expiry date.

3.15 Further Reading

The famous original paper that gave us the pricing formula (3.55) for vanilla options is Black and Scholes (1973), and the theory was expanded in Merton (1973). Those seeking a rigorous yet highly readable account of stochastic calculus for finance will be delighted by Shreve (2004), which is considered definitive by practitioners of quantitative finance. A further outstanding text is Baxter and Rennie (1996).

4 Dynamic Hedging and Replication

Up to now, we have seen how to assign a value to a derivative contract in such a way that there is no possibility of creating an arbitrage by trading in the underlying asset and bonds. We do not know if this value is unique, or failing that in any way optimal. With what we have learned so far, a trader could take on a new contract in a large notional amount and value it in a manner guaranteed to avoid arbitrage. All very well, but that does not help the bank manage the trade through its lifetime.

For example, let's suppose the trade is a contract that pays 1,000,000 dollars if spot ends up above a given strike in one year. Let's say this strike is the current one-year forward level, so that the probability the contract ends up in-the-money is around 50%. Then the arbitrage-free value of the contract will be around 500,000 dollars. But at expiry, the bank might have to pay out 1,000,000 dollars and so could easily lose a lot of money. If all the bank's trades happened to be in the same direction, as can easily happen, a large market move could bring down the bank.

Thus, up to now, we have fallen far short of the extravagant claims in the early part of this book. There we asserted that it is possible to trade in the underlying asset in just such a way as to have enough to pay the client at the time of expiry. This in spite of the fact that we can have no way of knowing where the spot price will end up.

Investment banks do not act like insurance companies. Banks do not take a premium based on a probability of winning or losing. They cannot because they could easily be decimated in a large market move. And in any case, as we shall now see, it is possible to do so much better.

4.1 Dynamic Hedging in the Absence of Interest Rates

Let's begin in a world in which interest and dividend rates are zero. As before, we assume that the real world process for the spot price of the asset is

$$\frac{dS}{S} = \mu \, dt + \sigma \, dW. \tag{4.1}$$

Our aim is to find a trading strategy so that we can exactly replicate the payout of a derivative contract when it expires. We will set up a portfolio containing some amount of the asset, and some cash. At any time during the life of the trade, we may convert asset into cash or vice versa. We may hold a negative amount of cash; this means we have borrowed money and have the obligation to pay it back in the future. Likewise, we may hold a negative amount of the asset, indicating that we have borrowed the asset and must repay it in the future. Technically, borrowing to hold negative amount of an asset is known as *going short* the asset, or simply as *shorting*.

Let's assume that at time t we hold α units of the asset, and β units of cash. Although we have not explicitly written it, α and β will depend on time t and spot level S_t. Then the value of the portfolio is

$$P = \alpha S + \beta. \tag{4.2}$$

The idea is that we are going to dynamically trade the asset in this portfolio in order to end up with exactly enough to pay our counterparty at expiry. We must not inject any cash into the portfolio except when we first set it up. If we did, then our replicating strategy would have failed so that we had to put more money in to meet our obligations. We call this a *self-financing portfolio*. Any change in its overall value must come about from changes in the asset value alone. Changes in α and β must exactly compensate each other. So the self-financing condition is

$$dP = \alpha \, dS. \tag{4.3}$$

At the risk of labouring the point, ordinarily the expression for dP would be obtained by applying Ito's lemma, and so equation (4.3) represents a condition on the derivatives of α and β that we could write down if we had the energy.

Instead, let's apply Ito's lemma to P directly:

$$dP = \frac{\partial P}{\partial t} dt + \frac{\partial P}{\partial S} dS + \frac{1}{2} \frac{\partial^2 P}{\partial S^2} (dS)^2 \tag{4.4}$$

$$= \frac{\partial P}{\partial t} dt + \frac{\partial P}{\partial S} dS + \frac{1}{2} \frac{\partial^2 P}{\partial S^2} S^2 \sigma^2 dt. \tag{4.5}$$

As usual the fundamental relation $(dW)^2 = dt$, implying $(dS)^2 = S^2\sigma^2 dt$, is what has allowed everything to work.

If we now compare (4.5) with (4.3), we see that we must have

$$\alpha = \frac{\partial P}{\partial S} \tag{4.6}$$

and

$$\frac{\partial P}{\partial t} + \frac{1}{2} \frac{\partial^2 P}{\partial S^2} S^2 \sigma^2 = 0. \tag{4.7}$$

The latter expression (4.7) is precisely the Black–Scholes equation when interest rates and dividend yields are zero. Let's assume that we have solved this equation with the boundary condition that the value $P(S_t,t)$ is equal to the payout of the derivative contract at the expiry time T. Then as long as at time 0 we set up the portfolio with value $P_0 = P(S_0,0)$, and we make sure that we always hold $\frac{\partial P}{\partial S}$ units of the asset, our portfolio is self-financing and we are guaranteed to have exactly the right amount to pay our counterparty at expiry.

Since we have successfully replicated the payout by following a dynamic trading strategy, the value of the derivative must be equal to the value of the portfolio. If we would charge less than this, the client could make money without risk by buying the contract and trading the opposite hedging portfolio. On the other hand, if we charged more, we could make money with zero risk by setting up the opposite hedging portfolio and dynamically trading in the asset.

4.2 Dynamic Hedging with Interest Rates

It is easy to add interest rates into the above argument. Our hedge portfolio will still contain α units of the asset and β units of cash

$$P = \alpha S + \beta. \tag{4.8}$$

But now the self-financing condition needs to be altered since we earn dividends at rate r_{yield} and interest at rate r_{dom}

$$dP = \alpha\,dS + r_{yield}\alpha\,S\,dt + r_{dom}\beta\,dt. \tag{4.9}$$

On the other hand, Ito tells us

$$dP = \frac{\partial P}{\partial t}dt + \frac{\partial P}{\partial S}dS + \frac{1}{2}\frac{\partial^2 P}{\partial S^2}S^2\sigma^2\,dt \tag{4.10}$$

and equating coefficients of dS we obtain

$$\alpha = \frac{\partial P}{\partial S} \tag{4.11}$$

so that the amount of cash in the portfolio is

$$\beta = P - S\frac{\partial P}{\partial S}. \tag{4.12}$$

Finally then, equating the coefficients of dt gives us the full Black–Scholes equation

$$\frac{\partial P}{\partial t} + \frac{1}{2}\frac{\partial^2 P}{\partial S^2}S^2\sigma^2 + (r_{dom} - r_{yield})S\frac{\partial P}{\partial S} - r_{dom}P = 0. \tag{4.13}$$

Let's summarise what we have learned. If the volatility σ is known, then a trader can ensure s/he has enough money to meet the obligations of any derivative contract by trading in the underlying asset through the life of the trade. The value of the contract with a given time to expiry and spot level is given by the solution to the Black–Scholes PDE with boundary condition given by the payout at expiry. Then the trick is to continuously buy and sell the asset so as to hold exactly $\partial P/\partial S$ units of the asset at all times.

In this chapter, we have not used any tricks of changing the measure associated with the alternative technique of arbitrage-free pricing with Martingales. But we still found that an option value is independent of the real world drift μ of the asset. Even if you are absolutely convinced that an asset is growing at a certain rate, so that, in your opinion, an option is very likely to end up in-the-money, its value is determined only by the interest rates and volatility.

4.3 Delta Hedging

If an option has value $C(S,t)$, the quantity

$$\Delta \equiv \frac{\partial C}{\partial S} \tag{4.14}$$

is known as the *delta* of the option. The hedging strategy that we have outlined in the previous sections amounts to adding enough of the asset into our portfolio to ensure that the Δ of the entire portfolio is zero. This is because a units of asset are worth aS and so have $\Delta = a$. So if we buy $\partial P/\partial S$ units of asset, that adds delta of $\partial P/\partial S$ to the portfolio.

This makes perfect sense. It seems like a very good idea to maintain the portfolio so that when spot moves the portfolio value remains unchanged to first order. But it is remarkable that following this strategy precisely allows us to replicate the final payout of the contract.

The strategy is known as *delta hedging*. It is absolutely fundamental to trading. Whether or not the trader believes the true dynamics are Black–Scholes, the very first thing he or she will do after putting on a trade is to put on the delta hedge. The delta will be calculated as the derivative with respect to spot of the contract valuation in the particular model, not necessarily Black–Scholes, that the trader uses to risk manage the book.

4.4 The Greeks

The delta, calculated via $\Delta = \partial C/\partial S$, is one example of what are endearingly known as *the Greeks*. Even if the bank's portfolio of trades is managed according to Black–Scholes valuation, which assumes that volatility and interest rates are constant, the reality is that all market parameters are stochastic. As well as staying neutral with respect to delta, the trader would like to ensure neutrality with respect to every market observable parameter. The derivatives of an option value with respect to market parameters are

Table 4.1. *Black–Scholes Greeks for a Vanilla Call Option*

Greek	Definition	Value in Black–Scholes
Delta, Δ	$\partial P/\partial S$	$e^{-r_{yield}T}N(d_1)$
Vega	$\partial P/\partial\sigma$	$e^{-r_{dom}T}F\dfrac{e^{-\frac{1}{2}(d_1)^2}}{\sqrt{2\pi}}\sqrt{T}$
Rho, ρ	$\partial P/\partial r_{dom}$	$Te^{-r_{dom}T}KN(d_2)$
Gamma, Γ	$\partial^2 P/\partial S^2$	$e^{-r_{dom}T}\dfrac{e^{-\frac{1}{2}(d_1)^2}}{\sqrt{2\pi}}\dfrac{1}{\sigma\sqrt{T}S}$
Theta, Θ	$\partial P/\partial t$	$-\frac{1}{2}S^2\sigma^2\Gamma + r_{dom}P - S(r_{dom}-r_{yield})\Delta$

known as the Greeks because they are denoted by Greek letters. After Δ, the next most important is *vega*,[11] which is the derivative with respect to volatility.

Table 4.1 shows the most fundamental of the Greeks. In the table, P is the premium of the option, S is the spot level, σ is the volatility and r_{dom} is the interest rate.

In practice, Greeks are usually quoted for a 1% move in the market parameter. This may be a percentage point move for volatility or interest rates, or a relative percent move for spot. So if a trader announces that he has a million dollars of vega he means that if volatility increases from say 10% to 11%, he will make one million dollars. On the other hand, if his colleague has a million dollars of delta, it means she will make that amount of money if spot increases by 1%.

4.5 Gamma, Vega and Time Decay

Gamma, Γ, is the second derivative of the premium with respect to spot, while theta, Θ, is the derivative with respect to time. Let's consider what happens if we own a portfolio that is long gamma, or in other words, which has $\Gamma > 0$. We see from Table 4.1 that this applies if we own a vanilla option. Assuming we always maintain zero delta by continuously trading in the asset, then a Taylor expansion tells us that if spot moves from S_0 to S, the value of the portfolio changes from $P(S_0)$ to

$$P(S) = P(S_0) + \tfrac{1}{2}(S - S_0)^2\Gamma + \cdots, \qquad (4.15)$$

which is always greater than $P(S_0)$ since $\Gamma > 0$.

What is wrong with the trading strategy of always staying long gamma? Every time spot moves, we make money.

The answer is that we had to pay a premium up front to own the option that makes our gamma position long. If, during the life of the trade, spot is not sufficiently volatile that we make enough money on our gamma position to cover the premium, we shall have lost money overall. Translating the derivatives in the Black–Scholes

---

[11] Alert readers will note that *vega* is not a real Greek letter.

equation (4.13) into their appropriate Greeks, and assuming we are delta-neutral, tells us

$$\Theta = -\tfrac{1}{2}S^2\sigma^2\Gamma + r_{dom}P. \tag{4.16}$$

The $r_{dom}P$ term just tells us how the time value of money (accumulating interest) applies to our portfolio. Assuming zero interest rates for a moment, we have that theta is proportional to minus gamma. If we own an option, then we will have positive gamma and negative theta. If spot moves during the day, we will make money because of the positive Γ. But if spot stays constant, we will lose money as time progresses because of the negative Θ. This is called time decay. An asset's volatility is usually concentrated into the normal trading hours in which markets are open. Therefore, if a model uses a constant volatility, a trader's portfolio appears to make money during trading hours and then lose money overnight and during the weekend. For this reason, it is common to hear a trader comment on how much money s/he expects to lose[12] overnight.

We can also see from Table 4.1 the relation

$$vega = e^{-r_{yield}}S^2\,T\Gamma, \tag{4.17}$$

which applies to all European options in Black–Scholes. Vega is proportional to Γ, and it is not possible to have vega without having gamma. (Though it is possible for very short dated options, for example a vanilla that expires tomorrow, to have gamma with little vega.)

4.6   Vega and Volatility Trading

Now we can understand our comment in Section 3.11 that buying an option is really taking a position in volatility.

The initial premium of the option depends on the market view of the volatility through the Black–Scholes formula. If the trader believes volatility will increase, or that volatility is priced too low (equivalently, vanilla options are too cheap) he or she can buy a vanilla option. An at-the-money option is usually chosen because it gives the largest vega (that is, exposure to volatility) and therefore the largest Γ. We recall from Section 3.11 that the value of an at-the-money vanilla option is roughly linear in volatility.

If the market price of volatility increases, then the trader can sell the option and make a profit. Or, if the market price of volatility does not increase, but the true volatility realised over the life of the trade is higher, then the trader will end up in profit after delta hedging the trade through its lifetime. This money is made through the trader's long Γ position because of the excessive movements of spot. On the other hand, if volatility turns out to be lower than expected, the money made from spot movements will not be enough to overcome the money lost due to the short Θ position causing time decay.

---

[12] Of course, on a short option position, one expects to make money overnight.

Of course, what starts out as an at-the-money option at the trade inception soon becomes an in- or out-of-the-money option as spot moves through the trade lifetime. If spot moves so that the option is far out-of-the-money, it will be worthless and the trader will have made his or her profit through delta hedging. On the other hand, if spot moves in-the-money so that the contract is very likely to pay out, the option has effectively become a forward contract, and is cancelled by the trader's delta hedge. Again, the profit will have been realised through the process of delta hedging.

Rather than attempt to keep track of all the contracts in the trading book, the trader will monitor the total vega of all contracts. If this is positive, it means that an increase in volatility will lead to a profit, and vice versa. An investment bank acting as a market maker in volatility is unlikely to want to take large vega positions. If the vega gets too large, traders will sell at-the-money options to reduce it. On the other hand, a hedge fund may deliberately take a position in vega to try and profit from future volatility movements.

We have given a rather idealised view of options trading. In practice, traders must contend with many difficulties. The most obvious of these are that in reality it is not possible to delta hedge continuously, and in addition, one must pay a spread for each hedging transaction. Nevertheless, this outline captures the essence of derivatives trading.

4.7 Key Points

- In a perfect Black–Scholes world having constant volatility and interest rates and zero transaction costs, it is possible to replicate the payout of a derivative contract by continuous trading in the underlying asset.
- The cost of following the replication strategy is exactly equal to the Black–Scholes price of the contract.
- The Greeks are the sensitivities of the derivative price to the various market parameters. Delta is the sensitivity to the spot rate.
- The Black–Scholes replication strategy is achieved by delta hedging, that is, buying and selling the asset to make sure that the portfolio has zero delta at all times.
- In practice, markets are not truly Black–Scholes. Volatility and interest rates may also change. Derivatives traders will hedge the associated Greeks where possible. For example, volatility risk (vega) can be hedged using at-the-money vanilla options.

4.8 Further Reading

Many derivatives traders have found Taleb (1997) invaluable for practical understanding of dynamic hedging. In practice, the implied volatility that derivatives traders use to value their books and then hedge their positions will not match the true volatility experienced. The impact of hedging with the wrong volatility is explained rather beautifully in Ahmad and Wilmott (2005).

5 Exotic Options in Black–Scholes

In this chapter we introduce some of the more common exotic option contracts, and show how to value them in Black–Scholes. The emphasis is on those contracts that can be valued analytically or semi-analytically. These formulas are all very useful for risk management. A typical portfolio of options managed by a single trader consists of thousands of trades. In order for the trader to understand his or her position, the entire book must be valued on a matrix of different spot, volatility and other market data. For this reason, pricing formulas that can be evaluated very fast are highly desirable. Even though Black–Scholes is known not to capture the full risk, many large investment banks still use Black–Scholes for parts of their risk-management process.

We will always work with the risk-neutral spot process with respect to the money market account of the natural pricing currency of the asset. That is, we will work with the spot process given by equation (3.42)

$$\frac{dS_t}{S_t} = [r_{dom}(t) - r_{yield}(t)]dt + \sigma(t)dW_t. \tag{5.1}$$

5.1 European Options

A European option is any contract whose payout depends only on the final spot level at the expiry time of the option. Using the trick outlined in Section 3.10 for replacing term structure rates and volatility with constant values, the distribution of spot at expiry is given by equation (3.43)

$$S_T(Z) = S_0 \exp\left[(r_{dom} - r_{yield} - \tfrac{1}{2}\sigma^2)T + \sigma\sqrt{T}Z\right], \quad Z = N(0,1) \tag{5.2}$$

where

$$r_{dom} = \frac{1}{T}\int_0^T r_{dom}(t)\,dt \tag{5.3}$$

$$r_{yield} = \frac{1}{T}\int_0^T r_{yield}(t)\,dt \tag{5.4}$$

$$\sigma^2 = \frac{1}{T}\int_0^T \sigma(t)^2\,dt. \tag{5.5}$$

Given any European style payout

$$P(S_T), \tag{5.6}$$

we can value the contract via

$$PV = e^{-rT} E[P(S_T)] \tag{5.7}$$

$$= e^{-rT} \int_{-\infty}^{\infty} \frac{e^{-\frac{1}{2}z^2}}{\sqrt{2\pi}} P(S_T(z))\, dz. \tag{5.8}$$

We have already seen that this integral can be evaluated in closed form for vanilla call and put options.

After vanillas, the next most popular contracts are digital options, which pay a fixed amount if spot ends up larger than strike. They come in two forms. The first form pays a fixed amount of cash, say one unit of the pricing currency. In this case the payout is

$$1_{S_T > K}. \tag{5.9}$$

The second form pays a fixed amount, say one unit, of the asset if it ends up in-the-money (that is, spot greater than strike). Then, since the asset is worth S_T at the expiry time T, the payout is

$$S_T 1_{S_T > K}. \tag{5.10}$$

It is left as a simple exercise for the reader to check that the values are respectively

$$e^{-r_{dom} T} N(d_2) \tag{5.11}$$

and

$$e^{-r_{dom} T} FN(d_1) \tag{5.12}$$

where F is the forward, and d_1, d_2 are given by equations (3.56) and (3.57).

5.2   Asian Options

The payout of an Asian option depends on the entire path taken by the spot, not just its level at expiry. The most common are average rate options which pay depending on the mean value of the spot level over some sample dates, usually every business day until expiry.

We define

$$A = \frac{1}{N} \sum_{i=1}^{N} S(t_i) \tag{5.13}$$

where t_i are the sample dates, and then the payout of a call struck at K is

$$P = (A - K)_+.$$ (5.14)

Since the average will be less volatile than the underlying spot, average rate options are cheaper than European options and can sometimes be more attractive to investors. If the trade is done to hedge a company's risk, it may well be that risk is better modelled by an average than a single cash flow in any case.

There is no closed formula for the value in Black–Scholes, but an approximation can be obtained as follows. We assume that the average can be approximated by a log-normal random variable

$$A \approx F_A e^{-\frac{1}{2}(\sigma_A)^2 T + \sigma_A \sqrt{T} X}, \quad X = N(0,1),$$ (5.15)

where F_A, the average forward, and σ_A, the average volatility, are constants to be determined.

To calculate F_A and σ_A we use *moment matching*. By taking the expectation of equation (5.15), the first moment is

$$E[A] = F_A$$ (5.16)

and on the other hand, we have

$$E[A] = E\left[\frac{1}{N}\sum_{i=1}^{N} S(t_i)\right]$$ (5.17)

$$= \frac{1}{N}\sum_{i=1}^{N} F_i$$ (5.18)

so this tells us that $F_A = \frac{1}{N}\sum_{i=1}^{N} F_i$ where F_i is the forward level to time t_i.

We can calculate σ_A by computing the second moment. First, taking the expectation of the square of equation (5.15), we obtain

$$E[A^2] = (F_A)^2 e^{(\sigma_A)^2 T}.$$ (5.19)

On the other hand, equation (5.13) gives

$$E[A^2] = \frac{1}{N^2}\sum_{i,j} E[S_i S_j]$$ (5.20)

$$= \frac{1}{N^2}\left\{2\sum_{i<j} F_i F_j e^{\sigma^2 t_i} + \sum_i (F_i)^2 e^{\sigma^2 t_i}\right\}$$ (5.21)

where, for simplicity, we have assumed constant volatility σ. To obtain equation (5.21) we used the Markov property to note that we can write

$$S_i = F_i e^{-\frac{1}{2}\sigma^2 t_i + \sigma\sqrt{t_i}X} \tag{5.22}$$

$$S_j = F_j e^{-\frac{1}{2}\sigma^2 t_j + \sigma\sqrt{t_i}X + \sigma\sqrt{t_j - t_i}Y} \tag{5.23}$$

with X and Y *independent* standard normal variables.

Together, equations (5.19) and (5.21) give us an equation for the volatility of the average, σ_A.

Now that we have modelled the average with a log-normal distribution, we can use the standard Black–Scholes formula to compute the value of the call option payout.

The averaging effect means that A will be less volatile than the underlying spot S, and therefore σ_A is smaller than σ. This makes an average rate option a cheaper alternative to a vanilla option. Quite often, a corporation's cash flows are spread over the year, and so an average rate option may also make more sense for hedging risk.

If we work with zero interest rates so that the F_i are all equal to current spot, and approximate the average with a continuous sampled average $A \approx \frac{1}{T}\int_0^T S_t dt$, then a simple calculation shows that

$$\sigma_A \sqrt{T} = \frac{1}{\sqrt{3}}\sigma\sqrt{T} + \mathcal{O}(\sigma^2 T). \tag{5.24}$$

The averaging effect reduces the volatility by a factor of approximately $\sqrt{3}$.

5.3 Continuous Barrier Options

Continuous barrier options are perhaps the most important contract at which the methods of this book are aimed. We will see that their valuation is dependent not only on the volatility smile, but also on the spot dynamic that causes the smile. It is for this reason that detailed understanding of the implied volatility smile is so important.

A continuous knock-out barrier option has an ordinary vanilla payout at expiry, but only pays if spot does not breach a given level (the barrier) at any time during the life of the trade. A knock-in barrier option only pays if the barrier is breached. If we have a portfolio of two options, one knock-in and one knock-out, this is equivalent to holding the underlying payout with no barrier, since one but not both will always pay. Therefore we have the replication formula

$$ko + ki = knockless \tag{5.25}$$

where *ko, ki* and *knockless* are respectively the prices of the option with knock-out barrier, the option with knock-in barrier, and the option without any barrier.

Barrier options can be valued analytically in Black–Scholes by using the *reflection principle* of Brownian motion together with a clever application of Girsanov's theorem. In addition to being beautiful in itself when applied to Black–Scholes, the reflection principle is important for understanding the valuation of barrier options in the presence of smile, as we will see in Section 9.5. A thoughtful presentation of the technique can be found in the excellent Joshi (2003), to which readers are referred for more detail.

5.3.1 The Reflection Principle

First, let's consider a simple model in which our spot level is a pure Brownian motion W_t. Consider a contract with a lower knock-in barrier at level l. That is, we have a vanilla payout at expiry time T, that pays as long as at some time between now and T, W_t goes below the barrier level l. If we define m_T to be the minimum value taken by the Brownian motion in the time interval $[0, T]$, then we can value our contract as long as we know the joint probability distribution

$$P(W_T > x, m_T < l) \tag{5.26}$$

of W_T (the final value of the Brownian motion) with m_T.

To compute the joint probability, it is helpful to consider the event that the Brownian motion touches the barrier at some time before T,

$$U = \{W_t = l, \text{ for some } t \in [0, T]\}. \tag{5.27}$$

Touching the barrier at some point is exactly equivalent to the minimum being at or below the barrier. Then we have, by the product rule,

$$P(W_T > x, m_T < l) = P(W_T > x, U) \tag{5.28}$$

$$= P(W_T > x | U) P(U). \tag{5.29}$$

The reflection principle will allow us to calculate $P(W_T > x|U)$. The condition on U tells us to consider only paths that touch the barrier. Let's suppose this happens at time t, and consider the path from t onwards. We are interested in a path that then moves back upwards and ends up with $W_T > x$. By the symmetry of Brownian motion, the path that is the exact reflection has identical probability so that $P(W_T > x|U) = P(W_T < 2l - x|U)$. This is illustrated in Figure 5.1. Then our joint probability becomes

$$P(W_T > x, m_T < l) = P(W_T < 2l - x | U) P(U) \tag{5.30}$$

$$= P(W_T < 2l - x, U) \tag{5.31}$$

$$= P(U | W_T < 2l - x) P(W_T < 2l - x). \tag{5.32}$$

But since $2l - x$ is the reflection of x in the barrier, it is certainly lower than the barrier and therefore the conditional probability of touching the barrier is $P(U|W_T < 2l - x) = 1$. This leaves us with a delightfully simple result

$$P(W_T > x, m_T < l) = P(W_T < 2l - x). \tag{5.33}$$

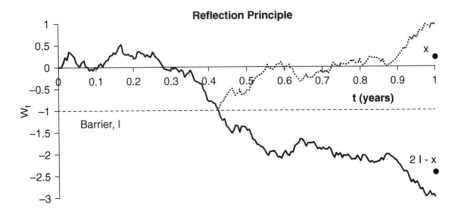

Figure 5.1   The reflection principle. Here there is a barrier with level $l = -1$. The Brownian motion that is the reflection of the original from the moment it touches the barrier has the same probability measure.

A problem depending on the full path of the Brownian motion has been reduced to a problem depending on the terminal value of a new Brownian motion constructed from the original and its reflection in the barrier. As W_T is normally distributed this gives

$$P(W_T > x, m_T < l) = N((2l - x)/\sqrt{T}) \qquad (5.34)$$

where $N()$ is the cumulative normal function. We can use this result with the ko/ki replication formula (5.25) to obtain any others we may need. For example, a knock-out barrier:

$$P(W_T > x, m_T > l) = P(W_T > x) - P(W_T > x, m_T < l) \qquad (5.35)$$
$$= N(-x/\sqrt{T}) - N((2l - x)/\sqrt{T}). \qquad (5.36)$$

Then by setting $x = l$ in equation (5.35), we obtain the probability distribution of the minimum alone

$$P(m_T > l) = N(-l/\sqrt{T}) - N(l/\sqrt{T}). \qquad (5.37)$$

This in turn allows us to obtain the formula for the joint probability that the minimum is greater than l and the Brownian motion ends up less than x

$$P(W_T < x, m_T > l) = P(m_T > l) - P(W_T > x, m_T > l). \qquad (5.38)$$

5.3.2 The Reflection Principle with Log-Normal Dynamic

Shortly, we will want to price a barrier option in Black–Scholes, and for this we need spot to follow the log-normal dynamic

$$d\log(S_t/S_0) = (\mu - \tfrac{1}{2}\sigma^2)dt + \sigma\,dW_t. \tag{5.39}$$

We will want to consider a lower barrier L on S_t, but this can be replaced by a barrier $l = \log(L/S_0)$ on $\log(S_t/S_0)$. Note that we are assuming constant drift μ and constant volatility σ.

Let's look at the simpler process

$$dB_t = v\,dt + dW_t. \tag{5.40}$$

Here we have set $B_t = \log(S_t/S_0)$, and replaced $\mu - \tfrac{1}{2}\sigma^2$ with v to simplify the notation. In addition, we have dropped the volatility σ from the dW term since it can easily be put back in the final formulas by checking the dimensions of the parameters.

One might guess that the drift term v will ruin the reflection principle. After all, we do not know at what time B will touch the barrier, and therefore we do not know how much longer the drift will apply to the reflected process, and this impacts the terminal distribution. The trick is to use Girsanov's theorem (from Section 3.7) to remove the drift from the process B_t. In addition to solving the problem at hand, this is a very useful exercise in understanding how to apply a measure change, and the meaning of a Radon–Nikodým derivative.

Looking back at Section 3.7, let's recall what Girsanov's theorem tells us. We begin with the Brownian motion W_t and then construct a Radon–Nikodým derivative

$$Z_T = \exp\left\{-\int_0^T v\,dW_t - \tfrac{1}{2}\int_0^T v^2\,dt\right\}. \tag{5.41}$$

Then we define a new probability measure by reweighting the probability of the path $\{W_t,\ t\in[0,T]\}$ by Z_T.

With respect to the new measure, the process $dB_t = dW_t + v\,dt$ is a Brownian motion (with zero drift). To change back to the original measure we use

$$Z'_T = \exp\left\{\int_0^T v\,dB_t - \tfrac{1}{2}\int_0^T v^2\,dt\right\}. \tag{5.42}$$

What is interesting for us is that, as v is a constant, Z'_T simplifies to

$$Z'_T = \exp\left\{vB_T - \tfrac{1}{2}v^2 T\right\}, \tag{5.43}$$

depending only on the terminal value of the new Brownian motion B_T.

The trick is to do all our calculations in the new measure (denoted with a prime $'$) so that B_t is a Brownian motion. However, we will use the Radon–Nikodým derivative Z'_T to ensure that the quantity we calculate is equal to the probability we require in the original measure.

We have

$$P(B_T > x, m_T < l) = E[1_{\{B_T > x, m_T < l\}}] \tag{5.44}$$

$$= E'[1_{\{B_T > x, m_T < l\}} Z'_T] \tag{5.45}$$

$$= E'[1_{\{B_T > x, m_T < l\}} e^{\nu B_T - \frac{1}{2}\nu^2 T}]. \tag{5.46}$$

Then we can use the reflection principle, and replace B_T with $2l - B_T$

$$P(B_T > x, m_T < l) = E'[1_{\{B_T < 2l - x\}} e^{\nu(2l - B_T) - \frac{1}{2}\nu^2 T}] \tag{5.47}$$

$$= e^{2l\nu} E'[1_{\{B_T < 2l - x\}} e^{-\nu B_T - \frac{1}{2}\nu^2 T}]. \tag{5.48}$$

In the $'$ measure B_T is normally distributed, and so this can be calculated directly. Alternatively, one can note that the factor $e^{-\nu B_T - \frac{1}{2}\nu^2 T}$ is the Radon–Nikodým derivative to transform to a probability measure in which B_t has drift $-\nu$. In either case, the result is

$$P(B_T > x, m_T < l) = e^{2l\nu} N((2l - x + \nu T)/\sqrt{T}), \tag{5.49}$$

and we can use this to write down the result for the Black–Scholes process (5.39)

$$P(\log(S_T/S_0) > x, m_T < l) = e^{2l(\mu - \frac{1}{2}\sigma^2)/\sigma^2} N\left(\frac{2l - x + (\mu - \frac{1}{2}\sigma^2)T}{\sigma\sqrt{T}}\right). \tag{5.50}$$

5.3.3 Valuing Barrier Options in Black–Scholes

In order to value a barrier option in Black–Scholes, we can use the elegant numeraire approach introduced in Section 3.13. Let's consider a call option with strike K and a knock-in lower barrier at level $L < K$. Then the payout is

$$P = (S_T - K)_+ 1_{m_T < L} \tag{5.51}$$

where $m_T = \min\{S_t : t \in [0, T]\}$. We split the payout into two parts

$$P = P_1 - P_2 \tag{5.52}$$

$$P_1 = S_T 1_{S_T > K, m_T < L} \tag{5.53}$$

$$P_2 = K 1_{S_T > K, m_T < L} \tag{5.54}$$

and the value of the second payout follows immediately from (5.50):

$$V_2 = e^{-r_{dom}T} E[P_2] \tag{5.55}$$

$$= e^{-r_{dom}T} K e^{2l\mu/\sigma^2 - l} N\left(\frac{2l - x + (\mu - \frac{1}{2}\sigma^2)T}{\sigma\sqrt{T}}\right) \tag{5.56}$$

where

$$l = \log(L/S_0) \tag{5.57}$$

$$x = \log(K/S_0). \tag{5.58}$$

As for the first payout, we can use the asset as numeraire and, following equation (3.88), obtain

$$V_1 = e^{-r_{dom}T} F_T E_{Asset}[P_2] \tag{5.59}$$

$$= e^{-r_{dom}T} F_T e^{2l\mu/\sigma^2 + l} N\left(\frac{2l - x + (\mu + \frac{1}{2}\sigma^2)T}{\sigma\sqrt{T}}\right). \tag{5.60}$$

Putting the results together gives value

$$V = e^{-r_{dom}T} \left(F_T e^{2l\mu/\sigma^2 + l} N(e_+) - K e^{2l\mu/\sigma^2 - l} N(e_-) \right) \tag{5.61}$$

where

$$e_\pm = \frac{2l - x + (\mu \pm \frac{1}{2}\sigma^2)T}{\sigma\sqrt{T}}. \tag{5.62}$$

So far we have considered single barrier options. That is, options with just one continuous barrier. There are a number of varieties of these since we can have all the combinations formed from call payouts, put payouts, upper barriers, lower barriers, knock-in barriers and knock-out barriers. Furthermore, the pricing formula differs depending on whether the strike is above or below the barrier level.

Formulas for the other varieties of barrier option can be obtained by following these methods, and they can be found in Haug (1997). As an example, we can write down the formula for an option with a knock-out lower barrier by using the ko/ki replication formula (5.25) together with the call option price (3.91)

$$V_{ko} = e^{-r_{dom}T} \left(F_T N(d_+) - KN(d_-) - F_T e^{2l\mu/\sigma^2+l}N(e_+) + Ke^{2l\mu/\sigma^2-l}N(e_-) \right)$$
(5.63)

where

$$d_\pm = \frac{-x + (\mu \pm \frac{1}{2}\sigma^2)T}{\sigma\sqrt{T}}.$$
(5.64)

5.3.4   Discretely Monitored Barrier Options

An alternative to the continuous barrier is a discretely monitored barrier for which the spot level is measured only at intervals (say once per day). The price is higher than a contract with continuous barrier at the same level since it is possible for the spot to breach the barrier for a short period in between monitoring instants. Broadie, Glasserman, and Kou (1997) provide a simple but high quality approximation for the price by moving the barrier away a little to account for this effect, and then pricing as a continuous barrier. The correction shifts the barrier away by a factor of $\exp(\beta\sigma\sqrt{\Delta t})$ where $\beta = 0.5826$, σ is the volatility and Δt is the time between monitoring instants.

5.4 Key Points

- Derivative contracts that depend on the underlying spot rate at a single date only are called European options. They can be valued in Black–Scholes by integrating the payout against the Black–Scholes probability density.
- Derivatives whose payout depends on the full path followed by the spot rate during the contract lifetime are called Asian options. A common example is the average rate option which has a vanilla style payout on the average of spot values sampled once per day during the trade lifetime. A good approximation to the Black–Scholes value can be obtained using the technique of moment matching in which the average is approximated by a log-normal variable.
- The most important exotic contracts are continuous barrier options. They have a standard vanilla payout at expiry, or may just pay a fixed cash amount. However, if the spot rate breaches the barrier level at any time during the contract lifetime, the trade ends worthless. They can be valued in Black–Scholes by using the reflection principle. This works by setting up a portfolio of vanilla options having value exactly zero on the barrier.

5.5 Further Reading

The closed form formula for a call option with knock-out lower barrier was provided in the seminal Merton (1973). Further works on barrier replication using the reflection principle include Rubinstein and Reiner (1991), Carr and Chou (1997a,b) and Andersen, Andreasen, and Eliezer (2002).

6 Smile Models

6.1 The Volatility Smile

Vanilla option prices are almost never quoted in a particular currency like pounds sterling or US dollars. Rather, prices are quoted in volatility terms. For this to work, both counterparties have first to agree on the values of the inputs to the Black–Scholes equation, namely the forward and interest rate. Then if the seller quotes a volatility of 10% for the given contract, the buyer will plug this into the Black–Scholes formula to get the price. Conversely, the Black–Scholes formula can easily be inverted numerically to obtain a volatility given a premium. The volatility one must plug into the Black–Scholes formula to get the true market price of a vanilla option is called the *implied volatility*.

In liquid markets, brokers will quote fairly tight two way prices[13] for vanilla options at several strikes. For example, in the foreign exchange markets you can get liquid quotes for five strikes at maturities from one day (overnight) to five or ten years. These five strikes correspond roughly to there being (risk-neutral) probabilities 10%, 25%, 50%, 75% and 90% that the option ends up in-the-money (worth something).

In Black–Scholes, there is a single constant volatility for the stochastic process followed by the spot. If the world is truly Black–Scholes, then the volatility quoted for each of these options will be identical. However, if you are able to get hold of some implied volatility quotes, and do the experiment of plotting them against strike, you will find this is not the case at all. The volatilities for strikes that are far in-the-money[14] or out-of-the-money are typically higher than the at-the-money volatility.

In foreign exchange markets, the shape of the curve is usually quite symmetrical around the at-the-money strike so that the volatility curve is smile shaped. For this reason, the plot is known as the volatility smile. In equity and interest rate markets, the volatility smile is often far from being symmetrical, but heavily skewed in one direction. In these markets, the smile is sometimes referred to simply as skew. Markets determine vanilla prices, which in turn determine implied volatilities. In addition to the strike dependence, the implied volatility for a given contract also depends on its expiry date T. When we want to emphasise this fact, we speak of the implied volatility *surface*, and write it as $\sigma_{imp}(K, T)$.

Figure 6.1 illustrates the implied volatility surface for the euro–dollar exchange rate as it was around January 2013. Smiles for vanilla options with various expiry dates are shown. The solid dots indicate the five market quotes corresponding roughly to

[13] That is, the buy and sell prices are close together.
[14] We recall that a vanilla contract that is likely to pay is termed *in-the-money* while a contract that is unlikely to pay is *out-of-the-money*. A vanilla having strike equal to the forward level is known as *at-the-money*.

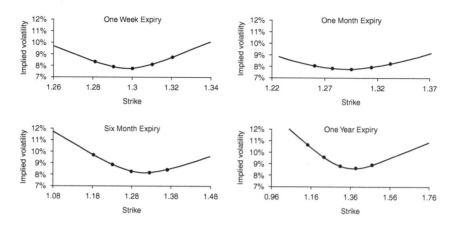

Figure 6.1 Implied volatility smiles for vanilla options on the euro–dollar exchange rate with various expiry dates.

market view probabilities of 10%, 25%, 50%, 75% and 90% of a put option ending up in-the-money.

The scale of the strike axis in Figure 6.1 is smaller for the shorter dated contracts because the spot rate has less time to move far from its initial level of 1.3. It is often useful to plot the smile against a rescaled strike to take account of this. A popular way of doing this is to plot against the quantity $\Delta_p = N(-d_1)$ where d_1 is the standard Black–Scholes variable defined in equation (3.56), but calculated using the smile volatility at the strike in question.

If the smile were flat so that we were in a Black–Scholes world, Δ_p would be the forward delta of a put option. That is, Δ_p would be the quantity of forward contracts one should buy to hedge the delta. It is equal to the standard spot delta, but with discount factor removed. We are not in Black–Scholes, and so it is only an approximation. Nevertheless, we will refer to it as the *Black–Scholes forward put delta*, or simply delta.

Delta has the nice property that it is between zero and one. Furthermore, the risk-neutral probability that spot ends up below a given strike is $N(-d_2)$ in Black–Scholes, which is approximately equal to Δ_p. Therefore Δ_p is a reasonable proxy for the market view of the probability distribution. For this reason, Δ_p is a much more reasonable scale for comparing smiles at different expiries than the raw strike is. The smiles from Figure 6.1 are replotted in delta space in Figure 6.2.

In the particular case of the volatility surface illustrated in Figures 6.1 and 6.2, the shorter dated one week and one month curves form classic symmetrical smile shapes, while the longer dated one-year curve is more skewed. These shapes are purely a function of the market quotes representing the prices that vanillas happen to be trading at. The best means of interpolating between the market quotes to provide the full implied volatility surface $\sigma_{imp}(K, T)$ is a source of constant debate among market practitioners. For our purposes, we will assume from now on that we are provided with a smooth implied volatility surface function, which we can query for an implied volatility at any particular strike and expiry we choose.

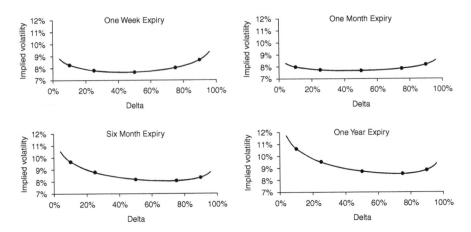

Figure 6.2 Implied volatility smiles for vanilla options on the euro–dollar exchange rate with various expiry dates. Strike axis rescaled into put option delta.

A call option and a put option at a given strike always have the same implied volatility. This is enforced by *put–call parity*. If we buy a call and sell a put, then the payout we are entitled to at expiry is

$$C - P = (S - K)_+ - (K - S)_+ \equiv (S - K), \qquad (6.1)$$

which is the payout of a forward contract struck at K. Since the forward can be replicated using the methods of Section 1.6, its value is independent of the volatility. If you write down the Black–Scholes prices of the call, the put and the forward you will see that this is indeed the case, but only if you use the same Black–Scholes volatility for the call and the put. Hence the call and put must have the same implied volatility to avoid arbitrage.

Why should there be a smile? Well the first answer is *why not?* The fact is that Black–Scholes is not the true process followed by the underlying, and therefore using the Black–Scholes formula to back out the volatility given prices seen in the market will not give a constant number.

It is interesting to think a little more deeply about what causes the smile. There are two ways of looking at this. The first is supply and demand of vanilla options. Volatility smiles for foreign exchange rate options are often fairly symmetrical, as in Figure 6.2 for euro–dollar. This is because euro investors see the market as the inverse of the way dollar investors see it. Literally, if the exchange rate is S dollars per euro to a company in the United States, what matters to a company in the Euro zone is that you can get $1/S$ euros per dollar. This explains the symmetry, but why do far out-of-the-money options and far in-the-money options have higher implied volatility than at-the-money options? Well, investors usually want to protect themselves from adverse moves in the exchange rate. So those people for whom a drop in the exchange rate would be bad buy out-of-the-money put options (which have low strikes) to protect themselves. Meanwhile, those for whom an increase in the exchange rate would hurt buy out-of-the-money call options (which have high strikes). Since there is greater demand from buyers than sellers, the prices are a little higher than you would otherwise expect, and as price increases with volatility, this means the volatilities at low and high strikes are higher.

A similar argument shows why it is that in equity markets the volatility smile is heavily skewed. Let's take the FTSE index of leading UK shares as an example. Investors in the FTSE are just that, *investors*. They buy into the index and expect its value to increase over time. However, a drop in its value would hurt and so they might buy out-of-the-money put options as protection. As there is greater demand to buy rather than sell, the implied volatility at low strikes is a little higher. Typical investors do not need to protect against increases in the index, and so there is a lack of demand for options at high strikes and the implied volatility is lower.

These arguments of supply and demand are not convincing when taken alone. Black–Scholes tells us we can replicate option payouts by delta hedging. So if the true dynamics are Black–Scholes with volatility 10% say, then no-arbitrage tells us that implied volatilities must be 10%. So if we have a volatility smile, this shows us that the true spot dynamics are not Black–Scholes. This means that if the supply and demand arguments were wholly true, the vanilla option market must have a big impact on spot movements. The mechanism by which this would happen is option traders delta hedging. But the fact is that this market is small compared to the pure spot market and so delta hedging cannot have such a large effect.

Let us look then at the second way of understanding volatility smile. This is that the true underlying dynamics are not Black–Scholes. What could they be? Well, if the underlying spot value S drops lower than one would normally expect, or goes higher than expected, this is probably because something has happened in the market and so volatility has increased. One could construct a model in which the volatility depends on spot so that large moves away from today's spot value cause the volatility to go higher. This idea is called *local volatility* and, as we shall see, leads to a volatility smile. Another idea is that volatility itself could be random. This idea is called *stochastic volatility*. If we make the volatility stochastic, we obtain a classic smile shape for the volatility surface. If we also make the stochastic process for the volatility correlated to the stochastic process for the underlying spot, we obtain a skewed smile. If we think about the FTSE index example, this makes sense. We expect volatility to be strongly anti-correlated with spot movements. When spot increases, the market is happy and volatilities are low. When spot decreases, the markets panic and volatilities increase. This can explain the skew of the FTSE volatility smile. It is also possible to construct models that are some way between local and stochastic volatility. These are known as *local stochastic volatility* models, or LSV.

Both suggestions we have outlined are good ways of understanding why the volatility smile is as it is. Investors' view of the market affects the way they trade in the spot as well as the vanilla hedges they put on. By no-arbitrage arguments, if it seems clear that volatilities should be higher at certain strikes for supply and demand reasons, then the true market dynamics must reflect this, and vice versa. One thing that can certainly be said is that volatility frowns (curves that take the shape of an inverted smile) are rare. Since the payout of a put option increases as strike increases it must be true that the value of a put option increases with strike, and the opposite is true for calls. This puts a constraint on the shape of smile curve that is possible without arbitrage.

6.2 Smile Implied Probability Distribution

We can make some progress without any knowledge of the true dynamic or model causing the implied volatility smile. Suppose we are interested in a particular expiry date T, perhaps because we have a European contract, that is, a contract only depending on the spot at T, and not on the path the spot takes between now and T. Let's say this contract has payout function $A(S_T)$ so that to price it we want to calculate

$$E[A(S_T)] = \int_0^\infty A(S)\, p_T(S)\, dS \tag{6.2}$$

where $p_T(S)$ is the probability density function for the spot level at time T under the usual risk-neutral measure.

The implied volatility smile tells us the price of vanilla call options at all strikes, and therefore we know

$$E[(S_T - K)_+] = B(F, K, T, \sigma_{imp}(K, T)) \tag{6.3}$$

where B is the Black–Scholes formula (3.55) but with discount factor $e^{-r_{dom}T}$ removed.

It is easy to check that differentiating the call option payout with respect to strike gives a step function[15] (a digital payout)

$$-\frac{\partial}{\partial K}(S - K)_+ = 1_{S>K} \equiv 1 - 1_{S<K}. \tag{6.4}$$

The expectation of a step function is equal to the cumulative probability distribution, which we denote $P(S_T < K)$, and therefore

$$P(S_T < K) = E[1_{S_T < K}] \tag{6.5}$$

$$= 1 - E[1_{S_T > K}] \tag{6.6}$$

$$= 1 + \frac{d}{dK} E[(S_T - K)_+] \tag{6.7}$$

$$= 1 + \frac{d}{dK} B(F, K, T, \sigma_{imp}(K, T)). \tag{6.8}$$

Then, we can differentiate the cumulative probability to get the probability density function

$$p_T(K) = \frac{d}{dK} P(S_T < K) \tag{6.9}$$

$$= \frac{d^2}{dK^2} B(F, K, T, \sigma_{imp}(K, T)). \tag{6.10}$$

---

[15] We use the notation $1_{S>K}$ to mean 1 if $S > K$ and 0 otherwise.

We have learned that, when we know the implied volatility smile at a given expiry, we can deduce the risk-neutral probability density function by using equation (6.10). Then we can go back to equation (6.2) and use our density function to price any European contract. Using vanilla prices in this way to determine the probability density is known as the Breeden and Litzenberger (1978) approach.

The very first contract we are likely to want to price is a digital option. We can write down the result using equation (6.8), and, remembering to put the discount factor back in,

$$e^{-r_{dom}T}E[1_{S_T>K}] = e^{-r_{dom}T}\left(-\frac{d}{dK}\right)B(F,K,T,\sigma_{imp}(K,T)) \qquad (6.11)$$

$$\equiv -e^{-r_{dom}T}\left(\frac{\partial B}{\partial K}+\frac{\partial B}{\partial \sigma_{imp}}\frac{\partial \sigma_{imp}}{\partial K}\right). \qquad (6.12)$$

The value of a digital option depends on the implied volatility at the option strike, and also the first derivative of the implied volatility at the option strike.

Digital payouts are difficult to risk manage because they are not continuous. If the spot ends up close to strike near the expiry date, one cannot know until the last moment whether the contract will pay out the full amount or nothing. Traders tackle this by using the fact that the digital payout can be obtained by differentiating a vanilla payout. One can approximate the differentiation in equation (6.4) using

$$1_{S>K} \approx \frac{(S-K-\epsilon)_+ - (S-K)_+}{\epsilon} \qquad (6.13)$$

with ϵ a small parameter, and risk manage the approximate payout instead of the true digital. The approximate payout is called a *call spread*, and has the impact of replacing the discontinuity with a continuous (albeit fairly steep) wedge, making risk management easier. By choosing the sign of ϵ, the trader can ensure that the call spread payout is greater than or less than the true digital payout. The additional premium required to risk manage the 'wrong' payout is passed on to the client, and represents the hedging cost of managing the discontinuity.

Next, let's suppose a counterparty has requested a particular payout $A(S_T)$, and this time we will assume that $A(S_T)$ is a smooth function. It is nice to know that we can obtain a fair price for the contract using equation (6.2), but how will we hedge the position once we do the trade?

The answer is that it is possible to replicate the payout from vanilla options. To see this, think of expanding the payout, with some infinitesimal weight $u(K)dK$ giving the amount of investment in the call option with strike K

$$A(S) = a + bS + \int_0^\infty (S-K)_+ u(K)\,dK. \qquad (6.14)$$

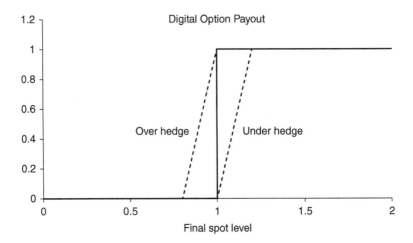

Figure 6.3   Approximating a digital payout with a call spread.

Differentiating a call option payout twice with respect to K gives a Dirac delta function, and so we have

$$A''(S) = \int_0^\infty \delta(S - K)u(K)\, dK \tag{6.15}$$

$$= u(S). \tag{6.16}$$

Then we choose $u(K) = A''(K)$, and pick the constants a and b so that $A(0)$ and $A'(0)$ are correct, giving the expansion

$$A(S) = A(0) + A'(0)S + \int_0^\infty (S - K)_+ A''(K)\, dK. \tag{6.17}$$

This tells us that we can perfectly replicate the European payout with an infinite portfolio of vanillas, plus a forward contract and a cash payment. It is also possible to use put payouts. Indeed, often it is necessary to use put payouts for part of the strike range and calls for the other part in order to keep the integral finite. In that case, the formula becomes

$$A(S) = A(\alpha) + A'(\alpha)(S - \alpha) + \int_\alpha^\infty (S - K)_+ A''(K)\, dK + \int_0^\alpha (K - S)_+ A''(K)\, dK, \tag{6.18}$$

where α is any conveniently chosen constant.

The replication formula (6.18) does not work directly for the digital option that we studied a moment ago, because with a payout $A(K) = (S - K)_+$, the second derivative $A''(K)$ does not exist. However, if we were to approximate the digital payout with a smooth function, we would end up with a replication formula approximating the call spread (6.13).[16]

Needless to say, it is not possible to go out and buy a continuum of vanilla options. In reality a trader would approximate the integral with a finite set of call and put options. We will discuss a classic case of this approach, the variance swap, in Section 10.2.3.

6.3 The Forward Kolmogorov Equation

If one writes down any stochastic differential equation for a spot process, it ought to be possible to work out the probability distribution for spot at a given time in the future. In this section we will show that the probability density function (PDF) is the solution of a PDE, and how to obtain that PDE. We work with a concrete example for the SDE, namely

$$\frac{dS}{S} = \mu dt + \sigma(S, t) dW. \tag{6.19}$$

This is a local volatility mode. The volatility σ depends on spot S and time t.

In order to find an equation for the PDF, we will take an arbitrary function $B(S)$ of S and examine its expectation at a given time t. It is convenient to assume B is a bump function, namely a smooth function that is zero outside some compact region.

If we apply Ito's lemma to B we obtain

$$dB = \frac{\partial B}{\partial S} dS + \frac{1}{2} \frac{\partial^2 B}{\partial S^2} dS^2 \tag{6.20}$$

$$= \frac{\partial B}{\partial S} S(\mu dt + \sigma(S, t) dW) + \frac{1}{2} \frac{\partial^2 B}{\partial S^2} S^2 \sigma(S, t)^2 dt \tag{6.21}$$

where we have used $(dt)^2 = 0$ and $(dW)^2 = dt$. Recall that dW is a random variable that is independent of the filtration $\mathcal{F}_t$, that is, independent of all information that can be known at time t. So in particular, dW is independent of $\frac{\partial B}{\partial S}(S)\sigma(S, t)$. In addition, since dW is normally distributed, we have $E[dW] = 0$, and by independence, $E[\frac{\partial B}{\partial S}(S)\sigma(S, t) dW] = 0$. Then taking the expectation of both sides of (6.21) we obtain

$$E[dB] = E\left[\frac{\partial B}{\partial S} S\mu dt + \frac{1}{2} \frac{\partial^2 B}{\partial S^2} S^2 \sigma(S, t)^2 dt\right] \tag{6.22}$$

which can be rewritten

$$\frac{d}{dt} E[B] = E\left[\frac{\partial B}{\partial S} S\mu + \frac{1}{2} \frac{\partial^2 B}{\partial S^2} S^2 \sigma(S, t)^2\right]. \tag{6.23}$$

---

[16] Readers who are happy with the meaning of the derivative of a delta function may go ahead and use formula (6.18) directly even for non-continuous payouts like the digital.

Now let's introduce the probability density that at time t spot takes the value s, and call this density $p(s, t)$. Then we can write the expectations in the previous equation as integrals over the density, and obtain

$$\frac{d}{dt}\int p(s, t)B(s)\,ds = \int p(s, t)\left(\frac{\partial B}{\partial s}s\mu + \frac{1}{2}\frac{\partial^2 B}{\partial s^2}s^2\sigma(s, t)^2\right)ds. \qquad (6.24)$$

On the left hand side we can take the total time derivative inside the integral by making it a partial derivative, and on the right hand side we can integrate by parts once for the first term and twice for the second. Since B is a bump function, boundary terms vanish and we obtain

$$\int B(s)\frac{\partial}{\partial t}p(s, t)\,ds = \int B(s)\left(-\frac{\partial}{\partial s}[s\mu p(s, t)] + \frac{1}{2}\frac{\partial^2}{\partial s^2}[s^2\sigma(s, t)^2 p(s, t)]\right)ds. \qquad (6.25)$$

Finally, since B is an arbitrary bump function, the following partial differential equation must be true

$$\frac{\partial}{\partial t}p(s, t) = -\frac{\partial}{\partial s}[s\mu p(s, t)] + \frac{1}{2}\frac{\partial^2}{\partial s^2}[s^2\sigma(s, t)^2 p(s, t)] \qquad (6.26)$$

and this is known as the *forward Kolmogorov* or *Fokker–Planck* equation.

Why is this a *forward* equation? Well the boundary condition is at time $t = 0$

$$p(s, 0) = \delta(s - S_0) \qquad (6.27)$$

where S_0 is the initial spot value. So to find the PDF at a future time t, one needs to solve this PDE forwards in time from $t = 0$. This is in contrast to the Black–Scholes pricing equation, which is a backwards PDE. When solving the Black–Scholes equation, we start at the expiry time of the option and the boundary condition is the payout of the option at that time. Then we solve backwards in time to find the value now at $t = 0$.

6.4 Local Volatility

As we have already hinted, one possible explanation for the volatility smile is that volatility is not constant, but depends on spot level S_t and time t. In the previous section, we derived the forward Kolmogorov equation for the probability density of spot in just such a model. Since we can look in the vanilla market and find prices or equivalently implied volatilities for vanilla options at any strike and expiry, a pressing question presents itself. Can we find the local volatility $\sigma_{local}(S_t, t)$ such that if spot follows the process

$$\frac{dS}{S} = \mu dt + \sigma_{local}(S_t, t)dW \qquad (6.28)$$

then the fair values of vanilla options exactly match the market?

The answer is emphatically yes, and gives us a powerful tool to price exotic option contracts in a model that is consistent with the vanilla market. For example, if we can find the function $\sigma_{local}(S_t, t)$ then we can solve a PDE derived from (6.28) to get an on-smile price for continuous barrier options. Whether or not we believe this model for the spot dynamics, what we really care about is that we use a model in which vanilla options are correctly repriced. Why? Well, let's take a simple example. Suppose we sell an option that has a vanilla payout and a continuous knock-out barrier. We do not have a smile model in place, so we price it in Black–Scholes and feel happy enough because we feel that as we hedge through the life of the trade, sometimes we will win and sometimes lose a bit, but on average over a number of contracts we will break even. However, the client we sell to notices that we sold at the Black–Scholes price, and immediately buys the same vanilla payout, but this time with a knock-in barrier. At expiry, one and only one of the contracts will have survived. If the barrier is hit, it will be the knock-in, and if not it will be the knock-out option. So the client is guaranteed the vanilla payout. We sold both at the Black–Scholes price, which is a little lower than a smile consistent price. The client immediately sold the corresponding vanilla option in the open market and received more than the cost of the two barrier options. So the client locks in immediate profit and has set up an arbitrage. If the vanilla option were sold back to us, we would have simply paid the client money for a set of contracts that amount to zero. Needless to say, this is a very bad situation. Suppose the client trades through an electronic platform. We could lose millions before anyone realises what is happening. In reality, no trader would be caught out by such a simple ruse. But it is not uncommon for a single deal to consist of a strip of hundreds of contracts, and it is crucial to price contracts in a way that avoids arbitrage, theoretical or otherwise.

Let us proceed then with calculating the local volatility $\sigma_{local}(S_t, t)$. The trick is to note that we can extract the risk-neutral probability density from the value of call options by differentiating with respect to strike. Let's work in the risk-neutral probability measure that has the natural pricing currency as numeraire. Then the value of the call option is

$$C(K, T) = e^{-r_{dom} T} E[(S_T - K)_+] \tag{6.29}$$

where K is the strike, r_{dom} the interest rate, and T the time to expiry. Differentiating the expectation twice with respect to K gives

$$\frac{\partial^2}{\partial K^2} E[(S_T - K)_+] = E[\delta(S_T - K)] \equiv p(K, T) \tag{6.30}$$

where $p(K, T)$ is the probability density that $S_T = K$ at time T. The idea is to rewrite the probability density as

$$p(K, T) = e^{r_{dom} T} \frac{\partial^2}{\partial K^2} C(K, T) \tag{6.31}$$

and then substitute into the forward Kolmogorov equation (6.26), giving

$$\left(r_{dom}+\frac{\partial}{\partial T}\right)\frac{\partial^2}{\partial K^2}C(K,T)=-\frac{\partial}{\partial K}\left(K\mu\frac{\partial^2}{\partial K^2}C(K,T)\right)$$
$$+\frac{1}{2}\frac{\partial^2}{\partial K^2}\left(K^2\sigma(K,T)^2\frac{\partial^2}{\partial K^2}C(K,T)\right). \quad (6.32)$$

We can rewrite the first term on the right hand side so that every term is a second derivative with respect to K,

$$\left(r_{dom}+\frac{\partial}{\partial T}\right)\frac{\partial^2}{\partial K^2}C(K,T)=-\frac{\partial^2}{\partial K^2}\left(K\mu\frac{\partial}{\partial K}C(K,T)-\mu C(K,T)\right)$$
$$+\frac{1}{2}\frac{\partial^2}{\partial K^2}\left(K^2\sigma(K,T)^2\frac{\partial^2}{\partial K^2}C(K,T)\right), \quad (6.33)$$

and then integrate twice

$$\left(r_{dom}+\frac{\partial}{\partial T}\right)C(K,T)=-K\mu\frac{\partial}{\partial K}C(K,T)+\mu C(K,T)+\frac{1}{2}K^2\sigma(K,T)^2\frac{\partial^2}{\partial K^2}C(K,T).$$
$$(6.34)$$

Finally then, we can read off what the local volatility must be by rearranging this equation,

$$\frac{1}{2}\sigma_{local}(K,T)^2=\frac{\frac{\partial}{\partial T}C(K,T)+K\mu\frac{\partial}{\partial K}C(K,T)+(r_{dom}-\mu)C(K,T)}{K^2\frac{\partial^2}{\partial K^2}C(K,T)}, \quad (6.35)$$

where, as a reminder, the drift is $\mu=r_{dom}-r_{yield}$ with r_{dom} the interest rate and r_{yield} the dividend yield of the stock.

So far, we have discovered that if we know the market prices of vanilla options, we can calculate the local volatility function using the formula (6.35). We have shown that if the underlying spot follows process

$$\frac{dS}{S}=\mu dt+\sigma_{local}(S_t,t)dW \quad (6.36)$$

then vanilla options are correctly repriced at all expiries and strikes. Let us complete the local volatility formulation by deriving the PDE to use for pricing. The derivation is identical to that of the Black–Scholes equation, but there is absolutely no harm in reminding ourselves by running through it again.

Let's suppose the value of a derivative contract at time t and given spot level S is $C(S,t)$. We use the bond which has value $B=e^{r_{dom}t}$ as numeraire, and study the quotient C/B, which must be Martingale to avoid arbitrage. Applying Ito's lemma gives

$$d(C/B) = dC/B - C/B^2 dB \tag{6.37}$$

$$= \frac{1}{B}\left(\frac{\partial C}{\partial t}dt + \frac{\partial C}{\partial S}dS + \frac{1}{2}\frac{\partial^2 C}{\partial S^2}(dS)^2 - Cr_{dom}dt\right) \tag{6.38}$$

$$= \frac{1}{B}\left(\frac{\partial C}{\partial t} + \frac{\partial C}{\partial S}S\mu + \frac{1}{2}\frac{\partial^2 C}{\partial S^2}S^2\sigma_{local}^2 - Cr_{dom}\right)dt \tag{6.39}$$

$$+ \frac{1}{B}\left(\frac{\partial C}{\partial S}S\sigma_{local}dW\right)$$

and for C/B to be Martingale, the drift must vanish, leading to the PDE

$$\frac{\partial C}{\partial t} + \frac{\partial C}{\partial S}S\mu + \frac{1}{2}\frac{\partial^2 C}{\partial S^2}S^2\sigma_{local}(S_t, t)^2 - Cr_{dom} = 0. \tag{6.40}$$

To summarise then, we have a formula that tells us how to calculate the local volatility function as long as we know the market value of vanilla options at all strikes and maturities, and we have a PDE that we can solve to price exotic contracts in the local volatility model. This model is heavily used in investment banks to price exotic options like barrier options because it eliminates any possibility of arbitrage against vanilla contracts. It is often known as the Dupire local volatility model.

6.5 Key Points

- Implied volatility is the volatility one must plug into the Black–Scholes formula to get the true market price of a vanilla option.
- In Black–Scholes, volatility should be constant. However, if one plots the implied volatility against the vanilla option strike, one sees a smile shaped curve. This is called the implied volatility smile.
- It is possible to determine the risk-neutral probability distribution of spot at a given expiry date from the market volatility smile. As a result, European contract valuation does not depend on the particular model causing the smile. However, this is not so for contracts that depend on the spot rate at more than one date.
- On the other hand, given a model defined by SDEs, it is possible to determine the model implied probability distribution by solving the forward Kolmogorov PDE forwards in time from the valuation date.
- One possible explanation for the implied volatility smile is that instantaneous volatility is not constant but depends on the spot level and time. This approach is called local volatility, and the local volatility function can be computed from market vanilla prices using Dupire's formula.

6.6 Further Reading

The smile implied probability distribution is due to Breeden and Litzenberger (1978). The replication formula for European payouts from calls and puts can be found in Carr and Madan (1998) where it is applied to the variance swap (which we will encounter in Chapter 10).

Local volatility as a means of reproducing the implied volatility smile was developed independently by Dupire (1994) and Derman and Kani (1994a,b) in the context of solving derivative pricing problems on a tree. At the same time, related work was presented in Rubinstein (1994). It was in Dupire (1994) that the celebrated local volatility formula (6.35) was first written down.

7   Stochastic Volatility

Another possible reason for the implied volatility smile is that instantaneous volatility is itself stochastic. As a model of the real world, this idea is attractive. We could measure the volatility of a stock or index like the FTSE over, say, a one month window and plot it over recent years. Alternatively, we could look at the one month volatility implied from at-the-money options over the last year. We would see that in both cases the volatility increases in times of political turmoil or uncertainty. As we cannot predict such events, it seems reasonable to model volatility itself as a stochastic process.

There are many possible choices of stochastic volatility model. In practice, irrespective of the model choice, making volatility stochastic introduces a smile with the right qualitative (smile) shape. Increasing the parameter that controls volatility of volatility (vol-of-vol) will increase the convexity of the smile. This can be understood by considering calls or puts that are so far out-of-the-money (as measured with respect to today's volatility) that they are worth almost nothing. If volatility can change randomly, then an increase in volatility could allow for larger spot moves so that these far strikes do become worth something. So adding vol-of-vol increases the implied volatility at far strikes. On the other hand, an at-the-money option is no more likely to end up worth something if we increase vol-of-vol. It still has roughly a 50% chance of ending in-the-money. The value of an at-the-money option depends on the expected volatility between now and expiry, and so increasing vol-of-vol has little effect on the implied volatility at the at-the-money strike.

One can add skew to the implied volatility smile by making the stochastic processes for the spot and volatility correlated. Why? Well, if when spot increases you also expect vol to increase, then you definitely want to sell out-of-the-money calls at a higher implied vol than out-of-the-money puts. If spot moves so that the calls expire in-the-money, the actual variance realised over the life time is likely to be higher and so the delta hedging costs greater.

A third property one should always consider in a stochastic volatility model is mean reversion. The fact is that volatility tends to have a typical background level. It may increase for a while or decrease for a while, but it is never going to go very high and stay high, nor collapse to zero. Rather, typically it will eventually relax to its background level. For example, foreign exchange rate volatilities are typically around 10%. During the delirious times in early 2007, pre-credit crunch, the Australian dollar to US dollar 3 month expiry implied volatility was as low as 7%. Following the Lehman bankruptcy, it peaked at nearly 30%. By early 2012, it had returned to around the 10% level.

Typically, the use of a stochastic volatility model proceeds as follows. First write down the model. Then calibrate the model by choosing its parameters so that vanilla options at a given maturity are correctly repriced at as many strikes as possible. Since we can control the smile convexity with the vol-of-vol, the skew with correlation, and the overall level with the starting volatility or mean reversion level, we might expect to calibrate to vanilla options at three strikes. We could make our parameters time dependent, and then attempt to calibrate the model to vanillas at more than one maturity. Finally, to value an exotic contract, solve the PDE implied by the model.

When deciding on a stochastic volatility model to use, an important consideration is ease of calibration. We need a model in which vanillas can be valued as fast as possible so that we can solve for the best model parameters. After calibration, one should consider realism. Specifically one should ask, am I ignoring any aspect of the dynamic to which I believe the contracts I wish to value are sensitive? Finally, once the model is calibrated and captures the risk, one should consider speed and stability of valuation.

7.1 Properties of Stochastic Volatility Models

Let's consider a fairly general stochastic volatility model, except that we will assume the spot and the volatility processes are uncorrelated. It has SDEs of the form

$$\frac{dS}{S} = \mu\,dt + \sigma\,dW_1 \tag{7.1}$$

$$d\sigma = f(\sigma, t)dt + g(\sigma, t)dW_2 \tag{7.2}$$

$$dW_1\,dW_2 = 0. \tag{7.3}$$

As we will see in sections that follow, the function f is often used to provide mean reversion to the volatility process, while g provides the form of the vol-of-vol.

We will value a vanilla option with expiry T, and define the total realised volatility $\sigma_{realised}$ (which is a random variable) via

$$\sigma_{realised} = \sqrt{\frac{1}{T}\int_0^T \sigma_t^2\,dt}. \tag{7.4}$$

Working in the risk-neutral measure as usual, the value of a call option is

$$P = e^{-r_{dom}T}E[(S_T - K)_+] \tag{7.5}$$

which we can rewrite by conditioning on the volatility path $\{\sigma_t\}$

$$P = e^{-r_{dom}T}E[E[(S_T - K)_+ | \{\sigma_t\}]], \tag{7.6}$$

using the standard nesting property of conditional expectations. Looking back to equation (3.61) in Section 3.10, we recall that when volatility is not stochastic but does have term structure, the Black–Scholes price of a vanilla option depends only on the total realised volatility. Since the spot and volatility processes are uncorrelated, and we have conditioned on the instantaneous volatility path, we are in the Black–Scholes world for the purpose of the inner expectation. Then the price becomes simply

$$P = E[P_{BS}(K, \sigma_{realised})] \qquad (7.7)$$

where P_{BS} is the Black–Scholes formula.

If the total realised volatility is constant, then we are in the Black–Scholes world and there is no smile. If we give some variance to the total realised volatility by using a stochastic volatility model, then we will get a convex smile. Adding more variance gives more convexity. Although we have considered a model without spot–volatility correlation, the same general behaviour applies when we include it, but now the smile will be skewed.

If we believe that stochastic volatility alone is the true cause of the implied volatility smile, then we might hope that the parameters that form the stochastic volatility model are roughly constant in time. Let's then remove the time dependence from the functions f and g defining our model and consider the implications. We will assume that the volatility process is mean reverting to some constant level.

Let us first consider contracts with short maturity. Taking the short maturity limit of the realised volatility,

$$\lim_{T \to 0} \sigma_{realised} = \sigma_0, \qquad (7.8)$$

gives us simply the initial volatility, which is a constant. Therefore, the smile is flat at short maturities. This can be understood as the instantaneous volatility not having time to move much.

Interestingly, we also see a flattening of the smile at long expiries. Assuming the volatility process is mean reverting, the instantaneous volatility wobbles around the mean reversion level. The total realised volatility (7.4) can be thought of as an average formed from many samples of the instantaneous volatility. If two samples of the instantaneous volatility are taken with enough time in between, they will appear independent of one another. When the expiry T increases, it is as if we have more independent samples contributing to the average and therefore we are likely to get a result closer to the true mean reversion level. Mathematically, the variance of the total realised volatility goes to zero as $T \to \infty$, and the smile flattens.

7.2 The Heston Model

7.2.1 What Makes the Heston Model Special

The Heston (1993) model is popular because vanilla options can be valued with a single numerical integration. This allows fast calibration to the implied volatility smile by repeatedly adjusting the model parameters and valuing vanilla options until they match the market. The model does have drawbacks when it comes to numerical simulation, and we will outline these in Section 7.2.3.

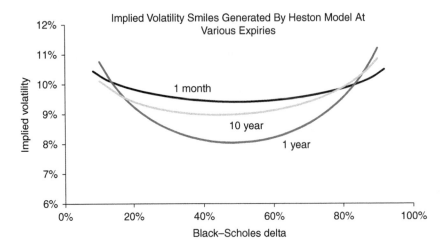

Figure 7.1   Implied volatility smiles generated by the Heston model at various expiries. The strike on the *x*-axis is expressed as put option delta.

First, let us write down the SDEs defining the model,

$$\frac{dS}{S} = \mu dt + \sqrt{v}dW_1 \tag{7.9}$$

$$dv = -\lambda(v - \bar{v})dt + \eta\sqrt{v}dW_2 \tag{7.10}$$

$$dW_1\, dW_2 = \rho\, dt. \tag{7.11}$$

Here we have a standard stochastic process for the spot rate S, driven by Brownian motion W_1. But the volatility $\sigma = \sqrt{v}$ is itself stochastic, driven by a second Brownian motion W_2. As usual, we work in a risk-neutral measure for pricing, and therefore the drift is $\mu = r_{dom} - r_{yield}$.

The model is initially appealing. It has stochastic volatility, with *volatility of variance* given by the parameter η. Increasing η increases the convexity of the smile generated by the model. There is mean reversion, with reversion rate λ and reversion level $\bar{v}$. If the stochastic variance v moves far from the reversion level $\bar{v}$, the mean reversion term $-\lambda(v - \bar{v})dt$ will tend to draw it back. Finally, it has correlation, ρ, between the spot and volatility processes that can be used to generate a skewed volatility smile.

Figure 7.1 shows the implied volatility smiles generated by the Heston model at three expiry dates. The Heston parameters used are mean reversion $\lambda = 1.15$, volatility of variance $\eta = 0.4$ and correlation $\rho = 0$. Both initial variance v_0 and the mean reversion level $\bar{v}$ are set to 0.01, corresponding to $\sqrt{0.01} \equiv 10\%$ in volatility terms. The range of strikes that is relevant at the various expiry dates varies considerably. At short expiries, spot has had little time to move and so a much smaller range of strikes is relevant than at long expiries. For this reason, we use the rescaling of strike space into delta space outlined in Section 6.1 for the purpose of the plot. Figure 7.1 shows the behaviour outlined in Section 7.1 very clearly. The smile generated for contracts with one-year expiry is much more convex than the short 0.1 year and long dated 10 year expiries.

The stochastic volatility process (7.10) is known as the Cox, Ingersoll, and Ross (1985) (CIR) model after its authors, who wrote it down initially for a model of stochastic interest rates. A moment's reflection provokes the question of why this particular form was chosen. Why, for example, does the volatility of variance v appear under a square root in the diffusion term of (7.10) while there is no square root in the mean reversion term? The answer is that this choice makes the Heston model easy to solve for valuing a number of contracts, including vanilla options.

Our aim then is to solve the Heston model (7.9) to compute vanilla prices as a function of the Heston parameters. We follow the original paper (Heston 1993), with some aids of exposition proposed in Gatheral (2006). We will first find the PDE for pricing in the Heston model, and then solve it to find the price of vanilla options. To obtain the pricing PDE, we follow the same argument that we used in Section 3.12 to obtain the Black–Scholes pricing PDE, and in Section 6.4 to obtain the local volatility PDE. Here though we need to deal with a model that has two rather than just one stochastic factor. Nevertheless, the derivation remains straightforward.

We suppose the value of a derivative contract at time t and given spot level S_t and instantaneous variance v_t is $V(S_t, v_t, t)$. As we have a fairly complex two-dimensional process to solve, we will take every opportunity to choose notation to simplify our work. To begin with, we are interested in valuing a call option with fixed expiry time $t = T$. Therefore, instead of using the rolling money market account for the numeraire as in previous sections, we choose the zero coupon bond expiring at T, having value $B_t = \exp(-r_{dom}(T-t))$. Then, as usual, our pricing equation will follow by ensuring the quantity $C(S_t, v_t, t) = V(S_t, v_t, t)/B_t$ is a Martingale. From now, we will work directly with C, which is of course the undiscounted price. We can always get back to the true value V of the option by multiplying by the discount factor given by B_t.

The step we have just taken will have the effect of removing the interest rate term from the PDE. If we work with the forward from t to T, given by

$$F_{t,T} = S_t e^{\mu(T-t)} \tag{7.12}$$

then we can get rid of the drift term μ too. A simple application of Ito's lemma shows that (7.9) becomes

$$\frac{dF}{F} = \sqrt{v} dW_1. \tag{7.13}$$

Finally, as $F_{t,T}$ is likely to behave much more like a log-normal than a normal variable, we'll work with

$$x_t = \log(F_{t,T}/K). \tag{7.14}$$

We have introduced a scaling constant K into this definition, and later it will be convenient to set this equal to the vanilla option strike.

After one more application of Ito's lemma to move from F to x, our original SDEs (7.9)–(7.11) become

$$dx = -\tfrac{1}{2}v\,dt + \sqrt{v}\,dW_1 \tag{7.15}$$

$$dv = -\lambda(v - \bar{v})dt + \eta\sqrt{v}\,dW_2 \tag{7.16}$$

$$dW_1\,dW_2 = \rho\,dt. \tag{7.17}$$

For the undiscounted price C to be Martingale, its drift must vanish. As usual, we apply Ito's lemma to C

$$dC = C_t\,dt + C_x\,dx + C_v\,dv + \tfrac{1}{2}\left(C_{xx}(dx)^2 + 2C_{xv}\,dx\,dv + C_{vv}(dv)^2\right) \tag{7.18}$$

$$= C_t\,dt + C_x(-\tfrac{1}{2}v\,dt + \sqrt{v}\,dW_1) + C_v(-\lambda(v-\bar{v})dt + \eta\sqrt{v}\,dW_2) \tag{7.19}$$

$$+ \tfrac{1}{2}\left(C_{xx}v\,dt + 2C_{xv}\eta v\rho\,dt + C_{vv}\eta^2 v\,dt\right).$$

Here, subscripts t, x and v represent partial differentiation with respect to those variables.

We gather up the coefficients of dt to obtain the drift, and set it to zero giving the pricing PDE

$$C_t - \tfrac{1}{2}vC_x - \lambda(v-\bar{v})C_v + \tfrac{1}{2}\left(C_{xx}v + 2C_{xv}\eta v\rho + C_{vv}\eta^2 v\right) = 0. \tag{7.20}$$

Remember that the boundary condition for this PDE is that at the expiry time $t = T$, the value must be equal to the option payout. Then we are going to solve the equation backwards in time from T to find the price at an earlier time t. For this reason it is helpful to change variables to work with τ given by

$$\tau = (T - t), \tag{7.21}$$

which is zero at the expiry. Then finally the PDE we will solve is

$$-C_\tau - \tfrac{1}{2}vC_x - \lambda(v-\bar{v})C_v + \tfrac{1}{2}C_{xx}v + C_{xv}\eta v\rho + \tfrac{1}{2}C_{vv}\eta^2 v = 0. \tag{7.22}$$

Looking at our pricing PDE (7.22), we can see what is so special about the process that allowed Heston to solve it: the coefficients are linear in the variance v. This was achieved at the outset in the SDEs (7.9)–(7.11) by ensuring that all dt terms are linear in v and all dW terms have factor $\sqrt{v}$ (so that when they are squared they give further dt terms linear in v).

7.2.2 Solving for Vanilla Prices

Heston's trick is to convert the pricing PDE into Fourier space and then make use of its linear form to guess the solution for vanilla prices. Readers who do not wish to get involved in the following technicalities may like to skip straight to the overall form of the solution in equation (7.47).

We aim to price a call option payout. Just as in Section 3.13, we can split it into two digital options

$$(S-K)_+ = S1_{S>K} - K1_{S>K}, \qquad (7.23)$$

the first paying an amount of the asset, and the second an amount of cash if spot ends up in-the-money. The cash digital $1_{S>K}$ has undiscounted value equal to the risk-neutral probability (with respect to the zero coupon bond numeraire). Similarly, the asset digital $S1_{S>K}$ has value equal to the risk-neutral probability obtained if one uses the asset itself as numeraire. Then it is clear that the undiscounted value of the call option takes the form

$$C(t,x,v) = FP_1(t,x,v) - KP_0(t,x,v), \quad x = \log(F/K) \qquad (7.24)$$
$$= Ke^x P_1(t,x,v) - KP_0(t,x,v) \qquad (7.25)$$

where P_1 and P_0 behave like probabilities. In particular, both are smooth functions increasing from 0 to 1 as x increases from $-\infty$ to ∞.

The values of the two digital contracts must also satisfy the pricing PDE. Therefore substituting $e^x P_1$ and P_0 into (7.22), we obtain

$$-P_{j,\tau} - (\tfrac{1}{2}-j)vP_{j,x} - [\lambda(v-\bar{v}) - j\rho\eta v]P_{j,v}$$
$$+\tfrac{1}{2}P_{j,xx}v + P_{j,xv}\eta v\rho + \tfrac{1}{2}P_{j,vv}\eta^2 v = 0. \qquad (7.26)$$

The boundary conditions at expiry $\tau = 0$ are the digital payout

$$P_j(0,x,v) = 1_{x>0}. \qquad (7.27)$$

We use a standard trick to solve (7.26) by moving to Fourier space. The Fourier transform is

$$\tilde{P}_j(\tau,w,v) = \int_{-\infty}^{\infty} e^{-iwx} P_j(\tau,x,v)\,dx. \qquad (7.28)$$

As the P_j do not vanish at infinity, care is needed in interpreting this integral. Indeed, the boundary condition at $\tau = 0$ gives us

$$\tilde{P}_j(0,w,v) = \int_{-\infty}^{\infty} e^{-iwx} 1_{x>0}\,dx \qquad (7.29)$$

$$= \tfrac{1}{2}\delta(w) + \frac{1}{iw} \qquad (7.30)$$

where $\delta(w)$ is the Dirac delta function, so that the Fourier transform is a distribution rather than a smooth function. This is no problem. All that matters is we construct a smooth solution for the P_j in the end.

By taking the Fourier transform, we remove the x-derivatives, replacing them with multiplications by iw. This removes one dimension from the PDE,

$$-\tilde{P}_{j,\tau} - iw\left(\tfrac{1}{2} - j\right)v\tilde{P}_j - [\lambda(v - \bar{v}) - j\rho\eta v]\tilde{P}_{j,v} - w^2\tfrac{1}{2}\tilde{P}_j v$$
$$+ iw\tilde{P}_{j,v}\eta v\rho + \tfrac{1}{2}\tilde{P}_{j,vv}\eta^2 v = 0. \tag{7.31}$$

Of course, we will pay for this later when we need to invert the Fourier transform to obtain the final result.

For now, we don't care about the factors of w appearing in (7.31), so we define

$$a = -w^2/2 - iw/2 + ijw \tag{7.32}$$
$$b = \lambda - \rho\eta j - \rho\eta iw \tag{7.33}$$
$$c = \eta^2/2, \tag{7.34}$$

and the PDE simplifies to

$$-\tilde{P}_{j,\tau} + v(a\tilde{P}_j - b\tilde{P}_{j,v} + c\tilde{P}_{j,vv}) + \lambda\bar{v}\tilde{P}_{j,v} = 0. \tag{7.35}$$

Now finally we can take advantage of the linear coefficients by trying a solution of the form

$$\tilde{P}_j = \exp\left[C(w,\tau)\bar{v} + D(w,\tau)v\right]\tilde{P}_j(0, w). \tag{7.36}$$

Here $\tilde{P}_j(0, w) \equiv \tilde{P}_j(0, w, v)$ is the boundary value calculated in equation (7.30), which fortunately is independent of v (since the option payout depends only on spot and not on instantaneous variance).

Substituting the proposed solution into (7.35) gives us ordinary differential equations for C and D

$$C_\tau = \lambda D \tag{7.37}$$
$$D_\tau = a - bD + cD^2 \tag{7.38}$$

with conditions $C(0, w) = D(0, w) = 0$. To solve (7.38), we can rewrite it in partial fractions which can be integrated directly

$$\left(\frac{1}{D - \alpha_-} - \frac{1}{D - \alpha_+}\right)dD = c(\alpha_+ - \alpha_-)d\tau \tag{7.39}$$

where

$$\alpha_{\pm} = \frac{b \pm \sqrt{b^2 - 4ac}}{2c}. \qquad (7.40)$$

Once D is obtained, C also follows by direct integration, and the result is

$$D_j(\tau, w) = \alpha_- \frac{1 - e^{-\sqrt{b^2 - 4ac}\tau}}{1 - (\alpha_-/\alpha_+)e^{-\sqrt{b^2 - 4ac}\tau}} \qquad (7.41)$$

$$C_j(\tau, w) = \lambda \left[\alpha_- \tau - \frac{2}{\eta^2} \log \left(\frac{1 - (\alpha_-/\alpha_+)e^{-\sqrt{b^2 - 4ac}\tau}}{1 - \alpha_-/\alpha_+} \right) \right]. \qquad (7.42)$$

In this way, we have completed our calculation of the Fourier transform of the P_j in equation (7.36)

$$\widetilde{P}_j = \exp\left(C_j(w, \tau)\bar{v} + D_j(w, \tau)v\right) \widetilde{P}_j(0, w) \qquad (7.43)$$

$$= \exp\left(C_j(w, \tau)\bar{v} + D_j(w, \tau)v\right) \left(\tfrac{1}{2}\delta(w) + \frac{1}{iw}\right) \qquad (7.44)$$

and it remains to apply the inverse Fourier transform

$$P_j(\tau, x, v) = \int_{-\infty}^{\infty} \frac{1}{2\pi} e^{iwx} \widetilde{P}_j(\tau, w, v)\, dw. \qquad (7.45)$$

The Dirac delta function makes the integration of the first term simple, and we are left with

$$P_j = \frac{1}{2} + \frac{1}{2\pi} \int_{-\infty}^{\infty} e^{iwx} \frac{\exp\left(C_j(w, \tau)\bar{v} + D_j(w, \tau)v\right)}{iw}\, dw. \qquad (7.46)$$

To see that this integral gives a real result, we note that replacing w with $-w$ in the integrand gives the complex conjugate. Then we can replace the integrand with its real part, and in that case the contributions from positive and negative w are identical, and so it is usual to write the result as

$$P_j(\tau, x, v) = \frac{1}{2} + \frac{1}{\pi} \int_0^{\infty} \mathrm{Re}\, \frac{\exp\left(C_j(w, \tau)\bar{v} + D_j(w, \tau)v + iwx\right)}{iw}\, dw. \qquad (7.47)$$

We are not quite done yet. Computation of the integrand requires a logarithm (and a square root) of complex numbers and therefore has multiple possible values. Strictly speaking, we should assign branch cuts in the complex plane and keep track of the winding number each time we cross the cut. In Heston's original paper, an equivalent formula for C is written slightly differently with a factor taken out of the logarithm. The result is that the principal value of the logarithm can be different, and lead to wrong valuation if one simply takes the principal value.

This meant that the practical implementation of (7.47) was tricky for some years. However, Albrecher et al. (2007) prove a conjecture that can be found in Gatheral (2006). As long as the formula for C is written as in (7.42), then the correct integral is obtained by taking the principal values of the logarithm and square root.

With this knowledge, the integral can be calculated fast numerically. Interested readers should consult Kahl and Jäckel (2005) as well as Albrecher et al. (2007) and Gatheral (2006).

7.2.3 The Feller Boundary Condition

While the use of the CIR process (7.10) has the advantage of leading to a semi-analytic formula for vanilla prices and therefore fast calibration, it also comes with disadvantages. If the stochastic variance v can go negative, that would be a major problem, giving imaginary volatility $\sqrt{v}$. Fortunately, this is not possible. To see why (at least heuristically) we can note that, when $v = 0$, the CIR process (7.10) becomes

$$dv = \lambda \bar{v} dt \tag{7.48}$$

so that if at any time the variance process touches zero, at that moment there will be no stochastic contribution, but only a deterministic pull back into positive territory.

However, for some values of the parameters in the CIR process, the variance can touch zero. To understand why, we follow the original paper by Feller (1951). Readers who do not wish to get involved in the technical details may skip straight to the result in equation (7.62).

We need to study the probability density function of the variance v_t at time t. Let's call this density function $u(t, v)$. Just as in Section 6.3, we can write down the forward Kolmogorov PDE satisfied by $u(t, v)$

$$\frac{\partial u}{\partial t} = -\frac{\partial}{\partial v}\{[\lambda(\bar{v} - v)]u\} + \frac{1}{2}\eta^2\frac{\partial^2}{\partial v^2}(vu). \tag{7.49}$$

To simplify notation, we can set $a = \frac{1}{2}\eta^2$, $b = -\lambda$, $c = \lambda\bar{v}$ and represent partial derivatives with subscripts. Then (7.49) becomes

$$u_t = (avu)_{vv} - ((bv + c)u)_v, \quad 0 < v < \infty. \tag{7.50}$$

Feller's method is to take the Laplace transform of (7.50). We'll seek a solution in which the Laplace transforms of both u and $(uv)_v$ exist, but we'll see that u may go to ∞ as v goes to zero, therefore we cannot assume the Laplace transform of u_v exists. To circumvent this problem, we write down a function which is the indefinite integral of the right hand side of (7.50)

$$v(t,v) = (avu)_v - (bv+c)u,$$ (7.51)

so that equation (7.50) becomes

$$u_t = v_x.$$ (7.52)

Then taking the Laplace transform (and denoting the Laplace transform of $u(t,v)$ by $w(t,s)$) we obtain

$$w_t(t,s) = -v(t,0) + s \int_0^\infty e^{-sv} v(t,v)\, dv.$$ (7.53)

If we define

$$f(t) = v(t,0),$$ (7.54)

and replace our definition of v, this becomes

$$w_t(t,s) = f(t) + s \int_0^\infty e^{-sv} [(avu)_v - (bv+c)u]\, dv.$$ (7.55)

All three Laplace transforms on the right hand side exist, and using standard methods we obtain

$$w_t = f(t) - s(as-b)w_s - csw.$$ (7.56)

Finally then we have a first order PDE, which can be solved using the method of characteristics. To do so, we need the initial condition, and define

$$\pi(s) = \lim_{t \to 0} w(t,s),$$ (7.57)

the Laplace transform of the PDF at time zero. The solution is

$$w(t,s) = \left(\frac{b}{sa(e^{bt}-1)+b} \right)^{c/a} \pi \left(\frac{sbe^{bt}}{sa(e^{bt}-1)+b} \right)$$

$$+ \int_0^t f(\tau) \left\{ \frac{b}{sa(e^{bt}-1)+b} \right\}^{c/a} d\tau.$$ (7.58)

The function $f(t)$ corresponds to the boundary condition on the probability density u where the variance is zero, $v = 0$. We hope for a solution in which the variance cannot hit zero so that $u(t,0) = 0$ and so we look for solutions with $f(t) \equiv 0$. Then using the usual property of Laplace transforms we can calculate

$$u(t,0) = \lim_{s \to \infty} s w(t,s). \qquad (7.59)$$

Since the argument of $\pi()$ goes to a constant, we need only examine the first factor in (7.58), and note that it goes to zero if $c/a > 1$, but goes to infinity if $c/a < 1$. Finally then, putting back our CIR parameters we obtain

$$u(t,0) = 0, \quad 2\lambda\bar{v} > \eta^2 \qquad (7.60)$$
$$u(t,0) = \infty, \quad 2\lambda\bar{v} < \eta^2. \qquad (7.61)$$

We have arrived at the *Feller condition*

$$2\lambda\bar{v} > \eta^2. \qquad (7.62)$$

If the Feller condition is satisfied, the stochastic variance can never touch zero. This will be so as long as the mean reversion λ is large enough compared to the volatility of variance η. However, when the mean reversion is large, it has the impact of reducing the stochasticity of the variance, since deviations from the mean reversion level $\bar{v}$ are quickly corrected. The result is that it can be hard to generate a sufficiently convex implied volatility smile without breaking the Feller condition.

A Heston model with CIR parameters not satisfying the Feller condition can be managed technically. The model is still well defined, though care is needed to use the Feller boundary condition

$$f(t) \equiv \lim_{v \to 0} [(avu)_v - (bv + c)u] = 0 \qquad (7.63)$$

when solving the forward Kolmogorov PDE. However, a volatility process that can hit zero is unpalatable financially. Furthermore, it causes problems when simulating the process in Monte Carlo on a discrete time grid. In that case the discretisation approximation can allow the variance to go below zero. This can be fixed by flooring the variance at zero, or reflecting in zero (using the absolute value), but convergence is rather poor and simulating the Heston model is considered tricky.

7.3 The SABR Model

The Heston (1993) model that we outlined in Section 7.2 is at once wonderful, because it can be solved, and flawed, because the volatility process can touch zero causing all sorts of problems in practical pricing. This statement is made in full deference to Heston's brilliant paper which introduced the model and solved it.

The SABR model was introduce in Hagan et al. (2002), nearly ten years later. If the $\beta = 1$ version of the model is used (see below), it suffers from none of the problems of Heston, but it comes with some of its own. These though, as we will see, are associated with how the model tends to be used rather than any fundamental flaw.

It is easier to write down the model in terms of the forward to a fixed expiry rather than in terms of a spot level. Therefore we choose a fixed T and write

$$F_t = S_t e^{\mu(T-t)} \tag{7.64}$$

so that

$$dF_t = e^{\mu(T-t)}(dS_t - \mu dt). \tag{7.65}$$

In terms of F, the Black–Scholes process

$$\frac{dS}{S} = \mu dt + \sigma dW \tag{7.66}$$

becomes

$$\frac{dF}{F} = \sigma dW \tag{7.67}$$

as a simple application of Ito shows.

SABR is practically the simplest extension of Black–Scholes to a stochastic volatility model that one can write down. It has SDEs

$$dF = \sigma F^\beta dW_1 \tag{7.68}$$
$$d\sigma = \nu\sigma dW_2 \tag{7.69}$$
$$dW_1 dW_2 = \rho dt \tag{7.70}$$
$$\sigma(0) = \alpha. \tag{7.71}$$

The parameters in the model are α, the initial volatility, ν, the vol-of-vol and ρ, the correlation between spot (forward) and volatility processes. In addition, in the forward process (7.68), the forward F is raised to a power β, which we will discuss in a moment. The model is named after three of its parameters: it is the stochastic-$\alpha\beta\rho$ (SABR) model.

Like the Heston model, SABR has a vol-of-vol parameter ν that controls the convexity of the implied volatility smile, and a correlation that controls the skew. There is no mean reversion, and this is a drawback compared to Heston as it means that when instantaneous volatility follows a path in which it becomes very large, it is likely to stay large.

Ordinarily, say in equity or foreign exchange markets, we would choose $\beta = 1$ so that the process is approximately log-normal in the limit of small vol-of-vol. On the other hand, interest rate traders are fond of SABR and do make use of the β parameter (according to Rebonato, Mckay, and White (2009), the interest rate market has settled on $\beta = 0.5$). We saw earlier that the skew of the implied volatility smile is controlled by the correlation between spot (or forward) and volatility. If we use a β not equal to 1, we could rewrite the process as

$$\frac{dF}{F} = \sigma F^{\beta-1} dW \tag{7.72}$$

so that the instantaneous 'log-normal vol' is $\sigma F^{\beta-1}$. In this way we add some dependence on the forward level to the volatility, and therefore β also impacts the skew. We can to some extent play off β and the correlation ρ against one another. However, β will also impact the convexity of the implied volatility smile. To see this, we could apply Ito to calculate the process followed by the effective volatility $\sigma F^{\beta-1}$ and see an additional contribution to the vol-of-vol.[17]

Caution is required in understanding the process when $\beta \neq 1$. In the special case of $v = 0$, for which the volatility σ is no longer stochastic, the process is known as *constant elasticity of variance* (CEV). This process is well studied, and rigorous results are provided in Andersen and Andreasen (1998):

1   For $\beta \geq 0.5$, the SDE (7.68) has a unique solution.
2   For $0 < \beta < 1$, the process can reach $F_t = 0$ but never go negative. When $\beta \geq 1$, the process can never reach $F_t = 0$.
3   For $\beta = 0$ the process is normal, and therefore F_t can go negative.
4   For $0 < \beta < 0.5$, the SDE only has a unique solution if one adds a boundary condition at $F_t = 0$. For the process to be arbitrage free, the boundary condition must be that when F_t hits zero it stays there.

SABR is popular because Hagan et al. (2002) were able to provide an approximate solution that is valid in the limit of small time to expiry T. We provide their result in the case $\beta = 1$. Rather than give the price of a call option with strike K, the implied volatility is given with the SABR formula

$$\sigma_{imp}(K, T) = \alpha \frac{z}{\chi(z)} \left[1 + \left(\frac{\rho\alpha v}{4} + \frac{2 - 3\rho^2}{24} v^2 \right) T \right] + \mathcal{O}(T^2) \tag{7.73}$$

where

$$z = \frac{v}{\alpha} \log F/K \tag{7.74}$$

---

[17] As the result is not instructive, we shall not pollute the text by writing it down, but leave it as an exercise for interested readers.

$$\chi(z) = \log\left(\frac{\sqrt{1 - 2\rho z + z^2} + z - \rho}{1 - \rho}\right).$$ (7.75)

The derivation of this formula is a little long, and we won't give it here. It works by starting with a clever guess for the form of the solution (a 'heat kernel') and then by writing the true solution as an expansion around this and solving term by term. Interested readers can consult the original paper Hagan et al. (2002) for the technique, and Obłój (2008) for an improvement to the approximation when $\beta \neq 1$.

For our purposes, the $\beta = 1$ version of the model is perfectly good. Later, we will add a local (spot dependent) component into the volatility that would allow for dynamics in which $\beta \neq 1$. For this reason, we will confine our discussion of the merits of SABR to $\beta = 1$, and call it log-normal SABR.

Log-normal SABR has a volatility process that cannot hit zero[18] and therefore it does not suffer from the numerical difficulties associated with Heston. Unlike the $\beta < 1$ version of SABR, log-normal SABR also has a spot process that stays positive. Therefore the only drawback with the process itself is the lack of mean reversion, allowing paths in which instantaneous volatilities become very large. For us, this is also not a problem. We can simply add in a mean reversion term to obtain the λ-SABR model:

$$dF = \sigma F dW_1$$ (7.76)

$$d\sigma = -\lambda(\sigma - \overline{\sigma})dt + v\sigma\, dW_2$$ (7.77)

$$dW_1\, dW_2 = \rho\, dt.$$ (7.78)

By including mean reversion, we lose the analytic approximation for the implied volatility smile in terms of our stochastic volatility parameters.[19] Fortunately, later when we build our local stochastic volatility smile models, it will not be particularly important to have an analytic formula for the volatility smile implied by the model parameters.

Then we have seen that the SABR or λ-SABR process itself is attractive. It is the asymptotic implied volatility formula that causes problems. The approximation is only valid at short expiries, and furthermore, it can imply negative probability densities at strikes that are far away from at-the-money. These are problems for people who want to use the SABR formula as a method to define or interpolate the implied volatility smile. The SABR formula has become a kind of market standard for marking smiles for interest rate products and therefore these defects have become prominent, and ways of 'fixing' the SABR formula continue to be the subject of research.

Fortunately, in this book we are concerned with smile modelling, and these issues will not cause us any problems.

---

[18] More correctly, the volatility process stays positive almost surely.

[19] In fact, there is an asymptotic approximation available even in this more complex case (Henry-Labordère 2005). However, the derivation is quite technical and not always used in practice.

7.4 The Ornstein–Uhlenbeck Process

Sometimes, an Ornstein–Uhlenbeck process is used to make volatility stochastic. The process is

$$dx_t = -\lambda(x_t - \bar{x})dt + v\,dW_t \qquad (7.79)$$

where λ is a mean reversion rate, $\bar{x}$ a mean reversion level and v a vol-of-vol parameter. It is a normal, as opposed to log-normal, process (since there is no x_t multiplying the dW_t), and therefore x_t can be negative. For this reason, when using the process to model a stochastic volatility, we do not use x_t directly, but instead some positive function of it. Typically this function will be an exponential so that we set $\sigma_t = e^{x_t}$ and the SDEs for the model become

$$\frac{dS}{S} = \mu\,dt + e^{x_t}\,dW_1 \qquad (7.80)$$

$$dx = -\lambda(x - \bar{x})dt + v\,dW_2 \qquad (7.81)$$

$$dW_1\,dW_2 = \rho\,dt. \qquad (7.82)$$

We call this the exponential Ornstein–Uhlenbeck model, or the Scott–Chesney model due to Scott (1987) and Chesney and Scott (1989).

The reason the Ornstein–Uhlenbeck process is interesting for us is that it has a simple solution. This is not a solution for the full model in equations (7.80)–(7.82), but just for the x_t that drive the spot volatility. Nevertheless, it will give us some useful understanding of the interplay between mean reversion and vol-of-vol.

To solve for x_t, we introduce a new variable u_t with

$$u_t = x_t e^{\lambda t}. \qquad (7.83)$$

Then, applying Ito's lemma, we obtain

$$du_t = \lambda x_t e^{\lambda t}\,dt + e^{\lambda t}\,dx_t \qquad (7.84)$$

$$= \lambda u_t\,dt + e^{\lambda t}\left(-\lambda(x_t - \bar{x})dt + v\,dW_t\right) \qquad (7.85)$$

$$= \lambda \bar{x} e^{\lambda t}\,dt + v e^{\lambda t}\,dW_t, \qquad (7.86)$$

which is a simple normal model with drift. The parameters are time dependent, but as we saw in Section 2.7 this presents no problem, and we can integrate to obtain a solution

$$\int_0^T du_t = \int_0^T \left(\lambda \bar{x} e^{\lambda t}\,dt + v e^{\lambda t}\,dW_t\right) \qquad (7.87)$$

$$u_T - u_0 = \overline{x}(e^{\lambda T} - 1) + v\sqrt{\int_0^T (e^{\lambda t})^2\, dt}\, Z, \quad Z = N(0,1) \tag{7.88}$$

$$= \overline{x}(e^{\lambda T} - 1) + \frac{v}{\sqrt{2\lambda}}\sqrt{e^{2\lambda T} - 1}\, Z \tag{7.89}$$

for u_T so that for x_T we have

$$x_T = e^{-\lambda T} x_0 + \overline{x}(1 - e^{-\lambda T}) + \frac{v}{\sqrt{2\lambda}}\sqrt{1 - e^{-2\lambda T}}\, Z \tag{7.90}$$

where $Z = N(0,1)$ is a standard normal variable.

This solution confirms our intuition about mean reversion. In the limit of large time T we obtain

$$X_T \sim \overline{x} + \frac{v}{\sqrt{2\lambda}} Z \tag{7.91}$$

so that x_T is normally distributed about the mean reversion level, even though it started at x_0 at time $t = 0$, which might be far from the mean reversion level.

This is good to know, but what is particularly interesting for us is that the variance becomes $v^2/(2\lambda)$ at large times. In contrast to normal or log-normal models without mean reversion (the pure SABR model for example) the variance of instantaneous spot volatility does not increase with time. The spot volatility remains under control over long time intervals when there is mean reversion. If there is no mean reversion, the variance grows with time so that spot volatility is likely to become very large or very small.

If we think of the implied volatility smile at a particular expiry date, we saw in Section 7.1 that it is the variance of the total realised volatility up to this date that gives the smile its convexity. That is, it is the variance of the quantity $\int_0^T \sigma_t^2\, dt$ that controls the convexity of the implied volatility smile at expiry T. Adjusting the parameters in our stochastic volatility model gives us control over the behaviour of the instantaneous volatility σ_t, and therefore over this total variance. Then we can play off mean reversion λ versus vol-of-vol v in order to achieve the required convexity of smile. This makes sense. If mean reversion rate is large, every time the Brownian motion moves the process away from its reversion level, it is quickly dragged back, and therefore it stays close to the reversion level, and the variance of the process is small.

When the time scale is not too large, the factor $\sqrt{1 - e^{-2\lambda T}}$ appearing in the variance in equation (7.91) is important. As it depends on the time T, it allows us to adjust the variance at two times, T_1 and T_2 say, by adjusting the two parameters λ and v. In this way, we can use mean reversion to control the convexity of smile at two expiries without needing to introduce time-dependent parameters into the model.

These features that are valid for the Ornstein–Uhlenbeck process can be assumed to apply qualitatively in other models having mean reversion in the same form. The λ-SABR model is an example. The mean reversion means that the process will not stray too far from the mean reversion level $\bar{\sigma}$, and the result is that, as an approximation, we can replace the λ-SABR volatility process (7.77)

$$d\sigma = -\lambda(\sigma - \bar{\sigma})dt + v\sigma\,dW_2 \qquad (7.92)$$

with the Ornstein–Uhlenbeck process

$$d\sigma = -\lambda(\sigma - \bar{\sigma})dt + v\bar{\sigma}\,dW_2. \qquad (7.93)$$

7.5   Mixture Models

Having examined the traditional stochastic volatility models, we will now briefly look at a more radical approach.

When valuing derivatives, one is not looking for the model that is closest to reality. Such an approach would be a fruitless task. Complex models have large numbers of parameters that must be calibrated with heavy numerical algorithms. Then when one comes to calculate the Greeks in order to understand one's risk, the chances are that the heavy numerics will lead to unstable results.

The Heston and SABR style models we have looked at so far are regarded as providing an acceptable balance between realism and simplicity. However, often they are not as fast nor as numerically stable as one would like in an ideal world.

The idea of a mixture model is to write down the simplest possible 'stochastic' volatility model. We imagine that we have a number of volatility states. In the simplest case, we might have just two states, σ_1 and σ_2. At time zero, that is, at the moment we perform the valuation, we toss a coin to decide which of the two volatility states will be used for the remainder of the contract.

Then the model is

$$\frac{dS}{S} = \mu\,dt + \sigma\,dW \qquad (7.94)$$

$$\sigma = \sigma_1, \text{ probability } p_1 = \tfrac{1}{2} \qquad (7.95)$$

$$\sigma = \sigma_2, \text{ probability } p_2 = \tfrac{1}{2}. \qquad (7.96)$$

In the simplest version, σ_1 and σ_2 might be constant (say 5% and 15% respectively). Alternatively, one can make them time dependent.

The seductiveness of a mixture model comes from its simplicity. After the initial coin toss, the spot follows a Black–Scholes process with volatility that is the outcome of the toss. Then, if we know the Black–Scholes formula $P_{BS}(\sigma)$ for any particular contract, we can evaluate the value in the mixture model via

$$P_{MM} = p_1 P_{BS}(\sigma_1) + p_2 P_{BS}(\sigma_2) \qquad (7.97)$$

where here we have assumed two volatility states having probabilities p_1 and p_2.

One can use the pricing formula (7.97) to value vanilla options at various strikes and then back out the corresponding implied volatilities. Readers who do this experiment will find that the smile generated is pretty convincing in spite of the simplicity of the model. The convexity of the smile is controlled by the spacing between the volatility states. If the volatility states are allowed to be time dependent, then one can control the convexity at various expiry dates.

An immediate drawback is that there is no spot–volatility correlation that could be used to add skew to the smile. If, however, one is modelling a smile that is not skewed, then there is nothing wrong with using the mixture model for European contracts. We saw in Section 6.2 that the value of a European contract depends only on the smile at its expiry date, and therefore as long as the smile is good, the dynamic causing the smile is irrelevant.

However, we would like to use our stochastic volatility model to value path dependent contracts, and here there is a major problem. All of the uncertainty in the volatility is concentrated into a single instant at the time of valuation. We do not truly believe that the smile will disappear after that instant. When we next come to value our contract a few seconds later, we will make the same assumption but this time concentrating the volatility uncertainty at the new valuation time.

In a delightfully elegant article, Piterbarg (2003) constructs a simple contract in which an exercise decision is made on a particular date. Valuation using a mixture model immediately before and immediately after the exercise gives two different prices, and therefore *the wrong exercise decision may be made.*

Piterbarg's example renders those mixture models that are expressed merely as distributions without actual arbitrage free dynamics useless and indeed dangerous for general path dependent derivative contracts. However, later in this book we will find them useful in extending our understanding of stochastic volatility pricing, and we will see that they can even be useful for valuing an important class of contracts. We will return to this in Section 9.5.3.

7.6   Regime Switching Model

At around the same time that the Heston model was published, Naik (1993) proposed a simpler *regime switching* model for option pricing. Regime switching is similar to the mixture model in that there are a small number of volatility states (say N). Again, in the simplest case, one might use just two states, σ_1 and σ_2. Unlike a mixture model, the process starts at time $t = 0$ in one predetermined state, but can then switch between the states at any time. For this reason, it does not suffer from the mixture model's problems, which were caused by concentration of all switching at time $t = 0$.

The process that the volatility follows is known as a continuous time Markov chain, and it works as follows. Given that the volatility is in state i at time t, the probability it will be in state j at a small time Δt later is

$$I_{ij} + Q_{ij}\Delta t \tag{7.98}$$

where I is the identity matrix, and Q is a matrix with rows that sum to zero,

$$\sum_{j=1}^{N} Q_{ij} = 0, \text{ for each } i. \tag{7.99}$$

We call Q the *transition matrix*.

To see that equation (7.98) makes sense, we can calculate the probability $P(t)_{ij}$ that the volatility is in state j at time t given it was in state i at time 0. To do so, we split the interval $[0, t]$ into n small segments $\Delta t = t/n$ and multiply up the probabilities using matrix notation

$$P(t) = \lim_{n \to \infty} \prod_{i=1}^{n} \left(I + Q \frac{t}{n} \right) \tag{7.100}$$

$$= \exp(Qt). \tag{7.101}$$

The result is the exponential[20] of the matrix Qt. To understand its meaning, one can think of the definition of the matrix exponential function as the Taylor series

$$P(T) = \exp(Qt) \equiv \sum_{r=0}^{\infty} \frac{1}{r!} (Qt)^r \tag{7.102}$$

with the powers computed using matrix multiplication. If we now sum over the ith row of P, equation (7.99) ensures for us that only the first term in the Taylor series contributes, and we obtain

$$\sum_{j=1}^{N} P(t)_{ij} = 1. \tag{7.103}$$

This shows that the total probability of being in one of the volatility states at time t is 1, and our system is well defined. The elements of the matrix Q are the transition rates (not probabilities) between the states. When $i \neq j$, Q_{ij} is the transition rate from state i to state j, and $-Q_{ii}$ is the total transition rate out of state i.

Having set up the Markov chain and decided on some values for the volatility states σ_i and transition matrix Q, we define the instantaneous volatility process σ_t by setting it equal to σ_i whenever the Markov chain is in state i. Then the SDE for the model is simply

$$\frac{dS}{S} = (r_{dom} - r_{yield})dt + \sigma_t dW. \tag{7.104}$$

---

[20] We take as given the result that the limit in equation (7.100) is equal to the matrix exponential.

As the instantaneous volatility σ_t follows a Markov chain rather than a stochastic process, we are left wondering how to write down a partial differential pricing equation for the model. The question is, how do we allow for the fact that the volatility can switch between states at any time?

The trick is to begin by discretising the times at which a volatility transition can occur. Then between these discrete time steps, volatility is constant and we must solve the standard Black–Scholes pricing PDE (3.72) for each volatility state,

$$-\frac{\partial C_i}{\partial t} = \mu \frac{\partial C_i}{\partial S} + \frac{1}{2}\sigma_i^2 \frac{\partial^2 C_i}{\partial S^2} - r_{dom}C_i. \tag{7.105}$$

Here $C_i(t,S)$ is the value of our contract at time t, given spot level S and volatility state i.

As usual, we start solving our PDE at the expiry time T of the option. Initially, we set each of the functions $C_i(T,S)$ equal to the option payout. We then solve backwards in time, eventually reaching the valuation time $t = 0$.

Let's suppose we have succeeded in solving backwards as far as time $t + \Delta t$. We can approximate the time derivative in equation (7.105) as

$$-\frac{\partial C_i}{\partial t} = \frac{C_i(t,S) - C_i(t+\Delta t,S)}{\Delta t} \tag{7.106}$$

and then convert (7.105) into an expression for the solution at the next time step

$$C_i(t_+,S) = C_i(t+\Delta t,S) + \Delta t \left(\mu \frac{\partial C_i}{\partial S} + \frac{1}{2}\sigma_i^2 \frac{\partial^2 C_i}{\partial S^2} - r_{dom}C_i \right). \tag{7.107}$$

Here t_+ indicates a time infinitesimally above t since we have not yet allowed for volatility transitions. To do so, we can use the Martingale property. The value immediately before the transition is the expected value immediately after the transition, and so

$$C_i(t,S) = \sum_j (I_{ij} + Q_{ij}\Delta t)C_j(t_+,S), \tag{7.108}$$

where we used the regime switching infinitesimal transition probability (7.98). It is helpful to think of the functions C_i as a vector and use matrix notation. To do so, we can define V to be the diagonal matrix having elements σ_i^2 on the diagonal

$$V = \mathrm{diag}(\sigma_1^2, \sigma_2^2, \cdots, \sigma_N^2). \tag{7.109}$$

Then putting (7.107) and (7.109) together gives

$$C(t,S) = (I + Q\Delta t)\left[C(t+\Delta t, S) + \Delta t\left(\mu\frac{\partial C}{\partial S} + \tfrac{1}{2}V\frac{\partial^2 C}{\partial S^2} - r_{dom}C\right)\right]. \qquad (7.110)$$

We can rearrange $C(t + \Delta t, S)$ back onto the left hand side and divide by Δt. Then taking the limit $\Delta t \to 0$ gives an expression for $\partial C/\partial t$

$$-\frac{\partial C}{\partial t} = QC + \mu\frac{\partial C}{\partial S} + \tfrac{1}{2}V\frac{\partial^2 C}{\partial S^2} - r_{dom}C. \qquad (7.111)$$

We have a arrived at a matrix PDE. In effect, there are N PDEs, one for each pricing function $C_i(t,S)$, corresponding to the N volatility states. Because the matrix Q is not diagonal, it causes the individual PDEs to interact with each other.

In Section 8.2 we will learn how to solve PDEs numerically. To solve the regime switching PDE (7.111), one can apply the methods of Section 8.2 to the Black–Scholes PDEs (7.105) for each volatility state, and allow them to interact at the discrete time steps by using equation (7.108). This technique is called interfacing.

When there are a large number of volatility states, a regime switching model with suitably chosen transition matrix may be the discretisation of a more conventional stochastic volatility model. However, regime switching is most useful with a small number of states. Then, the reduced complexity leads to faster pricing with better numerical stability than standard stochastic volatility models.

Like the mixture model, regime switching cannot generate a skewed smile since there is no spot–volatility correlation. Later, when we move to local stochastic volatility, this problem will be overcome by generating skew with a local volatility correction. In other respects, regime switching is rather attractive. As there is a finite set of volatility states, there is no risk that the volatility will go off to infinity or touch zero. If one has three or more states, one can set up the transition matrix so that the process tends to mean revert to the centre state.

Of course, the underlying assumption of a small set of volatility states is unrealistic. However, a trade that probes this feature is likely to have quite detailed dependence on the volatility process. Such a trade will have price that depends heavily on the details of any stochastic volatility model. This model risk means it may not be a suitable trade for an investment bank to have on its books, even with a more realistic model.

In the original paper, Naik (1993) provides a semi-analytic formula for valuing vanilla options in the simplest case in which there are two constant volatility states. This provides the two state model with the same advantage as Heston of fast vanilla option pricing.

7.7 Calibrating Stochastic Volatility Models

For our stochastic volatility model to be useful, we must choose its parameters so that it gives correct prices for vanilla options. That is, it must generate the correct implied volatility smile. The process of finding the best parameters is called calibration.

There are a small number of parameters, and it is only possible to exactly match a corresponding number of market prices. We have no option but to hope that once a small number of market prices are matched, the rest of the implied volatility smile will be reasonably approximated. This is a major disadvantage of using a stochastic volatility model versus Dupire's local volatility model.

The process of finding the best stochastic volatility parameters is a classic optimisation problem that we must solve numerically. We have a great deal of knowledge about the impact of the parameters on the valuation of vanillas, and we can use this knowledge to reframe the problem in a way that will help us solve it. Once this is done, one approach is simply to call a third party optimisation algorithm. However, we will illustrate calibration with a more direct approach.

The first step is to select the strikes and expiries for the market vanilla prices we wish to calibrate to. Then we take a trial set of parameters and use the model to value those contracts. We will get the wrong prices at first, so we must adjust the parameters to get an improvement. The process is repeated until the model gets the prices right to within a specified tolerance.

Let's consider the SABR model, defined in equations (7.68)–(7.71). We will use $\beta = 1$, and that leaves three parameters: α (the initial volatility), ν (the vol-of-vol) and ρ (the spot–volatility correlation). As there are three parameters, we have the opportunity to exactly match three market vanilla prices at a single expiry date. When calibrating a stochastic volatility model, we probably already have in mind a particular exotic contract we wish to value using the model. We should choose the expiry date to match this contract.

Certainly we should use the at-the-money option as one of the three contracts we calibrate to. The other two should be evenly spaced on either side of the at-the-money strike. A good choice is to take the market smile and use the methods of Section 6.2 to find strikes corresponding roughly to 25% and 75% risk-neutral probability. We will call the strikes K_{25}, K_{ATM} and K_{75} having respective implied volatilities σ_{25}, σ_{ATM} and σ_{75}.

The initial volatility α controls the overall level of volatility, and so we will use it to calibrate the at-the-money volatility σ_{ATM}. The vol-of-vol and the correlation control the convexity and the skew of the smile. Therefore it is helpful to reformulate the problem by defining

$$S = \tfrac{1}{2}(\sigma_{25} + \sigma_{75}) - \sigma_{ATM} \qquad (7.112)$$

$$R = \sigma_{75} - \sigma_{25}, \qquad (7.113)$$

which provide measures of convexity and skew respectively.[21]

If the expiry date is not too long, then we can use the analytic SABR approximation formula (7.73) to calculate vanilla prices given the model parameters. We could begin with, say, $\alpha = 10\%$, $\rho = 0$ and $\nu = 40\%$. Then, fixing ρ and ν we could solve to find α so that the at-the-money volatility is correct. At its simplest, this could be achieved

---

[21] The somewhat confusing notation S and R is inherited from foreign exchange conventions in which these parameters are known as the strangle and risk reversal.

with a bisection search. Next, fixing α and ρ, we could solve for ν to get the convexity S right. Finally, we can solve for ρ to get the skew R correct.

Each step in this solving process will break the previous steps. That is, once we have solved for ρ to get the skew right, the convexity and at-the-money volatility will no longer be perfect. But as we have chosen the calibration instruments to match roughly the impact of the three parameters, the error should not be too great. We can improve on it by repeating the process a few times until we are happy with the match for each of σ_{ATM}, S and R.

So far so good. We have successfully calibrated the SABR model to our smile at one expiry date. Having now understood this process, we can sit back and consider some of the major challenges in using pure stochastic volatility models for derivatives pricing.

Firstly, there is the problem that we have already touched on of the small number of parameters. In our SABR example, we were able to match three vanilla prices at a single expiry. By choosing the strikes for those three contracts carefully, we might hope that we achieve a reasonable approximation for the remainder of the smile at that date. This is not really good enough. We need something close to an exact match of market prices in order to avoid arbitrage.

One might hope that a stochastic volatility model with constant parameters would be a reasonable proxy for the true market. Sadly, this is not the case. We recall from Section 7.1 that at very short expiries, there has not been enough time for the instantaneous volatility to change much, and therefore the implied volatility smile generated is rather flat. On the other hand, at long expiry dates, a mean reverting process has little vol-of-vol, and so again the smile is flat. This means that if constant parameters are used, their values are heavily dependent on the expiry date chosen for the calibration, and the model implied volatility surface will be wrong elsewhere.

It is possible to calibrate to the smile at more than one expiry date by making the parameters time dependent. We might for example assume the parameters are piecewise constant between the expiry dates that we choose to calibrate to. This leads us to the next problem, relating to speed and stability.

In the simple SABR example, we were able to use the approximation formula. It allowed us to calculate vanilla prices analytically at each iteration of the calibration and therefore allowed the calibration procedure to complete in a reasonable time. Such luxury is only available for the simple SABR model, and even then it is only an approximation.

The next best thing to analytic evaluation of vanilla prices is a semi-analytic formula (that is, requiring only a numerical integration), like the Heston formula. Unlike the SABR approximation, the Heston formula is exact and includes mean reversion. This explains the popularity of the Heston model in spite of its drawbacks.

Failing a semi-analytic vanilla pricing formula, one is left with numerically solving the PDE. Remembering that this must be done numerous times by the calibration routine, such an approach is very slow. Furthermore, the heavy numerics involved mean that the results may be rather unstable to small changes in the market data, leading to potentially unstable results when calculating Greeks.

Overall, the challenges involved in attempting to calibrate a stochastic volatility model to a market implied volatility surface are too great, and stochastic volatility models are not useful for pricing exotic derivative contracts by themselves. However, we will see in Chapter 9 that they can be augmented with a local volatility component to provide a powerful pricing approach known as *local stochastic volatility*.

7.8 Key Points

- In Chapter 6 we looked at local volatility as one model able to generate the implied volatility smile. An alternative explanation for the smile is that instantaneous volatility is itself stochastic.
- There are many possible choices of stochastic volatility model, including Heston, SABR, λ-SABR and exponential Ornstein–Uhlenbeck models.
- Initial volatility and mean reversion level control overall implied volatility level. Vol-of-vol and mean reversion rate control smile convexity, and spot–volatility correlation controls the skew of the smile.
- Used alone, stochastic volatility models are hard (and slow) to calibrate, and struggle to generate a realistic implied volatility smile at more than one expiry date.
- However, in Chapter 9 we will see how stochastic volatility models form a building block in the powerful local stochastic volatility modelling framework.

7.9 Further Reading

The classic text on stochastic volatility models is Lewis (2000), and an illuminating work on the features of the different models is Jäckel (2004).

Hull and White (1987) developed the approach that we used in Section 7.1 when spot–volatility correlation is zero, and Stein and Stein (1991) introduced the Ornstein–Uhlenbeck process for volatility and solved for the resulting stock price distribution when correlation is zero.

Work on the volatility smile generated by stochastic models at long expiry dates can be found in Fouque, Papanicolaou, and Sircar (1999, 2000), and at short expiries in Lee (2001).

Calibration of the Heston model is discussed in Mikhailov and Nögel (2004), and suitable boundary conditions for solving the forward Kolmogorov PDE in the Heston model are discussed in Lucic (2012).

In Section 7.7, we noted that calibrating stochastic volatility models is particularly tricky when we allow time-dependent parameters in order to get the implied volatility smile right at more than one expiry date. A useful approach in this situation is provided by Piterbarg (2005b, 2007), who shows how to average over the time-dependent parameters up to a given expiry date in order to obtain an effective model with constant parameters that can be solved more easily.

8 Numerical Techniques

Now that we have seen a number of different models, we will take an interlude in our discussion of smile modelling. It is time to consider the numerical algorithms we can use to solve the model equations.

This is a subject that can be taken to almost any degree of detail and technicality. Our desire here is to give an introduction to the subject and, most importantly, to show that the equations in this book can be solved numerically with fairly straightforward algorithms.

When managing a portfolio of derivatives, a trader will want to see his or her risk frequently; perhaps many times a day. The risk means, of course, the value of the trades, but also the Greeks so that delta, vega and other hedges can be adjusted. Each Greek that the trader needs to see will require at least one additional valuation, with the market data in a slightly altered (bumped) state so that the derivative can be approximated numerically. In practice, we will want to see the sensitivity of the trade to all the market instruments that our model calibrates to, so that we can hedge each one if necessary. Since the yield curve will be built out of interest rate instruments with many expiries, and the volatility surface will be built out of vanillas with many expiries and strikes, there can quickly become a large number of instruments our valuation depends on. In addition to the trader's requirement to see Greeks for hedging, risk managers will also want to see how the value and Greeks of the trades change in various market scenarios in order to keep control of the risk position of the bank. The result is that the value of each trade must be evaluated in a large number of market states. Then, it is imperative that the numerical algorithms used be as fast as possible.

In addition to speed, numerical stability is essential. There may be small inaccuracies in the trade valuation caused by some numerical instability in the algorithm. These will be greatly amplified when one approximates a first or second order derivative numerically by bumping market data. For example, suppose there is noise of magnitude n in our present value calculation P. We might bump spot with a bump size ϵ in order to approximate the delta, and obtain

$$\Delta \approx \frac{P(S+\epsilon) - P(S) + n}{\epsilon} \tag{8.1}$$

so that the error in the delta calculation is of order n/ϵ. If we calculate a second order Greek, gamma for example, the error gets even larger, going like n/ϵ^2.

For these reasons, we always use an analytic formula if one exists. One of the very first things we are likely to want to do is calculate a vanilla option value using the Black–Scholes formula. Although there is no analytic representation of the cumulative normal function, excellent approximations exist and can be found in West (2009).

For this reason, we treat the cumulative normal function as available analytically. We would never solve a PDE numerically to value a vanilla option because we can simply plug the implied volatility into the Black–Scholes formula.

Inevitably, inverse cumulative normal functions also often appear in financial computations. Once one has implemented a decent approximation for the cumulative normal, the Newton–Raphson method can be used to invert it in a small number of iterations, perhaps using a polynomial approximation for the first step.

If no analytic solution exists, then the next best thing is usually a solution involving only numerical integration. For example, if we have a European payout, it may be that it can be replicated from a simple sum of vanilla payouts. If so, we would price it by valuing those individual vanillas using the Black–Scholes formula. If not, then we could use equation (6.2) to value it by integrating against the probability density function derived from the volatility smile. We could perform this integral numerically using the trapezium rule or quadrature.

If the contract we want to price is path dependent, then it cannot be reduced to depending on the implied probability distribution at a single expiry time only, and we are forced to solve the full pricing problem. We will keep in mind the local volatility example. As seen in equation (6.28), the stochastic process is

$$\frac{dS}{S} = \mu\, dt + \sigma_{local}(S_t, t)\, dW \tag{8.2}$$

and we assume that the drift μ has been chosen, via a measure change, to make the process risk-neutral. We will consider two methods of valuing a contract given a stochastic process. The first is Monte Carlo, which works by simulating the process. The second is the finite difference method, colloquially known simply as the PDE approach, in which we numerically solve the partial differential pricing equation.

8.1 Monte Carlo

8.1.1 Monte Carlo in One Dimension

As always, the fundamental fact we use to value the trade is that, for the price to be arbitrage free, it must be a Martingale when measured in units of the numeraire. We used this in equation (3.44) to get our first Black–Scholes valuation of a call option

$$\frac{C(S_0, 0)}{B_0} = E\left[\frac{C(S_T, T)}{B_T}\right]. \tag{8.3}$$

We can extend this to a more complex path dependent payout. If we use the money market account as our numeraire B_t, then $B_0 = 0$, and the $1/B_T$ factor is simply a discount factor e^{-rT}. Now let's suppose we have a payout $P(S_i)$ depending on a number of spot levels S_i that are the spot values at time T_i. During the lifetime of the trade, we keep a record of the spot levels S_i fixing at an agreed time on those dates, and at the final date of the trade, T, we make a payment of $P(S_i)$ to the counterparty.

Then using our Martingale pricing equation, this contract has value

$$V = E[e^{-r_{dom}T} P(S_i)]. \tag{8.4}$$

If interest rates are deterministic, the discount factor is known and can be taken outside the expectation, but we leave it in (8.4) in order to emphasise that the Monte Carlo technique works just as well when models include stochastic interest rates.

The idea of Monte Carlo is to compute a good approximation to the expectation in (8.4) by simulating the spot path many times and taking the average of the result. By the law of large numbers, this average will converge to the true risk-neutral expectation.

To achieve this, we discretise the time interval between valuation time and final expiry of the option, taking care that the times of interest T_i lie on our discretised time grid. Let's call the times on our grid $\{t_i\}$ with $t_0 = 0$ and $t_n = T$. For simplicity, let's extend our notation slightly so that now S_i are the spot levels at the times t_i. We can still write our payout $P(S_i)$.

Our task is to simulate a random spot path $\{S_i\}$. We begin at $t_0 = 0$ with the current spot level S_0, and we want to simulate S_1 at t_1, S_2 at t_2 and so on. The trick is to assume that the local volatility (and any other parameter in the SDE) is constant during the time interval from t_i to t_{i+1}. This makes sense if $t_{i+1} - t_i$ is small, and the local volatility function is well behaved. In that case, the process is approximately log-normal, and we have

$$S_{i+1} = S_i \exp \left((\mu - 0.5\sigma_{local}^2(t_i, S_i))(t_{i+1} - t_i) + \sigma_{local}(t_i, S_i)\sqrt{t_{i+1} - t_i} X_i \right) \tag{8.5}$$

$$X_i = N(0, 1) \tag{8.6}$$

where X_i is a standard normal variable. Effectively, we have discretised the original continuous Brownian process W_t. On our time grid, we replace dW_t with $\delta W_i = W_{t_{i+1}} - W_{t_i}$. The Brownian increments δW_i are independent and normally distributed with variance $t_{i+1} - t_i$.

Our aim is to simulate sequences of normally distributed random variables on a computer so that we can use equation (8.5) to obtain our random spot paths from the correct distribution. In order to do this, we first simulate random variables from a uniform distribution, and then convert them to normal variables.

There are a number of algorithms for generating sequences of pseudo-random numbers from a uniform distribution. They are called *pseudo*-random because there is no true randomness. They are really just a sequence of numbers generated by an algorithm. But when studied statistically, they display the characteristics of having been drawn from a uniform distribution. Many programming languages are shipped with such a random number generator. They are fine for trying out the ideas in this book, but usually not suitable for production quality pricers.

The problems we solve are high dimensional: we have to discretise the path into a large number of time steps, and in many cases we have more than one stochastic variable to simulate. Then we have to simulate a large number of random variables for each path. Rather than simulating a point in an interval, we are simulating a coordinate in a large-dimensional hyper-cube. Standard linear congruential generator algorithms do not sample the space properly, but instead put the points on a set of sub-planes of the hyper-cube. The result is that the probability space is not sampled properly, and the Monte Carlo algorithm may converge to the wrong value.

There is a high quality algorithm called Mersenne Twister which avoids these problems and is considered industry standard for generating pseudo-random numbers for Monte Carlo simulations. The algorithm was originally described by Matsumoto and Nishimura (1998), and implementations are available for a number of programming languages.

Once we have a series of uniform pseudo-random numbers, we need to convert them into standard normal variables. Given U (uniform) one could apply the inverse cumulative normal function to obtain

$$X = N^{-1}(U). \tag{8.7}$$

This is clearly normally distributed, but as the algorithm to invert the cumulative normal function will itself involve a number of operations, it is slow and may contribute numerical noise that accumulates during the Monte Carlo simulation.

A popular alternative is the Box–Muller transform. In its simplest version, one first simulates two independent uniform numbers U_1, U_2 in $(0, 1]$ and obtains two normal variables via

$$X_1 = \sqrt{-2\log U_1}\cos 2\pi U_2 \tag{8.8}$$

$$X_2 = \sqrt{-2\log U_1}\sin 2\pi U_2. \tag{8.9}$$

One can use a Jacobian to perform the two-dimensional change of variables and check that the resulting joint density of X_1 and X_2 is that of two uncorrelated normal variables. Faster and only slightly more complex variants of the Box–Muller algorithm are available, and can easily be found online.

This is all there is to a simple Monte Carlo algorithm. It can be used to price many types of derivative contract, and its simplicity is attractive. Once an implementation is tested and working on a set of simple contracts like vanilla options, it can be used to value arbitrarily complex trades with a good degree of confidence. Furthermore, any stochastic process can be modelled in Monte Carlo though, as with the Heston model (see Section 7.2.3), care is sometimes needed because of the need to approximate on a discrete time grid.

In addition to calculating the average of the option price during the Monte Carlo simulation, we can also compute the standard deviation s.d. Then the law of large numbers tells us that the average we calculate is normally distributed, and an unbiased estimate for the standard deviation of the average is

$$MC\ error = \frac{s.d.}{\sqrt{N-1}} \tag{8.10}$$

where N is the number of spot paths we simulate. The value we calculate will be within $2 \times (MC\ error)$ of the true value roughly 95% of the time.

This convergence is rather slow. If we want to halve the error, we need to quadruple the number of paths simulated. There are many ways of reducing the variance of the simulation, and therefore the error, and we will highlight the most important of these shortly. Nevertheless, accuracy is always an issue, and for production quality pricing and risk management, Monte Carlo is considered a last resort when other numerical techniques cannot be applied.

8.1.2 Monte Carlo in More than One Dimension

If there is more than one stochastic factor in our model, then we need to simulate correlated Brownian motions. For example, consider a simple SABR stochastic volatility model

$$\frac{dS}{S} = \mu\, dt + \sigma\, dW_1 \tag{8.11}$$

$$d\sigma = v\sigma\, dW_2 \tag{8.12}$$

$$dW_1\, dW_2 = \rho\, dt. \tag{8.13}$$

As before, we split the time between valuation and expiry of the option into a grid, and to simplify the notation, let's assume the spacing of that grid is constant δt. We will simulate approximate Brownian increments via

$$\delta W_1 = W_1(t_{i+1}) - W_1(t_i) = \sqrt{\delta t} X_1 \tag{8.14}$$

$$\delta W_2 = W_2(t_{i+1}) - W_2(t_i) = \sqrt{\delta t} X_2 \tag{8.15}$$

$$E[X_1 X_2] = \rho \tag{8.16}$$

where X_1 and X_2 are standard normal variables with correlation ρ.

The only question is how to simulate correlated normal variables. In two dimensions, it is easy. If Y_1 and Y_2 are independent normal variables, we can choose

$$X_1 = Y_1 \tag{8.17}$$

$$X_2 = \rho Y_1 + \sqrt{1 - \rho^2} Y_2. \tag{8.18}$$

Both X_1 and X_2 are clearly standard normal variables, and $E[X_1 X_2] = \rho$ so that they have correlation ρ. Of course this formula only works if the correlation is between -1 and $+1$, but that makes perfect sense.

However, it will not be long before we need to correlate three or more Brownian factors. For example, we might want to value a derivative contract depending on the spot levels of a number of different assets. In that case, a more systematic approach is required.

Suppose we have a matrix of correlations ρ_{ij} between X_i and X_j. For ρ to make sense as a correlation matrix, it must have 1s on the diagonal so that the correlation between each X_i and itself is 100%. Furthermore, it must be symmetric so that the correlation between X_i and X_j is equal to the correlation between X_j and X_i.

The trick to generating a set of correlated normal variables is to find a matrix C satisfying $C^T C = \rho$. Then we can begin with a vector Y of uncorrelated normal variables, and set

$$X = CY. \tag{8.19}$$

Then X will be a vector of standard normal variables with correlations ρ_{ij}. To see this, we calculate

$$E[X_i X_j] = \sum_{k,l} C_{ik} C_{jl} E[Y_k Y_l] \tag{8.20}$$

$$= \sum_{k,l} C_{ik} C_{jl} \delta_{kl} \tag{8.21}$$

$$= (C^T C)_{ij} \tag{8.22}$$

$$= \rho_{ij} \tag{8.23}$$

where δ_{kl} is notation for 1 if $k = l$ and 0 if $k \neq l$. A correlation matrix should have 1s on its diagonal, and so (8.23) tells us that $E[X_i^2] = 1$ and the X_i are indeed standard normal variables, and furthermore the correlation between X_i and X_j is ρ_{ij}.

The matrix C can be thought of as the square root of the correlation matrix ρ. Not every symmetric matrix can be decomposed in this way. If λ is an eigenvalue of ρ, with normalised eigenvector e, then $e^T \rho e = \lambda$. On the other hand, $e^T \rho e \equiv e^T C^T Ce \equiv (Ce)^T Ce \geq 0$. So the eigenvalues of ρ must be non-negative.

Conversely, if the eigenvalues are non-negative, we could diagonalise ρ, take the square root of the eigenvalues, and then undo the diagonalisation to find C. We conclude that, given ρ is symmetric, we can express $\rho = C^T C$ if and only if its eigenvalues are non-negative.

In the special case of $n = 2$, this reduces to our previous result that we must have $-1 \leq \rho_{12} \leq 1$. By extension, when $n > 2$, the positive eigenvalue condition can only be satisfied if all the elements in the matrix satisfy $-1 \leq \rho_{ij} \leq 1$.

In practice, diagonalising the correlation matrix is a particularly inefficient way of calculating C. Instead, we can use the Cholesky decomposition (which motivated the choice of the letter C). The aim is to choose C to be upper triangular. To compute C, we simply write out the terms arising from the matrix multiplication $C^T C = \rho$, and obtain simple formulas for the C_{ij} that can be solved starting from the top left corner of the matrix:

$$C_{jj} = \sqrt{\rho_{jj} - \sum_{k=1}^{j-1} (C_{jk})^2} \tag{8.24}$$

$$C_{ij} = \frac{1}{C_{jj}} \left(\rho_{ij} - \sum_{k=1}^{j-1} C_{ik} C_{jk} \right), \quad (\text{for } i < j) \tag{8.25}$$

$$C_{ij} = 0, \quad (\text{for } i > j). \tag{8.26}$$

Using the Cholesky decomposition to simulate correlated Brownian motions, our Monte Carlo algorithm has become a powerful tool that can be used for problems with any number of dimensions. The beauty of Monte Carlo is that, even when we have a problem with a large number of stochastic factors, the error still goes like $1/\sqrt{N}$ where N is the number of paths we simulate.

8.1.3 Variance Reduction in Monte Carlo

As Monte Carlo is rather slow to converge, a great deal of effort is put into reducing the error. A number of these are considered essential for any production quality Monte Carlo pricer, and we will give a brief introduction to those. As the error in Monte Carlo comes from the randomness in the simulated paths, they are known collectively as variance reduction techniques.

Antithetic Variates

A simple technique is to create an additional *antithetic* path for each original path simulated. In order to get our spot paths, we actually simulate a set of normal variables that represent the discretised Brownian motion. To get the antithetic path, we change the sign of each normal variable. The result is that the average drift of the simulated Brownian motion will be zero, exactly equal to its true expectation, even if only a small number of paths is used. In this way, a particularly important degree of uncertainty is removed from the simulation.

When using antithetic paths, one needs to take a little care with calculating the standard Monte Carlo error (8.10). If we simulate N paths, we will have $2N$ with the antithetics. However, as they are not independent of the original paths, we should use N and not $2N$ in our formula for the error

$$MC\ error = \frac{s.d.}{\sqrt{N-1}}. \tag{8.27}$$

The use of antithetics almost always significantly improves the convergence of a Monte Carlo simulation.

Calculating Greeks

The standard method to calculate Greeks is to perform the differentiation numerically by bumping the market data. For example, we might calculate delta as

$$\Delta \approx \frac{V(S+\epsilon) - V(S)}{\epsilon} \tag{8.28}$$

where V is the value returned by the Monte Carlo simulation.

A first crucial point is that most random number generators have a seed. This is an integer that is used to initialise the generator and tells it where to start the sequence of pseudo-random numbers. When doing two Monte Carlo simulations to calculate a value in the base state and the bumped state, it is imperative to use the *same* seed. If different seeds are used, the error will be the random Monte Carlo error divided by ϵ, which is bound to be huge. By using matching seeds, the impact of the market data bump is to change the paths only slightly. The error will have the same systematic bias as the unbumped value and their combined effect will be controlled.

Even so, Monte Carlo Greeks can be hard to stabilise. A classic illustration of the difficulties involves payouts with digital features. If we consider the simplest example of the payout $1_{S_T > K}$, we can image calculating the base price, and then bumping the initial spot to calculate the bumped price. If we use 100 paths (far too few, but enough to demonstrate the problem) then it may be that in the base valuation 48 ended up in-the-money so that the price of the contract came out as 0.48. Now suppose we decide to try and get a very good numerical approximation for the delta, so we bump spot by a tiny amount. It may be that one of the original paths was just on the cusp of being in-the-money, and the tiny bump tips it over so that the bumped price is 0.49. Then the calculated delta is $(0.49 - 0.48)/\epsilon$ and can be made arbitrarily large by taking ϵ arbitrarily small, which is clearly nonsense.

For this reason bump sizes should be chosen as large as possible without compromising the accuracy of the numerical differentiation. In addition, when a trade contains digital features, traders will often approximate it with a payout that has the digital part smoothed out, preferably in a conservative way. One way of doing this is the call spread outlined in Section 6.2. In addition to helping with the Monte Carlo Greeks, this also represents the fact that it can be expensive to manage a digital position, particularly if spot ends up close to the strike near expiry.

Low Discrepancy Random Numbers

Pseudo-random sequences behave just like true random numbers. By pure chance there will tend to be some regions with clusters of simulated points, and some without. They seem a rather inefficient way of sampling the probability space.

Naively, the alternative would be to start as before with uniform variables U_i, from which we eventually determine our sample Brownian motion, and choose their values to lie on a grid.

This is perfectly good in one dimension. It corresponds to using numerical integration after a sensible change of variables. However, our problem is multi-dimensional, since we need a random variable for each time step. To illustrate the problem, let's consider a simple two-dimensional case. In that case we need sample values for two variables, U_1 and U_2, both in $(0, 1)$ and we choose them on a square grid with N equal spacings in each direction.

Now let's suppose it so happens that our payout depends mainly on U_1 for some reason. If we project the two-dimensional square grid down onto the U_1 dimension, we have N sample points sitting on top of each other at each of our N one-dimensional grid points. As we ended up sampling N^2 points, we have completely wasted $N^2 - N$ of them.

This example illustrates why Monte Carlo is so much more efficient at evaluating large-dimensional problems than numerical integration. Indeed, as the dimension d

increases, numerical integration quickly becomes unfeasible, as the number of sample points goes like N^d. The payouts we trade must be simple enough that they can easily be understood by a human. In practice this means they are low dimensional, but in a coordinate system that we are unable to sample directly. We can think of Monte Carlo as making apparently high-dimensional integration feasible by taking advantage of this fact.

If only we could generate sequences of points that fill out the multi-dimensional space evenly in such a way that projections onto lower-dimensional spaces are also filled out evenly, then we could enjoy the best of both worlds.

This is made possible with *low discrepancy* sequences, also called *quasi-random numbers*. The most widely used is the Sobol sequence. Quasi-random sequences are only available up to fixed maximum dimension, and this dimension will often be exceeded in finance problems. One usually aims to use Sobol numbers for the 'most important' random factors, and to fill in the rest with pseudo-random numbers.

For our purposes, we are happy to know that we can replace our pseudo-random number generator with a generator using Sobol numbers, and significantly improve the convergence of our Monte Carlo. Full details are available in the comprehensive Jäckel (2002) and Glasserman (2003).

8.1.4 Limitations of Monte Carlo

Monte Carlo can be used to value complex trades in complex models easily as long as the payout can be expressed in the form $P(S_i)$. However, there are two trade features that are problematic: continuous barriers, and callability. We will give some pointers here on the issues and how they can be overcome.

Continuous Barriers

Beginning with continuous barriers, the problem is that the Monte Carlo simulates a discrete set of spot levels. It is easy to value a payout that has a barrier at discrete dates, but if the barrier does not knock out on those dates, there is still the possibility that the spot increased above the barrier level and then returned to below it at some point between two consecutive dates. This can be corrected for. At each time step t_i, we can multiply the payout by the probability that the barrier was not breached in the time t_{i-1} to t_i.

The trick is to assume the volatility is constant σ_i in the time interval $[t_{i-1}, t_i]$. Then we can calculate the probability using Black–Scholes theory in the manner of Section 5.3.2.

Let's suppose the spot levels simulated are s_{i-1} and s_i, and there is an upper barrier with level L. Since we are considering the time interval starting at t_{i-1}, we treat s_{i-1} as our current spot level, and denote the time interval from t_{i-1} to t_i by Δt. Then we need to calculate the probability that the barrier is not breached conditional on the final spot level, $P(M_{\Delta t} \leq L | S_{\Delta t} = s_i)$. Here $M_{\Delta t}$ is the maximum spot level in the time interval $[t_{i-1}, t_i]$ and $S_{\Delta t}$ is just another way of writing S_i.

By following the reflection principle method of Section 5.3.2, we can compute the joint probability distribution

$$P(M_{\Delta t} \leq L, S_{\Delta t} \leq s_i) = N\left(\frac{x - \mu\Delta t}{\sigma_i\sqrt{\Delta t}}\right) - e^{2\mu y/\sigma_i^2} N\left(\frac{x - 2y - \mu\Delta t}{\sigma_i\sqrt{\Delta t}}\right) \qquad (8.29)$$

where $x = \log(s_i/s_{i-1})$, $y = \log(L/s_{i-1})$ and μ is the drift as usual. To obtain the conditional probability, we can differentiate to obtain a density function, and then use the standard formula

$$P(M_{\Delta t} \leq L | S_{\Delta t} = s_i) = \frac{\frac{d}{ds_i} P(M_{\Delta t} \leq L, S_{\Delta t} \leq s_i)}{\frac{d}{ds_i} P(S_{\Delta t} \leq s_i)}. \tag{8.30}$$

After some algebra, this reduces to a particularly pleasing formula

$$P(M_{\Delta t} \leq L | S_{\Delta t} = s_i) = 1 - e^{2y(x-y)/(\sigma^2 \Delta t)}. \tag{8.31}$$

It is a simple matter to apply this formula at each time step in every simulated Monte Carlo path in order to correct for the use of a discrete barrier in place of the true continuous barrier.

Callable Trades

Trades with callable features provide a greater challenge. By callable, we mean that the counterparty, or the issuer, has the right to make an exercise decision that impacts the trade. This right might be available at any time, or only at a discrete set of dates.

One example would be a trade with a cancellation feature. On any of a set number of dates, the counterparty could choose to cancel the trade, and receive a cash payment as compensation. Another example would be a simple American vanilla option which, unlike a European contract, can be exercised at any time during its life.

To value this trade, the Monte Carlo needs to know whether it is optimal to exercise or not on each simulation date. To work this out, one must value the trade with and without the exercise, and pick the choice that gives the greatest value. So on the first possible exercise date, we have two additional simulations to perform. But each of these depends on exercise decisions at future dates, and the resulting tree of necessary simulations grows exponentially and will quickly become unfeasible.

There is a technique available that can be used for such trades. The idea is to pick a small number of variables that might explain the exercise decisions, and then to do a pre-simulation and use least squares regression to estimate the expected payout if the trade is continued conditional on the explanatory variables. Interested readers are referred directly to Longstaff and Schwartz (2001).

8.2   The PDE Approach

As we first saw in Section 3.12, if we begin with a stochastic process for the spot level, the Martingale condition leads to a PDE for the value of any derivative contract. The finite difference technique is a method to solve the PDE numerically. We often refer to it colloquially simply as the PDE approach.

To illustrate the method, we will again consider the local volatility process (8.2). We derived the corresponding partial differential pricing equation,

$$\frac{\partial C}{\partial t} + \frac{\partial C}{\partial S} S\mu + \frac{1}{2} \frac{\partial^2 C}{\partial S^2} S^2 \sigma_{local}(S,t)^2 - Cr_{dom} = 0, \tag{8.32}$$

in equation (6.40).

The contract has a final expiry date $t = T$, and (for now) we assume we know its payout as a function of the log-spot at that time. Our task is to solve the PDE backwards in time to the valuation date $t = 0$. Then we can read off from our solution the price $C(0, S)$ with S the spot at valuation date. As the heat equation is usually studied forwards in time, we will set $\tau = T - t$ so that we solve from $\tau = 0$ to $\tau = T$ rather than from $t = T$ to $t = 0$.

In addition, it is wise to change variables to $x = \log S$ in order to take advantage of the fact that S follows a process that is approximately log-normal. With these changes of variables, the PDE becomes

$$\frac{\partial C}{\partial \tau} = \left(\mu - \tfrac{1}{2}\sigma_{local}(x, \tau)^2\right) \frac{\partial C}{\partial x} + \tfrac{1}{2}\sigma_{local}(x, \tau)^2 \frac{\partial^2 C}{\partial x^2} - Cr_{dom}. \tag{8.33}$$

The trick to solving the PDE lies in its form

$$\frac{\partial C}{\partial \tau} = \mathcal{L}C \tag{8.34}$$

where $\mathcal{L}$ is a differential operator involving only x derivatives. If we know the solution at τ, we can calculate $\mathcal{L}C$. Then we can approximate the τ derivative

$$\frac{\partial C}{\partial \tau} \approx \frac{C(\tau + \Delta\tau, x) - C(\tau, x)}{\Delta\tau} \tag{8.35}$$

and use this to calculate the solution at the new time $\tau + \Delta\tau$

$$C(\tau + \Delta\tau, x) = C(\tau, x) + \Delta\tau \mathcal{L}C(\tau, x) + \mathcal{O}(\Delta\tau^2). \tag{8.36}$$

Starting with the known payout at $\tau = 0$, we repeat this process and build up the solution at all times τ.

To achieve this, we will discretise both the space x and time τ directions to form a two-dimensional pricing grid. The true bounds of x are $\pm\infty$, but to put the problem onto a computer, we choose some finite lower and upper boundaries x_l and x_u far enough away from current log-spot that the probability of reaching them in time T is small. This will ensure they have minimal impact on the solution. We might, for example, pick a measure of volatility (say, the at-the-money volatility at expiry T) $\bar{\sigma}$ and choose $x_{u/l} = x_0 + \mu T \pm 5\bar{\sigma}\sqrt{T}$ so that the grid boundaries are roughly five standard deviations away.

For simplicity, we will choose N equal spacings $\Delta\tau = T/N$ for the time direction, and M equal spacings $\Delta x = (x_u - x_l)/M$ for the space direction. We'll denote the time points $\tau_0 = 0, \tau_1, \cdots, \tau_N = T$, and the space points $x_0 = x_l, x_1, \cdots, x_M = x_u$.

We can approximate space derivatives via

$$\frac{\partial C}{\partial x} = \frac{C(t, x + \Delta x) - C(t, x - \Delta x)}{2\Delta x} + \mathcal{O}(\Delta x^2) \tag{8.37}$$

$$\frac{\partial^2 C}{\partial x^2} = \frac{C(t, x + \Delta x) - 2C(t, x) + C(t, x - \Delta x)}{\Delta x^2} + \mathcal{O}(\Delta x^2). \tag{8.38}$$

Note that in equation (8.37) we used a central difference scheme to approximate the first derivative in order to achieve the $\mathcal{O}(\Delta x^2)$ accuracy (which can be verified by Taylor expanding $C(t, x + \Delta x)$ and $C(t, x - \Delta x)$). Central differencing is always preferred, though at boundaries we may be forced to use one-sided differencing, which is only $\mathcal{O}(\Delta x)$ accurate.

We will use a lower case c to denote the value of the solution on the grid,

$$c_m^n = C(\tau_n, x_m). \tag{8.39}$$

Then for a fixed time slice τ_n, and space point x_m, the discretised PDE becomes

$$\frac{c_m^{n+1} - c_m^n}{\Delta \tau} = \left(\mu - \tfrac{1}{2}\sigma_{mn}^2\right) \frac{c_{m+1}^n - c_{m-1}^n}{2\Delta x}$$

$$+ \tfrac{1}{2}\sigma_{mn}^2 \frac{c_{m+1}^n - 2c_m^n + c_{m-1}^n}{\Delta x^2} - c_m^n r_{dom}, \quad (0 < m < M) \tag{8.40}$$

where we used the abbreviation $\sigma_{mn} \equiv \sigma_{local}(\tau_n, x_m)$.

Equation (8.40) gives us a simple formula to advance the solution by one time step in the interior of the space grid. However, it cannot be applied at the boundaries $m = 0$ and $m = M$ because that would involve knowledge of c_{-1}^n and c_{M+1}^n, each lying outside the grid.

This is the numerical manifestation of the fact from parabolic PDE theory that there is a unique solution only if we supply spatial boundary conditions (at $x = x_l, x_u$) in addition to the initial condition at $\tau = 0$. We need to supply some extra information to allow us to calculate the x derivatives at the boundaries.

One simple choice is to assume the solution is zero beyond the boundaries so that we effectively set $c_{-1}^n = c_{M+1}^n = 0$. As long as the boundaries are far enough away that the spot has no realistic chance of reaching them during the trade lifetime, this choice should not impact the value. We will call this the *zero price* boundary condition.

A more popular choice comes from noting that many option values behave roughly linearly when S is very large or small. The value of a vanilla payout $(S_T - K)_+$ is a clear example. Then it makes sense to choose

$$\frac{\partial^2 C}{\partial S^2} = 0 \tag{8.41}$$

at the boundary. We will call it the *zero gamma* boundary condition. In that case, the pricing equation simplifies to

$$\frac{\partial C}{\partial t} + \frac{\partial C}{\partial S} S\mu - Cr_{dom} = 0, \tag{8.42}$$

and if we change variables to x and τ, that becomes

$$\frac{\partial C}{\partial \tau} = \frac{\partial C}{\partial x}\mu - Cr_{dom} = 0. \tag{8.43}$$

We can use this to advance our PDE forwards at the boundaries

$$\frac{c_M^{n+1} - c_M^n}{\Delta \tau} = \mu \frac{c_M^n - c_{M-1}^n}{\Delta x} - c_M^n r_{dom} \tag{8.44}$$

$$\frac{c_0^{n+1} - c_0^n}{\Delta \tau} = \mu \frac{c_1^n - c_0^n}{\Delta x} - c_0^n r_{dom}. \tag{8.45}$$

Here we were forced by the boundary to use one-sided differencing to approximate the x derivative.

Equations (8.40), (8.44), (8.45) provide a simple formula allowing us to begin with the payout at $\tau = 0$, and advance the PDE step by step to get to the valuation date at $\tau = T$. We can then interpolate the solution from the grid to get the value at the true current spot level.

The scheme we have outlined is only one of many possible ways of discretising the PDE. It is called the *explicit* scheme, because the solution at τ_{n+1} is determined by a simple formula from the solution at τ_n.

The explicit scheme works as long as the time steps are small enough compared to the space steps. However, as we will soon see, for a small cost in additional complexity, we can set up schemes that are much better.

8.2.1 Stable and Unstable Schemes

In order to discuss alternatives to the explicit scheme, we will considering the simpler PDE

$$\frac{\partial C}{\partial \tau} = \frac{1}{2}\sigma^2 \frac{\partial^2 C}{\partial x^2}. \tag{8.46}$$

This will simplify our analysis of the schemes, but it should be noted that for practical implementation, the true pricing problem is hardly more complex.

Also for simplicity, we will work with the zero price boundary condition.

We can write the difference equation that is our original explicit discretisation of the PDE in matrix notation

$$\frac{c^{n+1} - c^n}{\Delta \tau} = \frac{\sigma^2}{2(\Delta x)^2} L c^n \tag{8.47}$$

where now each c^n is a vector, having elements c_m^n. For each fixed time τ_n, we are representing the solution, discretised in the x direction, by the vector c^n. Given that we have chosen zero boundary conditions, the matrix L is

$$L = \begin{pmatrix} -2 & 1 & & & & & \\ 1 & -2 & 1 & & & & \\ & 1 & -2 & 1 & & & \\ & & & \ddots & & & \\ & & & & 1 & -2 & 1 \\ & & & & & 1 & -2 \end{pmatrix} \tag{8.48}$$

and we note that it is tridiagonal.

Gathering the $(\Delta x)^2$ and $\Delta \tau$ into a single factor α simplifies the notation further

$$c^{n+1} - c^n = \alpha L c^n \tag{8.49}$$

where

$$\alpha = \frac{\sigma^2 \Delta \tau}{2(\Delta x)^2}. \tag{8.50}$$

The equation (8.49) gives the explicit scheme, but an alternative perfectly good discretisation of the PDE is

$$c^{n+1} - c^n = \alpha L c^{n+1} \tag{8.51}$$

where now we apply the x derivative operator L at the $n+1$ time step. The problem is that now we do not have a simple explicit equation for c^{n+1}, and (8.51) is called the *implicit scheme*.

To calculate c^{n+1} from c^n, we have a matrix equation that we must solve. Rearranging the implicit difference equation (8.51) gives

$$(I - \alpha L)c^{n+1} = c^n, \tag{8.52}$$

where I is the identity matrix, so that the solution is obtained by inverting the matrix $(I - \alpha L)$

$$c^{n+1} = (I - \alpha L)^{-1} c^n. \tag{8.53}$$

Fortunately, as the matrix is tridiagonal, calculating its inverse is not too hard. One can use the Thomas algorithm, which can easily be found online and is the straightforward result of solving the simultaneous equations by eliminating variables one by one in the usual way.

More generally, we could discretise the PDE using a combination of explicit and implicit methods

$$c^{n+1} - c^n = \alpha L[(1 - \theta)c^n + \theta c^{n+1}]. \tag{8.54}$$

When $\theta = 0$ we have the explicit method, while with $\theta = 1$ it is the implicit method. For general θ, the solution is

$$c^{n+1} = (I - \alpha \theta L)^{-1}(1 + \alpha(1 - \theta)L)c^n. \tag{8.55}$$

Shortly, we will see that the case of $\theta = \frac{1}{2}$ is special, and this is known as the Crank–Nicolson scheme (Crank and Nicolson 1947).

The true PDE has solutions that grow exponentially as well as solutions that decay. Consider

$$\frac{\partial C}{\partial \tau} = \frac{\partial^2 C}{\partial x^2}. \tag{8.56}$$

Both

$$C = e^{-\beta \tau} \cos(\sqrt{\beta} x) \tag{8.57}$$

and

$$C = e^{\beta \tau} e^{\sqrt{\beta} x} \tag{8.58}$$

are solutions for any $\beta > 0$. In practice, by applying boundary conditions, we pick out the financially realistic diffusive solutions (8.57).

However, when we discretise the PDE on a grid, our approximate solution may include small contributions from modes that grow exponentially. Locally, they are of the order of the discretisation error and therefore small. But because they grow exponentially as we solve the PDE, they will ruin the solution. Discretisation schemes displaying this bad behaviour are termed *unstable*, because tiny local errors blow up into huge errors in the solution.

If we denote the matrix operator in our general discretisation scheme by A, then the scheme is

$$c^{n+1} = Ac^n \tag{8.59}$$

where

$$A = (I - \alpha\theta L)^{-1}(1 + \alpha(1 - \theta)L). \tag{8.60}$$

This has solution

$$c^n = (A)^n c^0. \tag{8.61}$$

In words, we apply the matrix that evolves us through one time step n times. If a_i are the eigenvalues of A, then the modes grow like $(a_i)^n$, and we need $|a_i| < 1$ to be sure that errors decay away rather than blow up.

We can find the eigenvalues of A by finding the eigenvalues of L. Indeed, if e_i are the eigenvectors of L, with eigenvalues λ_i, then e_i are also eigenvectors of A, and the eigenvalues are

$$a_i = \frac{1 + \alpha(1 - \theta)\lambda_i}{1 - \alpha\theta\lambda_i}. \tag{8.62}$$

The eigenvalues of an $N \times N$ tridiagonal matrix of the form

$$T = \begin{pmatrix} b & c & & & & \\ a & b & c & & & \\ & a & b & c & & \\ & & & \ddots & & \\ & & & a & b & c \\ & & & & a & b \end{pmatrix} \tag{8.63}$$

are given by[22]

$$\lambda_i = b + 2\sqrt{ac}\cos\frac{\pi i}{N + 1} \tag{8.64}$$

---

[22] To reproduce this result, solve the difference equation implied by the eigenvalue problem, $e_{n+1} - 2e_n + e_{n-1} = \lambda e_n$, subject to the initial condition $e_0 = 0$, and then apply the other boundary condition $e_{N+1} = 0$.

with eigenvectors

$$e_i = \begin{pmatrix} \left(\frac{a}{c}\right)^{\frac{1}{2}} \sin \frac{1\pi i}{N+1} \\ \left(\frac{a}{c}\right)^{\frac{2}{2}} \sin \frac{2\pi i}{N+1} \\ \vdots \\ \left(\frac{a}{c}\right)^{\frac{N}{2}} \sin \frac{N\pi i}{N+1} \end{pmatrix}. \tag{8.65}$$

In our case, the eigenvalues of the matrix L are then

$$\lambda_i = -2 + 2\cos \frac{\pi i}{M+2} \tag{8.66}$$

and in particular we note that they satisfy

$$-4 < \lambda_i < 0. \tag{8.67}$$

Using (8.62), the stability condition is

$$\left| \frac{1 + \alpha(1-\theta)\lambda_i}{1 - \alpha\theta\lambda_i} \right| < 1, \tag{8.68}$$

and since $\lambda > -4$, it is easy to check that stability is *always* satisfied if $\theta \geq \frac{1}{2}$. This means that both the implicit scheme, and the Crank–Nicolson scheme are *unconditionally stable*. The explicit method ($\theta = 0$) does not have such a happy result. Then we only have stability when $\alpha < \frac{1}{2}$. Looking back at our definition (8.50) of α

$$\alpha = \frac{\sigma^2 \Delta\tau}{2(\Delta x)^2}, \tag{8.69}$$

we see that we need time steps to be small compared to space steps for the explicit scheme to be stable.

In order to have a scheme that is as stable as possible, we would like the largest eigenvalue of A (in absolute terms) to be as small as possible. Then errors will decay away faster. Examination of (8.68) shows that the fully implicit ($\theta = 1$) scheme is most stable.

However, there are good reasons for using Crank–Nicolson where possible. We have not yet discussed the order of convergence of the schemes. Let's go back to the definition of the general θ scheme (8.54),

$$\frac{c^{n+1} - c^n}{\Delta\tau} = \frac{\alpha'}{(\Delta x)^2} L[(1-\theta)c^n + \theta c^{n+1}]. \tag{8.70}$$

Here, we have unpacked the α parameter into a new parameter $\alpha' = \frac{1}{2}\sigma^2$ to give back the $\Delta\tau$ and $(\Delta x)^2$, making the approximation to the original PDE explicit. For fixed n, the c^n are vectors with element c_i^n representing the value of the numerical solution at the ith point on the spatial grid.

If we now represent a smooth function joining up the solution on the space grid by $c^n(x)$, we have

$$\frac{c^{n+1} - c^n}{\Delta\tau} = \alpha'[(1-\theta)c_{xx}^n + \theta c_{xx}^{n+1}] + \mathcal{O}(\Delta x^2) \qquad (8.71)$$

which is $\mathcal{O}(\Delta x^2)$ accurate since the operator L represents the central differencing approximation to the second derivative.

We are about to see that the scheme is also $\mathcal{O}(\Delta\tau^2)$ accurate only in the Crank–Nicolson ($\theta = \frac{1}{2}$) case. To see this, it is easier to do a Taylor expansion about a point mid-way between the points τ_n and τ_{n+1} on the time grid. Let us represent by $\bar{c}(\tau, x)$ a smooth function that joins up our approximate solution on the grid, and do a Taylor expansion around that point. Then the left hand side of (8.71) is a central difference, and so is the right hand side in the special case of $\theta = \frac{1}{2}$, and we obtain

$$\bar{c}_\tau = \alpha'[(1-\theta)\bar{c}_{xx} + \theta\bar{c}_{xx}] + \mathcal{O}(\Delta x^2) + (\theta - \frac{1}{2})\mathcal{O}(\Delta\tau) + \mathcal{O}(\Delta\tau^2) \qquad (8.72)$$

$$= \alpha'\bar{c}_{xx} + \mathcal{O}(\Delta x^2) + (\theta - \frac{1}{2})\mathcal{O}(\Delta\tau) + \mathcal{O}(\Delta\tau^2). \qquad (8.73)$$

Thus the Crank–Nicolson case, having $\theta = \frac{1}{2}$, is an $\mathcal{O}(\Delta\tau^2)$ scheme, while both the implicit ($\theta = 1$) and explicit ($\theta = 0$) are only $\mathcal{O}(\Delta\tau)$ accurate.

8.2.2   Choice of Scheme

Most of the time, it is best to use the Crank–Nicolson scheme as it is 'unconditionally stable'[23] and $\mathcal{O}(\Delta\tau^2)$ accurate. However it is imperative to keep the limitations of the above analysis in mind. Firstly, we considered a specific boundary condition (zero value). Similar analyses can be performed for other simple boundary conditions but, in general, the result should be considered a necessary but not sufficient condition for stability.

Furthermore, as the Crank–Nicolson scheme is exactly on the threshold of unconditional stability, there may be modes that have eigenvalue close to 1 and therefore oscillate, and decay very slowly. When there is a discontinuity in an initial or boundary condition, the discretisation error will be large at that point and can ruin the solution.

Similarly, though one would hope to take advantage of the higher order accuracy and use larger time steps in Crank–Nicolson, this must be balanced against larger time steps giving bigger discretisation errors that decay away only slowly.

For these reasons, it is common to use Crank–Nicolson, but to do a number of fully implicit steps after any discontinuity to allow those discretisation errors to decay away.

[23] We emphasise the fact that the terminology *unconditionally stable* can be misleading by using quotation marks here. From now, we shall use the terminology without further health warning.

This approach is often called Rannacher (1984) stepping, and a useful discussion is provided in Giles and Carter (2006).

8.2.3   Other Ways of Improving Accuracy

There are a number of other techniques that can significantly improve convergence of PDE solutions. Readers are referred to Tavella and Randall (2000) for detailed discussion of a number of these.

1   For simplicity, we have assumed an evenly spaced grid for the log-spot direction. However, nothing in the numerical method depends on this, and it can make significant improvements to accuracy if one uses more dense grid points close to points of interest. These might be the strike of an option, or a barrier level, and so on.
2   When calculating Greeks by bumping, stability can be greatly improved by keeping the grid fixed. For example, if spot is bumped to calculate a delta, the results will be more stable if the spatial grid points are not recalculated given the bumped spot.
3   When the payout is not smooth, as for example with a call option payout near the strike, improved convergence can be achieved by setting the payout value at the corresponding grid point to be the *cell averaged* value. That is, to consider the interval half a grid spacing either side of the grid point closest to the discontinuity, and to set the average payout value over that cell on to the grid at that point. This mitigates the dependence on exactly where the discontinuity falls compared to the grid.

8.2.4   More Complex Contracts in PDE

So far we have considered derivative contracts having a simple payout at an expiry date that we can use as our initial condition on the PDE grid. Clearly we are interested in more complex path dependent payouts.

Continuous Knock-out Barrier Options

Continuous barriers are handled by applying a zero price boundary condition at the barrier level on the PDE grid. If the barrier goes all the way from start date to expiry, then we only need a grid that goes out as far as the barrier position. If there are one or more window barriers (that is, with start and end dates between valuation date and expiry) then we will have some regions with zero price boundary condition at the barrier level, and some with zero gamma boundary condition as usual.

Discrete Barrier Options

Discrete barriers only apply at an instant. There may be one or many, applying say at 3pm every business day for a month. They can be priced on PDE by ensuring the discrete barriers lie on the grid, and applying zero price boundary conditions at those points, plus zero gamma conditions as usual elsewhere.

Callable Contracts

Contracts that have exercise features are easy to handle on PDE because the technique works backwards in time.

Consider an American vanilla option. It can be exercised at any time between the valuation date and expiry. We begin with the standard vanilla payout at the expiry date as usual, and then solve backwards. Let's assume we have solved all the way back and know the price at time τ_n. In order to compute the price at τ_{n+1}, we first step the PDE solver, and then compare the result at each space point with the value if the option were exercised. Then the value we choose is the maximum of those two, since a rational investor would exercise if it is optimal to do so.

Continuous Knock-in Barriers

Simple knock-in barrier options can be replicated from knock-out options since the price of a contract with knock-in barrier plus the price with knock-out barrier must be equal to the price when there is no barrier. This is often expressed as

$$knock\text{-}out + knock\text{-}in = knockless. \tag{8.74}$$

In more complex cases, we may need to use two PDE solvers. The first calculates the price of the overall contract, and includes the continuous barrier. The second solver calculates the price of the thing we will get if we touch the barrier, and is used at each time step to provide the boundary condition at the barrier for the first solver.

Asian Options

Asian options have a payout that depends on the spot level at a number of dates prior to the final expiry. An example would be an average rate option, in which we have some spot fixings S_i at given dates t_i, and use them to form an average

$$A = \frac{1}{N} \sum_{i=1}^{N} S_i. \tag{8.75}$$

Then, at the expiry date, the payout might be a vanilla, but on the average

$$P = (A - K)_+. \tag{8.76}$$

Here we have a difficulty. Given only the spot level at the final expiry date, we cannot know the value of the average and therefore the payout. This means we cannot follow our usual approach and use the option payout as the initial condition for the PDE solver.

To solve this, we add a new spatial dimension to the problem to represent the average. Then instead of a vector representing the value of the option at a given time step, we have a two-dimensional array. One dimension, x, represents the log-spot at that time, and the other, A, represents the part of the average (or log-average) that is undetermined.

The PDE solver can be advanced step by step as usual, using the standard one-dimensional approach applying to the log-spot dimension, until it reaches a fixing date t_i for the average. From that point, we introduce a new spatial variable

A' representing the part of the average that has the spot fixing S_i (which we can now determine from the grid) removed.

Since we have solved back as far as t_i, we know the value of the contract given A and $S \equiv S_i$. Then we can calculate the value on our new grid representing A' and log-spot x. This may involve interpolation because the A determined from S_i and A' on the new grid is unlikely to fall exactly on the original grid.

Then we can continue and step back to the next fixing date t_{i-1}. Eventually, we reach the first fixing date t_1, and from there the problem reduces to the standard one-dimensional case.

This technique is called the *method of planes*, since we add a new dimension (plane) to the pricing problem. The process of updating the solution on a new grid at a fixing date is known as *interfacing*. The introduction of the additional dimension means that the solution will be slower and more memory intensive. Nevertheless, it works well and is widely used.

8.2.5 Solving Higher Dimension PDEs

If volatility is stochastic, or if we have a contract on more than one spot rate, then we will need to solve a PDE with more than one dimension.

In two dimensions, the general problem we may need to solve is of the form

$$\frac{\partial C}{\partial \tau} = a_1(x,y,\tau)\frac{\partial^2 C}{\partial x^2} + a_2(x,y,\tau)\frac{\partial^2 C}{\partial y^2} + a_3(x,y,\tau)\frac{\partial^2 C}{\partial x \partial y}$$

$$+ a_4(x,y,\tau)\frac{\partial C}{\partial x} + a_5(x,y,\tau)\frac{\partial C}{\partial y} + a_6(x,y,\tau)C, \tag{8.77}$$

but to ease our notation, we will consider the simpler problem

$$\frac{\partial C}{\partial \tau} = \frac{\partial^2 C}{\partial x^2} + \frac{\partial^2 C}{\partial y^2} + \frac{\partial^2 C}{\partial x \partial y}. \tag{8.78}$$

It is straightforward to put back the missing a_i factors and first derivative terms when one comes to implement a solver in code.

As we have two spatial dimensions x and y, we need a two-dimensional array c_{ij} to approximate the solution at a fixed time step. Then we can use central differencing to discretise the pure x and y derivatives in the usual way

$$\frac{\partial^2 C}{\partial x^2} = \frac{c_{i+1,j} - 2c_{i,j} + c_{i-1,j}}{(\Delta x)^2} + \mathcal{O}(\Delta x^2) \tag{8.79}$$

$$\frac{\partial^2 C}{\partial y^2} = \frac{c_{i,j+1} - 2c_{i,j} + c_{i,j-1}}{(\Delta y)^2} + \mathcal{O}(\Delta y^2) \tag{8.80}$$

$$\frac{\partial^2 C}{\partial x \partial y} = \frac{c_{i+1,j+1} - c_{i-1,j+1} - c_{i+1,j-1} + c_{i-1,j-1}}{(\Delta y)^2} + \mathcal{O}(\Delta x^2, \Delta y^2). \tag{8.81}$$

Although the c_{ij} form an array, we could easily rearrange the elements into a vector, and then write down the explicit discretisation scheme

$$c^{n+1} - c^n = L_{xx}c^n + L_{yy}c^n + L_{xy}c^n, \tag{8.82}$$

where the matrices L_{xx}, L_{yy}, L_{xy} represent the discretisations (8.79)–(8.81) respectively. To keep the notation simple, we have absorbed the factor $\Delta\tau/(\Delta x)^2$ into L_{xx}, and similar for L_{yy} and L_{xy}.

Needless to say, we would prefer an implicit scheme in order to get unconditional stability, but here we have a problem. A moment's perusal of the discretisation equations (8.79)–(8.81) shows that the element $c_{i,j}$ interacts with eight other elements of the array c, and therefore the matrix $L = L_{xx} + L_{yy} + L_{xy}$, is not tridiagonal, but has elements on nine diagonals. Implicit schemes require inversion of the matrix, and we have lost the nice tridiagonal form from the one-dimensional case that made this easy. The matrix L is sparse, and we could look up a sparse matrix inverter from Press et al. (1992), or attempt to solve the simultaneous equations by hand, but this would be hard, and we can do much better.

Because of the diffusive property of the PDE, any discontinuity in the solution is quickly smoothed out as we step the PDE solver forward in time. Therefore, let's assume that the array $c_{i,j}$ is the discretisation of a smooth function. In that case, since the L matrices are all equal to $\Delta\tau$ multiplied by the discretisation of spatial derivatives, we have $Lc = \mathcal{O}(\Delta\tau)$.

For a moment, let's look at the case in which $L_{xy} = 0$. This corresponds to zero correlation between the two spatial factors x and y. Then an implicit finite difference scheme is

$$c^{n+1} - c^n = (1-\theta)L_{xx}c^n + \theta L_{xx}c^{n+1} + (1-\theta)L_{yy}c^n + \theta L_{yy}c^{n+1} + \mathcal{O}(\Delta\tau^2). \tag{8.83}$$

As before, the parameter θ controls the scheme, with $\theta = 0$ being explicit, and $\theta = 1$ fully implicit.

We rewrite the scheme gathering the c^{n+1} terms on the left hand side

$$(I - \theta L_{xx} - \theta L_{yy})c^{n+1} = [I + (1-\theta)L_{xx} + (1-\theta)L_{yy}]c^n + \mathcal{O}(\Delta\tau^2), \tag{8.84}$$

and our problem is that we need to invert the matrix $I - \theta L_{xx} - \theta L_{yy}$. However, since L_{xx} and L_{yy} are both $\mathcal{O}(\Delta\tau)$, we have $L_{xx}L_{yy} = \mathcal{O}(\Delta\tau^2)$. Then we can factorise the matrix operators on the left hand side and right hand side of (8.84) and still retain the $\mathcal{O}(\Delta\tau^2)$ accuracy

$$(I - \theta L_{xx})(I - \theta L_{yy})c^{n+1} = [I + (1-\theta)L_{xx}][I + (1-\theta)L_{yy}]c^n + \mathcal{O}(\Delta\tau^2). \tag{8.85}$$

Now we are in business. For each fixed y direction index, j, the matrix operator L_{xx} only acts on the x direction index, i, of the solution array $c_{i,j}$. As L_{xx} is tridiagonal, we can quickly invert $(I - \theta L_{xx})$ using the Thomas algorithm. The same applies to L_{yy}, and so we have a simple scheme that we could write

$$c^{n+1} = (I - \theta L_{yy})^{-1}(I - \theta L_{xx})^{-1}[I + (1 - \theta)L_{xx} + (1 - \theta)L_{yy}]c^n + \mathcal{O}(\Delta\tau^2). \quad (8.86)$$

This technique is called the *factorisation method*.

There are many ways in which we can factorise our overall central differencing operator. Each alternative factorisation works by dropping a different $\mathcal{O}(\Delta\tau^2)$ term. As we apply operators separately in the x and y directions, the methods are collectively known as *alternating direction implicit* (ADI) schemes. Each needs to be studied individually for its stability and convergence properties. We will not go into those details here, but simply quote results.

We begin with our simple ADI scheme (8.86). Our next task is to add in the cross derivative term L_{xy}, which we excluded until now. Unfortunately, further reflection on the discretisation (8.81) shows that L_{xy} can never be made tridiagonal. Therefore it appears we are stuck with treating it explicitly.

Fortunately, there is a way around this. We do a first predictor step, treating the cross derivative term explicitly, and then use the result to calculate the cross derivative term to use in a second corrector step. This scheme will only be of interest to us in the fully implicit $\theta = 1$ case, so we assume that here to keep the formulas simple

$$c^* = (I - L_{yy})^{-1}(I - L_{xx})^{-1}(I + L_{xy})c^n \quad (8.87)$$

$$c^{n+1} = (I - L_{yy})^{-1}(I - L_{xx})^{-1}(c^n + L_{xy}c^*). \quad (8.88)$$

This technique is known as the *predictor–corrector* method. Though it is easy to put θ back in, unfortunately it remains an $\mathcal{O}(\Delta\tau)$ scheme even when $\theta = \frac{1}{2}$. Still, it is very useful when one needs to do some fully implicit steps to damp errors after a discontinuity in initial or boundary conditions.

While the Crank–Nicolson method was invented remarkably early in 1947, it was not until Craig and Sneyd (1988) that we were provided with an unconditionally stable $\mathcal{O}(\Delta\tau^2)$ method that works in two and three dimensions. Here, we provide the two-dimensional version of the *Craig–Sneyd* scheme

$$(I - \tfrac{1}{2}L_{xx})(I - \tfrac{1}{2}L_{yy})c^* = [(I - \tfrac{1}{2}L_{xx})(I - \tfrac{1}{2}L_{yy}) + L_{xx} + L_{yy}]c^n \quad (8.89)$$
$$+ L_{xy}c^n$$

$$(I - \tfrac{1}{2}L_{xx})(I - \tfrac{1}{2}L_{yy})c^{n+1} = [(I - \tfrac{1}{2}L_{xx})(I - \tfrac{1}{2}L_{yy}) + L_{xx} + L_{yy}]c^n \quad (8.90)$$
$$+ \tfrac{1}{2}L_{xy}(c^n + c^*).$$

In the first predictor step, one computes c^* by inverting the two matrices on the left hand side of (8.89). Then, in the corrector step, c^{n+1} is computed, again by inverting two matrices. The extensions to three (and higher) dimensions are provided by the natural extension of (8.89) and (8.90).

In a practical implementation, each of the predictor and corrector steps can themselves be split into ADI steps. For example, we can write the predictor step (8.89) as

$$(I - \tfrac{1}{2}L_{xx})c^{**} = (I - \tfrac{1}{2}L_{xx})c^n + (L_{xx} + L_{yy} + L_{xy})c^n \tag{8.91}$$

$$(I - \tfrac{1}{2}L_{yy})c^* = c^{**} - \tfrac{1}{2}L_{yy}c^n \tag{8.92}$$

with c^{**} a new intermediate solution.

If the grid is discretised into N_x steps in the x direction, and N_y steps in the y direction, then each time step requires $\mathcal{O}(N_x N_y)$ operations. For example, we have to invert the matrix $(I - \tfrac{1}{2}L_{xx})$, which is $N_x \times N_x$, and this can be done with $\mathcal{O}(N_x)$ operations using the Thomas algorithm. Then we must apply the result to each of the N_y x-vectors that make up the array $c_{i,j}$.

The Craig–Sneyd scheme reduces to Crank–Nicolson in the one-dimensional case and, like Crank–Nicolson, it is an $\mathcal{O}(\Delta\tau^2)$ scheme. It is unconditionally stable, at least in two and three dimensions. Three dimensions are often considered the limit for numerical solution of PDEs. The amount of memory required, and the number of operations needed, to advance the solution for a four- or higher-dimensional problem mean that Monte Carlo is usually preferred. Therefore the fact that Craig–Sneyd is unconditionally stable only up to three dimensions does not cause further restriction.

8.3 Key Points

- When derivative pricing problems are too complicated to be solved analytically or semi-analytically, there are two approaches available: Monte Carlo simulation and numerical PDE solution.
- Monte Carlo works by simulating random spot paths in order to estimate the expectation in the Martingale pricing formula.
- The PDE approach works by discretising the partial differential pricing equation on a grid, and solving it backwards in time from the final payout to the valuation date.
- Monte Carlo is useful for valuing complex or bespoke payouts, or when there are a large number of stochastic factors in the model.
- The PDE approach is preferred over Monte Carlo when there are a small number of stochastic factors (up to three) because it is faster and gives more stable Greeks.
- Monte Carlo can easily value path dependent trades but callable trades are tricky.
- The PDE approach can easily value callable trades. Path dependent trades require the addition of planes to the problem, which act as an additional factor and therefore slow down the solution.

8.4 Further Reading

For the Monte Carlo approach, the books by Jäckel (2002) and Glasserman (2003) are strongly recommended. The original reference is Metropolis and Ulam (1949).

A classic reference for the PDE approach is Wilmott, Dewynne, and Howison (1993), and a pleasingly concise introduction is Tavella and Randall (2000). The PDE problems that we solve in finance are rather simple compared to those in medicine and engineering. The finite difference approach seems well suited to derivative pricing, but more sophisticated approaches are well known outside quantitative finance. One that may be useful is the method of wavelets, reviewed in Dempster and Eswaran (2001).

We noted in Section 7.2.3 that simulation of the Heston model in Monte Carlo is tricky. Discussion of approaches for simulating stochastic volatility processes can be found in Kahl and Jäckel (2006) and Andersen (2008).

The method of planes for valuing Asian options in PDE was introduced by Rogers and Shi (1995) for a continuously sampled average, and is provided in Benhamou and Duguet (2003) when there is discrete sampling. An unusual and fascinating use of an implicit PDE solver is provided by Andreasen and Huge (2011), who use it to create an arbitrage-free volatility surface interpolation from a set of market vanilla prices.

9 Local Stochastic Volatility

So far, we have looked at two modelling approaches to explain the implied volatility smile: local volatility and stochastic volatility. If we choose a stochastic volatility approach, we have seen that there are many possible models, each having the ability to generate a smile. This is rather unsatisfactory since it leaves us wondering which approach or which particular model we should use. There are further questions we have touched on but not yet answered. What if our stochastic volatility model does not perfectly match our smile at all strikes? As we only have a small number of stochastic volatility parameters, what can we do about getting the smile right at a number of different expiry dates? Do all the contracts we care about even have well-defined prices in the model we choose?

All of these questions will be addressed soon. We will learn that we need a new kind of model that is some way between local volatility and stochastic volatility. We will discover that, for many contracts we care about, it doesn't matter too much which particular process we use to generate the stochastic volatility component of the model, and we will see that we can set up our model so that it perfectly matches the implied volatility smile at all expiry dates. Much excitement lies ahead.

We will work by first setting up our local stochastic volatility model, and only then go into the detail to answer these questions.

Let's step back for a moment and remind ourselves of what we would like to achieve. We have an asset in mind. Let's say it is gold. We would like to price an exotic derivative contract that depends on the gold price over a period of time. For example, it might be a knock-out barrier option which has an ordinary vanilla payout at an expiry date one year from now, but only pays if the gold price never goes below a certain level between now and that date. In the market, there are a lot of contracts traded liquidly. There is spot gold itself, then there are forward contracts at multiple expiry dates, and there are vanilla contracts at multiple strikes and expiries. Indeed, as usual, we will assume that a full implied volatility smile can be deduced from the vanilla market at any expiry date.

Our model must price all these liquid instruments correctly, otherwise we are exposed to arbitrage. For example, if it doesn't get vanilla prices right, then a smart counterparty could trade a knock-out barrier option and a knock-in barrier option (the latter giving the vanilla payout only if the barrier is breached). Since one or other of these contracts always gives the vanilla payout, the two contracts together are identical to the pure vanilla option. If our model gets the vanilla price wrong, the counterparty will be able to make money with no risk by trading the two barrier options and the opposite vanilla.

The task appears immense because the constraints of repricing all vanilla contracts are so tight. It is not as if they are constraints on the instantaneous model parameters at a given time. Rather, they insist that the cumulative effect of the model parameters from the start date to the expiry time in question exactly conspire to price vanillas correctly at all strikes. And furthermore, the same must be true at all expiry times.

9.1 The Fundamental Theorem of On-smile Pricing

It is a beautiful theorem due to Gyöngy (1986), coupled with Dupire's work on local volatility, that makes everything possible. So important is Gyöngy's theorem that in this book we have called it the fundamental theorem of on-smile pricing. We will first state the theorem in Gyöngy's original form.

   Let ξ_t be a stochastic process satisfying

$$d\xi_t = \beta_t + \delta_t \, dW_t \tag{9.1}$$

where W_t is a Brownian motion with filtration $\mathcal{F}_t$ and β_t, δ_t are bounded stochastic processes adapted to $\mathcal{F}_t$. Then there exists a stochastic differential equation

$$dx_t = b(t, x_t)dt + \sigma(t, x_t)dW_t \tag{9.2}$$

with non-random coefficients with a solution x_t having the same one-dimensional probability distribution as ξ_t for every t. The coefficients b and σ satisfy

$$\sigma(t,x)^2 = E[\delta_t^2 \,|\, \xi_t = x] \tag{9.3}$$

$$b(t,x) = E[\beta_t \,|\, \xi_t = x]. \tag{9.4}$$

In the statement of the theorem, β_t and δ_t are arbitrary random processes. For example, δ_t could be any of the stochastic volatility processes we have discussed, and might also contain dependence on ξ_t itself. Similarly, the theorem allows for a stochastic drift term β_t. All that we need to assume about the processes is that they are adapted to the filtration, that is, that they respect the same concept of time as the Brownian motion W_t. The assumption that the processes are bounded is no constraint on us as financial engineers. If we are working with a stochastic volatility process, say, that is not bounded, we can simply add in a bound at a large enough level that the probability of reaching it is small and it won't concern us.

   We will recouch the theorem in terms that are weaker but will be most useful to us, and then show why it is true. In the following, it is helpful to keep in mind that σ is shorthand for σ_t, the stochastic instantaneous volatility at time t.

   Suppose $dS/S = \mu dt + \sigma \, dW$ and the volatility σ follows a stochastic process with the property that the vanilla market is repriced everywhere. Then

$$E[\sigma^2 \,|\, S] = \sigma_{local}^2(S, t) \tag{9.5}$$

where $\sigma_{local}(S,t)$ is Dupire's local volatility function calculated from the market implied volatility surface.

Here we have not bothered with a stochastic drift. We will be applying the theorem to risk-neutral spot processes in which the drift is given by the difference between deterministic interest rate and yield. Since we know from Section 6.2 that knowledge of the vanilla market is equivalent to knowledge of the probability distribution of spot at any fixed time, we have replaced the statement that one-dimensional probabilities are matched with the statement that vanilla options are correctly repriced. Finally, we have already seen from the construction in Section 6.4 that a local volatility process with matching one-dimensional probability distributions exists, and so we have reduced the theorem to the calculation of the local volatility function from the stochastic parameters.

We provide the nice financial proof due to Derman and Kani (1998). Take the random variable call payout $(S-K)_+$ and differentiate (by applying Ito's lemma)

$$d(S-K)_+ = 1_{S>K}\,dS + \tfrac{1}{2}\delta(S-K)S^2\sigma^2\,dt. \tag{9.6}$$

Take the expectation

$$dE[(S-K)_+] = E[S1_{S>K}]\mu\,dt + \tfrac{1}{2}E[\delta(S-K)S^2\sigma^2]\,dt \tag{9.7}$$

$$\tfrac{1}{2}E[\delta(S-K)S^2\sigma^2] = E[S1_{S>K}]\mu - dE[(S-K)_+]/dt. \tag{9.8}$$

The expectations on the right hand side of (9.8) are the undiscounted values of European contracts, and therefore can be determined from the vanilla market. The left hand side is

$$\tfrac{1}{2}K^2\,E[\sigma^2|S=K]\,E[\delta(S-K)] \tag{9.9}$$

and again the $E[\delta(S-K)]$ can be determined from the vanilla market. The conclusion is that $E[\sigma^2|S]$ depends only on the vanilla market, so is the same for all choices of process, including Dupire local volatility. The result follows.

9.2 Arbitrage in Implied Volatility Surfaces

A useful consequence of Gyöngy's theorem is that it gives us a way of checking whether our implied volatility surface could be the result of a reasonable stochastic spot process. If not then we will be on the look out for a possible arbitrage. Imagine we are a market making vanilla option dealer. We see prices in the market at a particular set of strikes and expiry dates, either from brokers, or from trades that are dealt. We plug these into our interpolator in order to obtain the surface of implied volatilities at all expiries and all strikes. The thing is, the prices we build our smile from may not be perfectly consistent. How do we know that the implied volatility surface we obtain does not give vanilla prices that can be used to create an arbitrage?

The very first thing we should do is check that call option prices behave sensibly as strike increases from 0 to ∞

$$\lim_{K \to 0} C(K, T) = e^{-rT} E[(S_T - 0)_+] = e^{-rT} F_T \tag{9.10}$$

$$\lim_{K \to \infty} C(K, T) = 0 \tag{9.11}$$

$$\frac{\partial}{\partial K} C(K, T) < 0. \tag{9.12}$$

Then, we can calculate the local volatilities from our vanilla prices using equation (6.35),

$$\tfrac{1}{2}\sigma_{local}(K, T)^2 = \frac{\frac{\partial}{\partial T} C(K, T) + K\mu \frac{\partial}{\partial K} C(K, T) + (r_{dom} - \mu) C(K, T)}{K^2 \frac{\partial^2}{\partial K^2} C(K, T)}. \tag{9.13}$$

If the Dupire local volatility function $\sigma_{local}(S, t)$ is everywhere positive then certainly there is a stochastic process (the local volatility process) giving those vanilla prices using the usual absence of arbitrage argument, and we are done. But what if the local volatility is bad (imaginary or undefined) somewhere? Then there cannot be any stochastic volatility process giving those vanilla prices either, because if there were, Gyöngy's theorem tells us that there would also be a good local volatility function.

This is satisfying. We can eliminate the possibility of arbitrage opportunities in our implied volatility surface simply by calculating the local volatilities and checking they are well defined.[24] If they are not, we may be able to go further and find a trade to take advantage of the arbitrage.

For the local volatility to go bad, either the numerator or the denominator must be non-positive in equation (9.13). Considering the denominator first, we recognise the risk-neutral probability density calculated in equation (6.10),

$$p(K, T) = e^{r_{dom} T} \frac{\partial^2}{\partial K^2} C(K, T). \tag{9.14}$$

This is the undiscounted value of a security having the Dirac delta function $\delta(S_T - K)$ as its payout, and should have positive value in an arbitrage-free world as the payout is everywhere positive or zero. In order to lock in the arbitrage, we could choose three strikes close to K and use them to approximate the second derivative so that our arbitrage portfolio is the right hand side of

$$\frac{\partial^2}{\partial K^2} C(K, T) \approx \frac{C(K + \epsilon, T) - 2C(K, T) + C(K - \epsilon, T)}{\epsilon^2}. \tag{9.15}$$

---

[24] Note that it is allowable for the denominator in (9.13) to go to zero while the numerator is finite in certain circumstances and so the local volatility function may blow up, but it must always stay real and non-negative. See Cont and Gu (2012) for spot processes with jumps.

This portfolio has a positive triangular shaped payout that is non-zero in the region $(K - \epsilon, K + \epsilon)$. As long as the region in which the implied probability density is negative includes this, the payout is assigned negative value and therefore represents an arbitrage.

The second way the local volatility can go bad is if the numerator of (9.13) is negative. If the interest rate and asset yield were zero, this would correspond simply to $\partial C(K,T)/\partial T < 0$. In order to lock in the arbitrage, one can do a calendar spread

$$C(K, T+\epsilon) - C(K, T), \tag{9.16}$$

which the market is valuing negative. If we do this trade, then suppose the call option happens to be out-of-the-money when we get to the expiry T so that $S_T < K$. In that case, our portfolio is worth

$$C(K, T+\epsilon) - 0 \tag{9.17}$$

which is positive since during the time between T and $T+\epsilon$, spot may move to be in-the-money.

On the other hand, if the call option is in-the-money, we can use put–call parity

$$C(K, T+\epsilon) - C(K, T) \equiv P(K, T+\epsilon) + (F_{T+\epsilon} - K) - P(K, T) - (F_T - K). \tag{9.18}$$

As rates are zero we have $F_{T+\epsilon} = F_T$, and as the call at T is in-the-money, the put is out-of-the-money, and we obtain

$$C(K, T+\epsilon) - C(K, T) = P(K, T+\epsilon) + 0 \tag{9.19}$$

which, again, is positive.

In this way, we have set up a portfolio whose value at T is guaranteed positive, but which is valued negative now, and we have achieved the arbitrage. If rates are not zero, then adjustments are needed to take into account the time value of money (and the time value of the asset) and this explains the full form of the numerator of equation (9.13)

$$\frac{\partial}{\partial T} C(K, T) + K\mu \frac{\partial}{\partial K} C(K, T) + (r_{dom} - \mu) C(K, T). \tag{9.20}$$

In this case, the arbitrage can be set up by choosing strikes and expiries to approximate the derivatives in (9.20).

The calendar spread argument presented here assumes interest rate and yield rate are deterministic, since the arbitrage portfolio we set up depends on the rates. We shall treat this as good enough for our purposes, since we assume deterministic rates throughout this book. A more formal approach is provided in Carr and Madan (2005).

9.3 Two Extremes of Smile Dynamic

We have looked at two types of smile model: local volatility, and the family of stochastic volatility models. However, other than practicalities of implementation, we have not considered which type of model is most appropriate. In Section 9.7, we will see that the choice of model can give quite a dramatic impact on the price of some important contracts. For now, as a primer, we will look at how the choice of model affects the dynamic followed by implied volatility. That is, we will look at how the implied volatility smile changes when the underlying spot moves.

9.3.1 Sticky Strike Dynamic

One possible smile dynamic is that, when the underlying spot moves, the implied volatility smile measured in strike space $\sigma_{imp}(K, T)$ remains unchanged. This is known as the *sticky strike* dynamic.

To test a model for sticky strike behaviour, we would use it to value vanilla options at various strikes given a number of different initial spot values. Then we would back out the corresponding implied volatilities and check if $\sigma_{imp}(K, T)$ depends on the initial spot level.

The local volatility model produces a smile that is sticky strike to a fair approximation. To see this, we can look back to the local volatility formula (6.35)

$$\tfrac{1}{2}\sigma_{local}(K, T)^2 = \frac{\frac{\partial}{\partial T}C(K, T) + K\mu\frac{\partial}{\partial K}C(K, T) + (r_{dom} - \mu)C(K, T)}{K^2\frac{\partial^2}{\partial K^2}C(K, T)}. \quad (9.21)$$

Given vanilla call option prices $C(K, T)$, it tells us how to calculate the local volatility function so that our model prices the vanillas correctly.

Since implied volatility tells us the price of vanilla options (by applying the Black–Scholes formula), we can recast (9.21) into a formula relating the local volatility function to the market implied volatilities. The result

$$\sigma_{local}(K, T)^2 = \frac{\sigma_{imp}^2 + 2\sigma_{imp}T\left(\partial_T\sigma_{imp} + \mu\partial_x\sigma_{imp}\right)}{1 + \sigma_{imp}T\left[\left(\frac{2d_1}{\sigma_{imp}\sqrt{T}} - 1\right)\partial_x\sigma_{imp} + \partial_x^2\sigma_{imp} + \frac{d_1 d_2}{\sigma_{imp}}(\partial_x\sigma_{imp})^2\right]}, \quad (9.22)$$

obtained by changing variables using the chain rule, is pleasingly simple. Here $\sigma_{imp} = \sigma_{imp}(K, T)$ is the implied vol at time T and strike K, and $x = \log K$. The standard Black–Scholes parameters d_1 and d_2, defined in equations (3.56)–(3.57), can be rewritten

$$d_1 = \frac{\log(S/K) + (\mu + \tfrac{1}{2}\sigma_{imp}^2)T}{\sigma_{imp}\sqrt{T}} \quad (9.23)$$

$$d_2 = \frac{\log(S/K) + (\mu - \tfrac{1}{2}\sigma_{imp}^2)T}{\sigma_{imp}\sqrt{T}} \quad (9.24)$$

in order to make their dependence on the spot level more explicit.

The two terms in the denominator of (9.22) depending on d_1 and d_2 provide the only dependence of that formula on the spot level S. If we assume that the volatility smile is not too strongly skewed so that $\partial_x \sigma_{imp}$ is small, then those terms disappear and the relation between local and implied volatility is indeed approximately independent of the spot level.

9.3.2 Sticky Delta Dynamic

Another possible implied volatility dynamic would allow the implied volatility smile to *float* in strike space. That is, to move in strike space along with any spot move. Another way of putting this is that if we choose to write the implied volatility as a function of strike divided by spot, $\sigma_{imp}(K/S, T)$, then this function would remain unchanged if spot moves.

In some markets (notably foreign exchange), it is common to express implied volatility as a function of Black–Scholes delta rather than of strike. Looking back to Table 4.1, we see that the delta is a function of d_1

$$\Delta = e^{-r_{yield}T} N(d_1). \tag{9.25}$$

Given a strike, we can use the implied volatility smile to get the volatility, and then calculate the delta. Conversely, given a delta, we can find the corresponding strike, and so write the implied volatility as $\sigma_{imp}(\Delta, T)$. Since the formula for Δ depends on the spot S only through S/K, a floating smile model will leave the implied volatility smile expressed in Δ terms unchanged after a spot move. For this reason, the floating smile dynamic is often known alternatively as the *sticky delta* dynamic.

A stochastic volatility model having zero correlation between the spot and volatility processes exhibits sticky delta behaviour. To see why, consider the general (zero correlation) model

$$\frac{dS}{S} = \mu\,dt + \sigma\,dW_1 \tag{9.26}$$

$$d\sigma = \alpha(\sigma, t)dt + v\beta(\sigma, t)dW_2 \tag{9.27}$$

$$dW_1\,dW_2 = 0, \tag{9.28}$$

and imagine pricing a vanilla call option with payout

$$\frac{(S_T - K)_+}{K}. \tag{9.29}$$

The Black–Scholes formula for the price of this contract is

$$e^{-r_{dom}T}\left(\frac{S_0 e^{\mu T}}{K}N(d_1) - N(d_2)\right). \tag{9.30}$$

If we now perform the transformation

$$S_t \to \lambda S_t \tag{9.31}$$

$$S_0 \to \lambda S_0 \tag{9.32}$$

$$K \to \lambda K \tag{9.33}$$

then equations (9.26)–(9.30) are all left invariant, and therefore so must be the implied volatility that we would back out of the Black–Scholes formula (9.30).

This shows that stochastic volatility models display sticky delta dynamics as long as the correlation is zero. If there is a non-zero correlation, then the argument breaks down. In that case, volatility process moves are linked to spot moves, so we can't keep the initial instantaneous volatility σ_0 constant while performing the scaling transformation. In the extreme case of $\pm100\%$ correlation, instantaneous volatility moves are governed entirely by the same process W_1 that drives the spot moves, and the model behaves similarly to a local volatility model.

9.4   Local Stochastic Volatility

We are now ready to look at the triumph of modern derivatives pricing: *local stochastic volatility* (LSV). The technique resolves, at a stroke, two major problems, that we will now outline.

The first problem applies to stochastic volatility models. Suppose we decide that the SABR model is the right model to use to explain the volatility smile and value exotic contracts. We choose a vanilla expiry date, say six months from now, and calibrate the model parameters to match vanilla option prices at three strikes at that date, as discussed in Section 7.7. The difficulty we have is that we will not match the vanilla market at other strikes, let alone at other expiry dates. LSV solves this problem by including a local volatility component which exactly fixes the pricing at expiries and strikes away from the original calibration data.

The second problem is the choice of a stochastic or local volatility model to explain the smile. While, assuming perfect calibration, both types of model get vanilla prices right, exotic contracts like barrier options will be priced very differently. LSV allows us to set up a model in which the smile is explained partly by a local volatility component, and partly by stochastic volatility. We begin with a stochastic volatility model explaining, say, 60% of the steepness of the smile, and then add in a local volatility correction that fills in the difference. By choosing the *mixing* between stochastic and local volatility, we can control the price of exotic contracts while always correctly pricing the vanilla smile.

The technique that makes the calculation of the local volatility correction possible is known as *forward induction*. It is remarkable in that, while it is a purely numerical technique, the result is so perfect that it is considered mathematically beautiful in its own right.

Let us write down the model without further ado. First, we need to choose an underlying stochastic volatility process. Any of the models from Chapter 7 will do, and indeed there are many other possible choices. For the purpose of our presentation, we will use the λ-SABR process defined in equation (7.77). Our spot process will be of standard log-normal style, with the instantaneous volatility composed partly of the stochastic λ-SABR volatility σ_t, and partly of a local volatility correction function $A(S, t)$. Then the SDEs defining the model are

$$\frac{dS}{S} = \mu\, dt + A(S, t)\sigma\, dW_1 \tag{9.34}$$

$$d\sigma = -\lambda(\sigma - \overline{\sigma})dt + v\sigma\, dW_2 \tag{9.35}$$

$$dW_1\, dW_2 = \rho\, dt. \tag{9.36}$$

With our choice of underlying stochastic volatility model, the parameters are vol-of-vol, v, mean reversion, λ, mean reversion level, $\overline{\sigma}$, and spot–vol correlation, ρ. We assume they are fixed at the outset, and then our problem is that we need to calculate the local volatility correction function $A(S, t)$.

To achieve this, we apply the fundamental theorem of on-smile pricing (Gyöngy's theorem) from Section 9.1. Applying equation (9.5) tells us

$$E[(A(S, t)\sigma_t)^2 \mid S] = \sigma_{local}^2(S, t), \tag{9.37}$$

where $\sigma_{local}(S, t)$ is the Dupire local volatility function, and can be calculated from vanilla prices using the formula (6.35), or directly from the implied volatility smile by using (9.22). The expectation on the left hand side of equation (9.37) is conditional on S, and therefore, for the purpose of this expectation, the function $A(S, t)$ is not random and we can take it outside. Then we have the formula

$$A(S, t)^2 = \frac{\sigma_{local}^2(S, t)}{E[\sigma_t^2 \mid S]}, \tag{9.38}$$

and the problem has been reduced to calculating $E[\sigma_t^2 \mid S]$.

As the process for S is dependent on the process for σ, the conditional expectation $E[\sigma_t^2 \mid S]$ depends on the function $A(S, t)$ and so one might think that we are stuck with a difficult non-linear problem to compute the function A.

The trick is to write down the forward Kolmogorov PDE. As in Section 6.3, we apply Ito's lemma to a test function, take the expectation, and then integrate the partial derivative terms by parts. The result is the PDE satisfied by the joint probability density at time t, $p(t, S, \sigma)$, of the spot S and stochastic volatility component σ,

$$\frac{\partial}{\partial t}p = -\frac{\partial}{\partial S}(S\mu p) - \frac{\partial}{\partial \sigma}[(-\lambda)(\sigma - \overline{\sigma})p] + \frac{1}{2}\frac{\partial^2}{\partial S^2}[S^2 A(S, t)^2\sigma^2 p]$$

$$+ \rho\frac{\partial^2}{\partial S\partial \sigma}[vSA(S, t)\sigma^2 p] + \frac{1}{2}\frac{\partial^2}{\partial \sigma^2}(v^2\sigma^2 p). \tag{9.39}$$

If only we knew the local volatility correction function $A(S,t)$, we could solve the PDE numerically using the finite difference technique of Section 8.2.5. To do so, we would discretise the problem on a grid having two spatial dimensions (for S and σ) plus the time dimension. In practice, as usual, we would transform both spatial variables to log space allowing the distribution of points on the grid to better sample the solution.

The initial condition for the problem should be a delta function

$$p(0,S,\sigma) = \delta(\sigma - \sigma_0)\delta(S - S_0) \qquad (9.40)$$

since at $t = 0$, both S and σ are equal to their initial values with probability 1. This is discretised on the grid in the obvious way with

$$p(0,S,\sigma) = \begin{cases} 1/(\Delta S \Delta \sigma), & S = S_0, \sigma = \sigma_0 \\ 0, & \text{otherwise,} \end{cases} \qquad (9.41)$$

where ΔS and $\Delta \sigma$ are the grid spacings. As the initial condition is discontinuous, it is essential to use an implicit scheme (the scheme in equations (8.87)–(8.88) for example) for the first few steps.

A small technical detail is that the coefficients in the PDE (9.39) appear inside the partial derivatives rather than outside as was assumed in Section 8.2. A moment or two's reflection on the finite difference method shows that this is no obstacle, and the ADI technique works with little modification.

All this is well and good, but our problem is that, without knowledge of the function $A(S,t)$, we cannot step the PDE solver forward. Let's assume, however, that we have managed to compute $A(S,t)$ on the grid all the way from $t = 0$ up to the nth time step t_n. Then we can approximate $A(S,t)$ as $A(S,t_n)$ in the entire interval $[t_n, t_{n+1})$, and step the PDE solver forward to the next time step. This gives us the joint density function $p(t_{n+1},S,\sigma)$ at time t_{n+1}.

Looking back to equation (9.38), we recall that we can calculate $A(S,t_{n+1})$ as long as we can calculate $E[\sigma_t^2|S]$. But as we have the joint density function approximated on the grid, this is available to us through the formula

$$E[\sigma_{t_{n+1}}^2|S] = \frac{\int \sigma^2 p(t_{n+1},S,\sigma)\,d\sigma}{p(t_{n+1},S)}. \qquad (9.42)$$

The integral in the numerator of the right hand side is calculated, in the natural way, by summing over the grid points in the σ direction. The PDF in the denominator could similarly be obtained by $p(t_{n+1},S) = \int p(t_{n+1},S,\sigma)\,d\sigma$. Alternatively, we recall from Section 6.2 that the Breeden–Litzenberger approach allows us to read off the spot density function $p(t_{n+1},S)$ directly from the implied volatility surface we are calibrating to.

In this way, if we know the local volatility correction at time t_n, we can compute it at t_{n+1} by stepping a finite difference PDE solver forward one time step. We begin with a sensible choice at $t_0 = 0$ along the lines of

$$A(S,0) = \frac{\sigma_{local}(S,0)}{\sigma_0}. \qquad (9.43)$$

Then the entire local volatility correction function $A(S,t)$ can be calculated on the grid by running the PDE solver through one forward sweep.

This technique, known as forward induction, works beautifully. One can use the local volatility correction so calculated either directly on a matching PDE grid for pricing, or by interpolation if the spatial grid differs. To test if the method has worked, one should then value vanilla options at various strikes and maturities by solving the pricing PDE, and check that they match the implied volatility smile to which the model was calibrated.

One might worry that the discretisation of the Dirac delta function at $t = 0$ would cause problems, perhaps because it is too challenging for the PDE solver to remain stable. However, the model is remarkably robust, providing correct vanilla repricing to a high degree of accuracy. As of 2012, most (if not all) investment banks are using local stochastic volatility calibrated via forward induction in their production pricing systems.

9.5 Simplifying Models

We have seen that there are a plethora of stochastic volatility models. Every financial institution has its own, and therefore one would expect that it would be hard to agree on the price of exotic contracts. In fact, spreads are remarkably tight on first generation exotic options, that is, vanilla or digital payouts with continuous barriers from start to expiry. We will refer to these trades simply as *barrier options*.

In a moment, we will argue that barrier options are insensitive to almost all the details of the stochastic volatility model that underlies the local stochastic volatility model. The first step will be to suggest that there is little point in including a correlation between the spot and volatility processes, because the effect of such a correlation can be mimicked with the local volatility correction. This argument will not be made precise mathematically except in a specific example. Those readers who feel uncomfortable with this can treat it as an empirical observation by looking at the specific examples in Section 9.7. Then the next step is to show that, in a pure stochastic volatility model without correlation, barrier option prices are determined purely by the probability distribution of the total variance between valuation date and expiry, and therefore details of the exact process causing this distribution are irrelevant. This argument is mathematically rigorous, though it involves an approximation.

9.5.1 Spot–Volatility Correlation

We begin then with a fairly general stochastic volatility model but, for simplicity, we assume interest rates are zero so that the process for S is

$$\frac{dS}{S} = \sigma \, dW_1 \qquad (9.44)$$

$$dσ = a(σ,t)dt + b(σ,t)dW_2 \qquad (9.45)$$

$$dW_1 dW_2 = ρdt, \qquad (9.46)$$

with $a(σ,t)$ and $b(σ,t)$ functions of the instantaneous volatility that determine the exact form of the mean reversion and vol-of-vol.

As the Brownian processes W_1 and W_2 are correlated with correlation $ρ$, we can rewrite

$$dW_2 = ρdW_1 + \sqrt{1-ρ^2}dW_2' \qquad (9.47)$$

where W_2' and W_1 are uncorrelated. Then, whenever there is a change dW_1 causing a change in the spot level, this will feed into W_2 through the term $ρW_1$ and so cause a change in the instantaneous volatility $σ$. This is a 'local volatility like' effect. An increase in spot causes an increase in the volatility. There is still the effect from the dW_2' contribution to the process for $σ$ left over, so that, if this happens to be bigger and in the opposite direction, then the volatility may decrease. That's fine. The volatility is only correlated to the spot process, not entirely dependent on it.

The idea then is that we can obtain a similar dynamic with an alternative model of the form

$$\frac{dS}{S} = A(S,t)σ\,dW_1 \qquad (9.48)$$

$$dσ = \tilde{a}(σ,t)dt + \tilde{b}(σ,t)dW_2 \qquad (9.49)$$

$$dW_1 dW_2 = 0. \qquad (9.50)$$

Here the two Brownian motions driving $σ$ and S are uncorrelated, but there is a local volatility function $A(S,t)$ so that the true instantaneous volatility is

$$\bar{σ} = A(S,t)σ. \qquad (9.51)$$

If the volatility and spot are positively correlated, then $A(S,t)$ will be upward sloping as a function of spot, while negative correlation corresponds to a downward sloping local volatility function. As we explained in Section 6.1, equity markets tend to have negative correlation between spot and volatility, since share prices dropping leads to uncertainty and high volatility. In this case, if spot goes down, then $A(S,t)$ will increase, and the volatility increases. Again, it may be that simultaneously, a particularly large move in the volatility process W_2 causes the volatility to increase overall. That's fine. As before, the volatility is only correlated to the spot process, not entirely dependent on it.

The argument we have made is heuristic. In almost all cases, it is not exactly mathematically true that one can achieve an identical effect by replacing a spot–volatility correlation with a local volatility correction. One can begin to make counter arguments and point out that in a local volatility model, if spot goes down and stays there, volatility will go up and stay there, while a strongly correlated stochastic volatility model can include mean reversion so that even if the spot stays low, volatility is likely to mean revert back down again. This argument happens to be flawed because a large mean reversion reduces the volatility of σ and therefore a larger vol-of-vol is needed to achieve the convexity of the market smile thereby overcoming the mean reversion effect. But it shows that caution is required when considering the naive presentation we have made. After chasing these arguments around for a while, one is well advised to take a pragmatic approach and look at numerical examples. We will look at one example in Section 9.7. Practically speaking, including correlation in one's local stochastic volatility model appears to have little impact on barrier pricing.

To illustrate our point, let us take one particular example of a stochastic volatility model, having stochastic differential equations

$$\frac{dS}{S} = \sigma \, dW_1 \tag{9.52}$$

$$d\sigma = \tfrac{1}{2}(\alpha - v\sigma^2)dt + v\sigma \, dW_2 \tag{9.53}$$

$$dW_1 \, dW_2 = dt. \tag{9.54}$$

Like the λ-SABR model of equations (7.76)–(7.78), this model is an extension of SABR to include a mean reversion term. However, the mean reversion term involves σ^2 instead of σ, and the rate of mean reversion has been chosen as exactly half the vol-of-vol v. Furthermore, we have written down SDEs with $dW_1 \, dW_2 = dt$ so that there is perfect correlation between the spot and volatility processes: we could write $dW_1 = dW_2 \equiv dW$.

This model was chosen carefully. Consider now the local volatility model

$$\frac{dS}{S} = (v \log S/A + \tfrac{1}{2}\alpha t)dW. \tag{9.55}$$

The local volatility is

$$\sigma(S,t) = (v \log S/A + \tfrac{1}{2}\alpha t), \tag{9.56}$$

where A is some constant determining the initial volatility at time 0 and initial spot S_0. We can apply Ito's lemma to this volatility, and note that the process it follows is

$$d\sigma = \tfrac{1}{2}(\alpha - v\sigma^2)dt + v\sigma \, dW, \tag{9.57}$$

identical to the stochastic volatility process in equation (9.53). This is a contrived example of a stochastic volatility model for which the correlation can be replaced by a local volatility correction. Although it is not true for the general case, it does lend weight to the claim that the impact of correlation can be well approximated by a local volatility correction.

9.5.2 Term Structure Vega for a Barrier Option

It is a fascinating fact that the vega of a barrier option is mostly concentrated at its expiry. To be more precise, in Black–Scholes, let's allow a time-dependent volatility σ_t, and define the terminal volatility $\sigma = \frac{1}{T} \int_0^T \sigma_t^2 \, dt$. Then, to a very good approximation, the value of a barrier option expiring at time T is dependent only on σ and not on the full term structure σ_t. In a normal, rather than log-normal, model this is exactly true.

This is a consequence of the reflection principle from Section 5.3.1. We begin with the normal model

$$dS_t = \sigma_t \, dW_t. \tag{9.58}$$

To value a barrier option, we need to know the joint probability distribution of the spot at expiry and the minimum of spot between now and the expiry. The fact that σ_t is time dependent has no bearing on the reflection principle, and we have as usual

$$P(S_T \geq K, m_T \leq L) \equiv P(S_T \leq 2L - K) \tag{9.59}$$

where

$$m_T = \min_{0 \leq t \leq T} \{S_t\}. \tag{9.60}$$

Then, in a *normal* model, the value of the barrier option depends only on the probability distribution of S_T, the spot at expiry. Looking back to Section 2.7, we recall this implies the value can be expressed in terms of the σ alone.

Just as in Section 5.3.2, a constant drift can be included in the model, and the reflection principle applied with only minor adjustment. In our case though, we would like to include a time-dependent drift ν_t,

$$dS_t = \nu_t \, dt + \sigma_t \, dW_t. \tag{9.61}$$

This would allow us to apply our results to the log-normal model, by taking advantage of the relation

$$d \log S_t = -\tfrac{1}{2} \sigma_t^2 \, dt + \sigma_t \, dW_t. \tag{9.62}$$

To understand why this is *not* possible, let us follow the argument for a constant drift, and see where it goes wrong.

We can use dimensional analysis to put the volatility back in later, so we will work with the process

$$dB_t = \nu_t \, dt + dW_t \tag{9.63}$$

having unit volatility. As in Section 5.3.2, we use a measure change to remove the drift of B_t. The Radon–Nikodým derivative is

$$Z_T = \exp\left\{-\int_0^T v_t \, dW_t - \frac{1}{2}\int_0^T v_t^2 \, dt\right\} \tag{9.64}$$

and to change back requires

$$\tilde{Z}_T = \exp\left\{\int_0^T v_t \, dB_t - \frac{1}{2}\int_0^T v_t^2 \, dt\right\}. \tag{9.65}$$

Then the probability can be expressed as an expectation under the new measure (indicated with a tilde $\tilde{\ }$) in which B_t is a pure Brownian motion without drift

$$P(B_T \geq k, m_T \leq l) = \tilde{E}[1_{\{B_T \geq k, m_T \leq l\}} e^{-\frac{1}{2}\int_0^T v_t^2 \, dt + \int_0^T v_t \, dB_t}]. \tag{9.66}$$

Here we have used the lower case letters $k = \log K$ and $l = \log L$ to remind us that we aim to apply our results to the log process.

We can define B_t' to be the Brownian motion that is equal to B_t until the moment it touches the barrier, and is its reflection in the barrier thereafter. Then the reflection principle tells us that we can replace the joint condition $\{B_T \geq k, m_T \leq l\}$ with a single condition on the reflected process $\{B_T' \leq 2l - K\}$, giving

$$P(B_T \geq k, m_T \leq l) = \tilde{E}[1_{\{B_T' \leq 2l-k\}} e^{-\frac{1}{2}\int_0^T v_t^2 \, dt + \int_0^T v_t \, dB_t}]. \tag{9.67}$$

If v_t is constant $v_t = v$, then this simplifies to

$$P(B_T \geq k, m_T \leq l) = \tilde{E}[1_{\{B_T' \leq 2l-k\}} e^{-\frac{1}{2}v^2 T + v B_T}] \tag{9.68}$$

$$\equiv \tilde{E}[1_{\{B_T' \leq 2l-k\}} e^{-\frac{1}{2}v^2 T + v(2l - B_T')}], \tag{9.69}$$

as in Section 5.3.1. In this special case, the random variable inside the expectation depends only on the terminal value B_T' and we are done.

In the general case in which we put back the time dependence of v_t, the argument goes wrong. The two random variables

$$X = \int_0^T v_t \, dB_t \tag{9.70}$$

and

$$Y = B_T \sqrt{\frac{1}{T} \int_0^T v_t^2 \, dt} \tag{9.71}$$

have matching probability distribution, but they are *not* equal to each other.

Nonetheless, as long as v_t is everywhere of the same sign and not strongly varying, X and Y are strongly (anti-)correlated to each other. Indeed, their correlation is

$$\frac{E[XY]}{\sqrt{\mathrm{Var}[X]\mathrm{Var}[Y]}} = \frac{\frac{1}{T} \int_0^T v_t \, dt}{\sqrt{\frac{1}{T} \int_0^T v_t^2 \, dt}}, \tag{9.72}$$

which is just the quotient of two measures of the average of v_t. We define the quantity

$$\bar{v} = \left| \frac{1}{T} \int_0^T v_t \, dt \right| \tag{9.73}$$

and make the approximation

$$\sqrt{\frac{1}{T} \int_0^T v_t^2 \, dt} \approx \bar{v}. \tag{9.74}$$

This is a reasonable assumption for our case in which $v_t = -\frac{1}{2}\sigma_t^2$ is the log-normal drift adjustment, and we do not expect the instantaneous volatility σ_t to vary too wildly from its mean reversion level. Then, in our approximation, we can replace the random variable X in equation (9.67) with $-Y$ since they are now perfectly anti-correlated. This leads to the approximate formula

$$P(B_T \geq k, m_T \leq l) \approx \tilde{E}[1_{\{B_T' \leq 2l-k\}} e^{-\frac{1}{2}\bar{v}^2 T - \bar{v}(2l - B_T')}]. \tag{9.75}$$

Now that our expectation depends only on the terminal value of the Brownian motion B_T', and the quantity $\bar{v} \equiv \frac{1}{2}\sigma^2$, we see that, in our approximation, the joint probability depends only on σ and not on the full term structure of σ_t.

It is worth noting that the above argument can be made to go wrong more easily when considering the drift caused by interest rates, since this drift can be both positive and negative. To demonstrate this, we can artificially set up a model in which there is almost no volatility, but a strongly varying term structure of interest rates causing the forward to breach the barrier and then come back again. If the term structure of rates were ignored, the value would have almost no impact from the barrier, while taking them into account, the contract would almost certainly knock out and have zero value.

In any case, our conclusion is that, to a good approximation, the Black–Scholes price of a barrier option is independent of the term structure, but depends only on the terminal volatility $\sigma^2 = \frac{1}{T}\int_0^T \sigma_t^2 \, dt$. This explains why the term structure vega of a barrier option is concentrated at its expiry.

9.5.3 Simplifying Stochastic Volatility Parameters

Let us now return to the stochastic volatility model from equations (9.44)–(9.46) that we might wish to use to underlie our local stochastic volatility model. Later, we will be able to use a local volatility correction to provide an effect like spot–volatility correlation, and so we work with a model having zero correlation

$$\frac{dS}{S} = \sigma \, dW_1 \tag{9.76}$$

$$d\sigma = a(\sigma,t)dt + b(\sigma,t)dW_2 \tag{9.77}$$

$$dW_1 dW_2 = 0. \tag{9.78}$$

The undiscounted price of a barrier option is given by

$$I = E[(S_T - K)_+ 1_{\{m_T > B\}}] \tag{9.79}$$

$$= E[E[(S_T - K)_+ 1_{\{m_T > B\}} | \{\sigma_t\}]] \tag{9.80}$$

where we used the standard nesting property of expectations to condition on the stochastic volatility path $\{\sigma_t\}$. As there is zero spot–volatility correlation, the Brownian motion W_1 is independent of the volatility so that, conditional on $\{\sigma_t\}$, the problem reduces to a term structure Black–Scholes model. Then, using the results of the previous section, we can approximate the undiscounted value as an expectation over the terminal volatility

$$I \approx E[BS(K,B,\sigma)] \tag{9.81}$$

where BS is the Black–Scholes formula for the barrier option price, and the terminal volatility is $\sigma = \sqrt{\frac{1}{T}\int_0^T \sigma_t^2 \, dt}$.

This means that all that concerns us is the probability distribution of the terminal volatility. Whether the volatility process is normal or log-normal, and the details of the mean reversion and vol-of-vol: all are irrelevant.

We can represent the PV by

$$I = \int f(\sigma)BS(K,B,\sigma)\,d\sigma, \tag{9.82}$$

which can be approximated using numerical integration by

$$I \approx \sum_{i=1}^{N} w_i BS(K, B, \sigma_i) \tag{9.83}$$

for a set of N discrete volatilities σ_i and weights w_i. Remarkably, this is exactly the pricing formula for the mixture model from Section 7.5. Furthermore, if a Gauss–Hermite approach is used to choose the w_i and σ_i, excellent results can be achieved with rather a small number of integration points N, and we have arrived at a mixture model with a small number of states. We had rejected mixture models for path dependent contracts because the dynamic is too unrealistic. Now we see that, like European options, continuous barrier options can provide an exception to this rule.

9.5.4 Risk Managing with Local Stochastic Volatility Models

We have considered the kind of pure stochastic volatility models that we might use to underlie our local stochastic model. We began by arguing that there is little point in including a spot–volatility correlation, because a similar effect on the spot dynamic can be achieved with the local volatility correction alone. Then, given a general stochastic volatility model with zero correlation, we saw that barrier option prices depend only on the probability distribution of the *terminal* volatility, at least to a good approximation. This allows us to replace our original arbitrarily complex stochastic volatility process with a much simpler model. As long as our simple model gives a good approximation for the terminal volatility distribution, it can be used in place of the original. In practice, the terminal volatility will usually be well approximated by a normal variable, at least close to the mid point of the distribution. The only real degree of freedom is the amount of vol-of-vol injected into the terminal volatility by the stochastic process. This can be controlled by adjusting the vol-of-vol parameter in whatever form it appears in the underlying model.

It is important to emphasise that we have made a financial engineering argument rather than anything approaching a rigorous proof. Nevertheless, it shows how it is that all investment banks can agree on barrier prices even though they have different stochastic volatility processes underlying their local stochastic model. The instruments that are liquid in the market are continuous barrier options (also called first generation exotic options). All that really matters for valuing these contracts is the amount of vol-of-vol in the underlying stochastic volatility model, and this parameter can be tuned by traders. We will see in Section 9.7 that it is possible to take quite large liberties with the underlying stochastic volatility model. Even a mixture model with only a very small number of states can still provide good results for first generation exotic options.

The arguments we have made break down if we wish to value products with more complex path dependence. The most obvious example would be a trade with a continuous *window* barrier. That is, a barrier that does not extend all the way from the start date to expiry of the trade, but is only live for a fraction of that period (the window). Here, a cool head and some pragmatism is required.

Let's imagine we wish to trade a window barrier option. We calibrate our local stochastic volatility model and, in so doing, achieve an exact match to market vanilla prices at all expiry dates. Furthermore, by tuning a term structure of vol-of-vol parameter, we can get an excellent match to first generation exotic options at a range of expiries, strikes and barrier levels. In this way, our model correctly prices all the instruments we might possibly use to hedge with. We have nailed our boots quite firmly to the ground by correctly matching so many contract prices. As a window barrier trade is not too dissimilar from an ordinary barrier trade, it is unlikely that changing the model will alter the value by much.

Care is needed when considering contracts with more complex payouts. Consider, for example, a forward starting call option having payout

$$(S_{T_2} - S_{T_1})_+. \tag{9.84}$$

Here $T_2 > T_1$ are two future times, say six months and one year from now, and S_{T_1}, S_{T_2} are the spot levels measured at those dates. It is very much like a call option paying at T_2 except that the strike is not known until T_1, at which point it is set to the spot level S_{T_1}.

The forward starting contract (9.84) depends on the term structure of volatility, and therefore on the structure of mean reversion and vol-of-vol in the underlying stochastic volatility model. One might think it is necessary to set up a complex model to capture this. In practice, the necessity to match the implied volatility surface and barrier prices places quite a heavy constraint on forward start prices, and it is possible that a simple model may be good enough even for these contracts.

For more complex contracts, caution is certainly required. It is easy to construct contracts to exploit flaws in any given model. For example, consider a mixture model having two volatility states at 5% and 10%. We could set up a contract to exploit the fact that the volatility can only take two discrete values in the model. We could sample the spot level at frequent regular intervals, and at expiry calculate a realised volatility from the spot samples. Then our contract could pay out only if the realised volatility is between 6% and 9%. In our model, this contract has zero value, which is clearly absurd.

The fact is that it is easy to criticise almost any model this way. Derivatives modelling is not about trying to set up a spot dynamic that is as close to reality as possible. Not only is that impossible, it is not desirable. Nobody really believes that the true spot dynamic is a mixing between Dupire local volatility and stochastic volatility. No, given a contract we wish to price, our aim is to find a model in which as many as possible of the contracts that could be used to hedge are valued correctly. In this way we avoid arbitrage. By calculating risk (Greeks) to the parameters that define the prices of the hedging instruments, we can use trades available in the market to offset our risk. Or at the very least, we can avoid building up positions with large exposure to any particular risk.

When understood this way, we see that it makes sense to use the simplest possible model that captures all the risk for the trade in question. Put another way, our model needs to correctly reprice all the useful hedging instruments. It is helpful for exotic option traders to have an armoury of models at their disposal. If a contract has value that varies significantly in the different models without good explanation, that indicates it is not a safe trade to put on the books.

9.6 Practical Calibration

Once we have decided on the stochastic volatility (SV) model to underlie our LSV model, we need to choose its parameters. For example, if we use the λ-SABR model as in equations (9.34)–(9.36), the parameters are the mean reversion rate, mean reversion level, vol-of-vol, correlation and also the initial volatility that applies at time 0.

Once the SV parameters are fixed, we use the forward induction technique, explained in Section 9.4, to compute the local volatility correction. When this is done, vanilla options are guaranteed to be priced correctly at all strikes and expiries. Therefore the aim of calibration is to choose the SV parameters so that exotic option prices are correct. The most liquid, and therefore most important, exotics are barrier options.

We can look at a contract that pays 1 if a continuous barrier is hit and 0 otherwise. This is called a one-touch option. It will have a particular time to expiry T, say three months from now. We can pick the barrier level so that it has probability roughly 50% of the barrier being touched. Experience shows that when the parameters are tuned to match the market price of this contract, prices of the other possible barrier options with varying barrier level and different payouts at expiry will be correct to good approximation. We saw in Section 9.5 some indication of why this is so. Therefore, if we only have one expiry date in mind, we need tune only one of the SV parameters.

The appropriate parameter to tune is the vol-of-vol. When this is zero, the stochastic volatility is deterministic because there is no contribution from the Brownian motion dW_2. Then when the local volatility correction is applied, the model will exactly match Dupire's local volatility. On the other hand, as the vol-of-vol increases towards a value that generates a smile as steep as the market smile, the model approaches a pure stochastic volatility model. Mean reversion impacts the effective vol-of-vol over a given time interval, and it is also possible to play mean reversion and vol-of-vol off against each other to some extent.

There are two approaches to determining the SV parameters. The first approach is to leave them as user inputs and allow traders to choose them. Traders will quickly build up an intuition for how to adjust the parameters in order to match the barrier option prices they wish to calibrate to. The advantage of this approach is that it is fast: all that is required is the forward induction PDE sweep. However, it is not particularly intuitive. For example, one cannot look at the SV parameters and easily comment on whether the market is more sticky strike, or more sticky delta.

In the second approach, one first calibrates the underlying SV model to the vanilla market, as in Section 7.7, to obtain an initial set of SV parameters. This involves repeatedly valuing a set of vanilla options that are considered important, and adjusting the SV parameters until the valuations are correct. Then, a mixing parameter m is introduced. In any SV model, one can find a parameter representing the vol-of-vol, or equivalently controlling the convexity of the smile generated. In the λ-SABR model, this is the parameter v. Then the vol-of-vol is replaced with a new value that is reduced by a factor of 1 minus the mixing,

$$v' = (1 - m)v. \tag{9.85}$$

The other SV parameters are left alone.

With this scheme, a mixing of zero leaves the original vol-of-vol untouched so that the underlying SV model reprices the set of vanillas to which it was calibrated. Usually, these will be at three strikes so that the overall level, convexity and skew of the volatility smile are correct in the SV model. Then the local volatility correction, calculated via the forward induction, will make small adjustments to ensure an exact fit to the input volatility surface. Thus, with mixing zero, the LSV model is close to pure stochastic volatility.

On the other hand, if the mixing is set to 1, the vol-of-vol used will be zero so that the stochastic component of the model volatility is actually deterministic. In this case, the local volatility correction will act to make the LSV model identical to Dupire local volatility.

The down side of this second approach is that it requires the calibration step of the underlying SV model. If there is no analytic solution for the value of vanilla contracts, this requires numerical techniques and therefore may be slow and potentially unstable.

However, this is not nearly such a problem as at first it seems. Rather than insist on an exact calibration for the underlying SV parameters, an approximation can be used. It does not need to be a particularly good approximation because the local volatility correction will cover up any errors in vanilla pricing, and the mixing parameter can be adjusted to allow for any errors in barrier pricing. For example, if SABR is used, the standard SABR approximation of Section 7.3 is perfectly good. If one wishes to include mean reversion, an approximation can be found in Henry-Labordère (2005), or one could temporarily approximate by an Ornstein–Uhlenbeck process, as in Section 7.4, for the purpose of the mean reversion and vol-of-vol calibration.

The beauty of this approach is that traders can express the stochastic volatility versus local volatility (or sticky delta versus sticky strike) nature of the market by choosing the mixing parameter. The most developed markets for barrier option trading are foreign exchange. There, one finds that mixing parameters have remained notably stable, typically around 40%. This is important for traders because they want to know that they can price and risk manage their exotic trades even when markets are moving fast.

9.7 Impact of Mixing on Contract Values

Until now, we have merely asserted that local volatility and stochastic volatility models value path dependent contracts differently without showing any examples. In the language of Section 9.6 we would like to understand how contract values depend on the mixing, with mixing 1 corresponding to a pure local volatility dynamic, and mixing 0 corresponding to stochastic volatility. One-touch options are often the most liquid of the first generation exotics, and as we noted in Section 9.6, are useful for calibration of the SV parameters or mixing.

Figure 9.1 shows a classic one-touch plot giving the impact of the dynamic on the valuation. We recall that a one-touch contract has an expiry date, and a continuous barrier from the start date to expiry. If spot breaches the barrier at any time during the

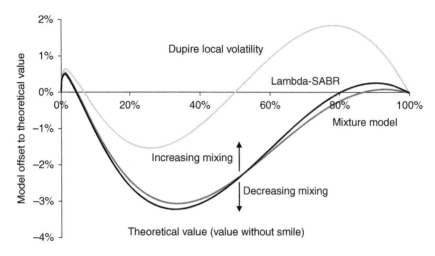

Figure 9.1   One-touch plot (upper barrier) with λ-SABR mixing 0.4.

life of the trade, the contract pays 1 at the expiry date. If not, it pays 0. The trades in Figure 9.1 have an expiry date one year from the trade inception.

An important concept in smile pricing is the *theoretical value* (TV), or *off-smile* value. To obtain the TV, we take the volatility surface and switch off the smile. In practice, this means we use the at-the-money volatility for all strikes. We do still allow a term structure of volatility (and interest rates), so the at-the-money volatility can vary for different expiry dates. Any sensible smile model will reduce to Black–Scholes when the smile is switched off, and so the TV can be thought of as the Black–Scholes price, using term structure at-the-money volatility.

Traders almost always like to see the TV alongside the smile price. This is because it is model independent and so allows for easy sense checking of the valuation. It is quite normal for exotics traders to ensure that they agree on the TV with the counterparty before trading. Although the trade will transact at the smile price, matching TVs ensures both parties have set up the same trade correctly.

In Figure 9.1, we have chosen to plot one-touch prices against the TV rather than the barrier level. We have chosen to look at trades with an upper barrier. Clearly if the barrier level is equal to current spot, the (undiscounted) trade value is 1, while when the barrier is moved to ∞, the value goes to zero. By plotting against TV instead of barrier level, we can display valuations for the full range of barriers.

On the *y*-axis are plotted the offset of the value of the one-touch compared to the TV. These valuations happen to have been obtained using the volatility surface displayed in Figure 6.1 and market interest rates. However, the overall two-humped shape of the plot is classic for all volatility surfaces.

Valuations in three models are shown, each calculated by running a PDE solver. The Dupire local volatility model can be considered the base case, and corresponds to mixing 1. The λ-SABR LSV model has the stochastic process defined in equations (9.34)–(9.36) with parameters given in Table 9.1. They were chosen to correspond to a mixing of roughly 0.4.

Table 9.1. *λ-SABR Parameters Used To Generate Figure 9.1*

Parameter	Value
Mean reversion rate, λ	0.7
Mean reversion level, $\overline{\sigma}$	8.62%
Initial volatility, σ_0	9.11%
Vol-of-vol, ν	60%
Spot–vol correlation, ρ	−16%

Table 9.2. *Mixture Model Parameters Used To Generate Figure 9.1*

Volatility State	Probability
5.1%	1/6
8.4%	2/3
14.0%	1/6

Finally, a three state mixture model is included for comparison. The spacing of the states was chosen so that the one-touch valuation matches the λ-SABR model when the TV is around 50%. The volatility states and probabilities are given in Table 9.2.

The two underlying stochastic models we have tried could not be more different from one another. The λ-SABR model has a full dynamic for the stochastic volatility including mean reversion and spot–volatility correlation, while the mixture model involves only the toss of a (three sided) coin at the start. Nevertheless, as we expect from the discussion in Section 9.5, the valuations in the two LSV models are close at all barrier levels.

If we increase the mixing parameter towards 1, both LSV models become closer and closer to pure Dupire local volatility, and the plots move upwards as indicated by the arrow in Figure 9.1. On the other hand, if the mixing parameter is decreased towards zero, the LSV values move downwards, away from the local volatility valuations.

The shapes of the plots in Figure 9.1 are absolutely characteristic. Although not a formal proof, we can understand why a one-touch contract is cheaper under stochastic volatility dynamics than local volatility as follows.

The underlying principle we are going to use is that a one-touch contract is worth roughly twice as much as a digital contract with strike matching the barrier level. To see why this is, we first consider a normal model

$$dS = \sigma\, dW \tag{9.86}$$

(to keep things simple, we will assume zero interest rates). Imagine the one-touch has a continuous upper barrier at level B, and pays 1 at expiry time T if the barrier is touched, so that the payout is

$$O(B) = 1_{\{M_T > B\}},\tag{9.87}$$

where $M_T = \max_{0 \le t \le T}\{S_t\}$ is the maximum spot level between now and the expiry time.

At a moment t when spot touches the barrier, the one-touch is worth 1. Let's now consider a digital option having payout

$$D(B) = 1_{\{S_T > B\}}.\tag{9.88}$$

If we look at the value of this digital at the instant t when spot touches the barrier, the digital is worth exactly 0.5 because there are equal chances of ending up above or below the barrier at the expiry T.

Therefore we can follow a trading strategy to replicate the one-touch payout. At the inception of the trade, we buy two units of the digital. If spot never touches the barrier during the life of the trade, both the one-touch and the digital expire worthless at time T. But if spot touches the barrier, we can immediately sell the digital contract and receive 1, matching the payout of the one-touch. For the strategy to work, it is essential to close out the digital contracts when spot touches the barrier, otherwise if spot ends up lower than the barrier we will have lost all the value of the hedge.

This argument shows that the price of a one-touch in the normal model is equal to twice the digital price, which we can represent with risk-neutral expectations of the payouts

$$E[O(B)] = 2E[D(B)].\tag{9.89}$$

Really, this is just another way of looking at the reflection principle. We used the fact that in a normal model there is perfect symmetry about the current spot level to see that the value of the digital is exactly 0.5.

The method can be extended to the log-normal (Black–Scholes) case. A glance back to Sections 3.10 and 3.13 reminds us of the standard Black–Scholes formulas. The value of the digital at time t is now $N(d_2)$ with

$$d_2 = \frac{\log(S/B) - \frac{1}{2}\sigma^2(T-t)}{\sigma\sqrt{T-t}}.\tag{9.90}$$

At the instant spot touches the barrier, we have $S = B$ giving digital value

$$N(-\tfrac{1}{2}\sigma\sqrt{T-t}).\tag{9.91}$$

This is close, but not exactly equal, to 0.5. For example, when there is one year left to expiry, and the volatility is 10%, this gives value around 0.48. We cannot simply adjust the notional of the digital to get our hedge, because this value depends on the touch time.

However, looking back to equations (3.55)–(3.57), we note that when spot touches the barrier, $S = B$, d_2 and d_1 are related simply by $d_2 = -d_1$, and a vanilla call payout $C(B) = \frac{1}{B}(S_T - B)_+$ with strike B has value

$$N(-d_2) - N(d_2) \equiv 1 - 2N(d_2) = 1 - 2D(B). \tag{9.92}$$

Then, at the moment spot touches the barrier, we can replicate the one-touch price using a call option and two units of the digital, and following the same trading strategy as before shows that the value of the one-touch is

$$E[O(B)] = 2E[D(B)] + E[C(B)]. \tag{9.93}$$

When we include volatility smile, the argument goes wrong again. Let's assume that the barrier is first touched at time $t = \tau$. We can value the call option using the Black–Scholes formula with the at-the-money implied volatility that we see at that time

$$E[C(B)] = BS(B, \sigma_{ATM}). \tag{9.94}$$

We cannot simply use the at-the-money volatility to calculate the digital price. By definition, implied volatility is *that volatility we plug into the Black–Scholes formula to get the correct vanilla price*, and we cannot directly use implied volatilities to value contracts other than vanillas. However, we recall from equation (6.4) that the digital payout can be obtained from a vanilla payout by differentiating with respect to strike

$$1_{S>K} = -\frac{\partial}{\partial K}(S-K)_+. \tag{9.95}$$

Then the value of the digital is

$$E[D(B)] = -\frac{d}{dB}BS(B, \sigma_{imp}(B))\bigg|_{\sigma_{imp}=\sigma_{ATM}} \tag{9.96}$$

$$= -\frac{\partial}{\partial B}BS(B, \sigma_{ATM}) - \frac{\partial}{\partial \sigma}BS(B, \sigma_{ATM})\frac{d}{dB}\sigma_{imp}(B) \tag{9.97}$$

$$= N(d_2) - Vega \times Skew \tag{9.98}$$

where

$$Vega = \frac{\partial}{\partial \sigma}BS(B, \sigma_{ATM}) \tag{9.99}$$

$$Skew = \left. \frac{d}{dB}\sigma_{imp}(B)\right|_{\sigma_{imp}=\sigma_{ATM}} \tag{9.100}$$

and d_2 is evaluated using the at-the-money volatility.

Then, at touch time τ we have

$$E[O(B)] = 2\left\{E[D(B)] + E[Vega(\tau) \times Skew(\tau)]\right\} + E[C(B)] \tag{9.101}$$

where, since unlike the other terms they are not the values of market instruments, we have emphasised the dependence of the vega and skew on the touch time. The digital and vanilla components of equation (9.101) are European payouts that can be set up at the trade inception. Therefore (recalling from Section 6.2) their values are dependent only on the smile and not on the model that causes the smile. Then, to understand the model dependence of our one-touch price, we can concentrate on the contribution from the term

$$I = E[Vega(\tau) \times Skew(\tau)]. \tag{9.102}$$

Looking back to the result of Section 3.11, an at-the-money option is linear in volatility to a very good approximation, and therefore the vega is independent of the volatility. By differentiating equation (3.64), the vega is

$$Vega(\tau) = \frac{1}{\sqrt{2\pi}}B\sqrt{T-\tau} \tag{9.103}$$

when the spot level is equal to barrier level B. Then we can rewrite our model dependent term as

$$I = \frac{B}{\sqrt{2\pi}}E[\sqrt{T-\tau}\,Skew(\tau)]. \tag{9.104}$$

In this way, we see that the model dependence of the one-touch price depends only on the *forward skew Skew(τ)* experienced in the model. Now we can use our intuition to understand why a one-touch is more expensive in local volatility than stochastic volatility.

First, we recall that when the market volatility surface is skewed, we need to include spot–volatility correlation in our stochastic volatility model to achieve that skew. But the impact of spot–volatility correlation in a stochastic volatility model is very similar to a local volatility correction. Therefore, we will consider a nice symmetrical smile shaped volatility surface without skew.

Now let's consider what happens if spot moves far enough to touch the barrier. In the local volatility model, the local volatility function is smile shaped like the implied volatility. This is a consequence of equation (9.22) which shows that the leading order term in the calculation of the local volatility function is the implied volatility function. Then, if spot moves up to touch the barrier at level B, it has moved from a flat region of local volatility to a positively skewed region. If we were to use the local volatility function to calculate the prices of vanillas as seen from there, we would see a positively skewed implied volatility surface.

On the other hand, in the stochastic volatility model, spot is not correlated with volatility. Therefore if spot moves up to touch the barrier, the model looks just the same as from the original spot level, and generates a new implied volatility surface without skew.

Therefore our intuition tells us that the forward skew at a random future touch time τ satisfies

$$Skew(\tau)_{loc} > Skew(\tau)_{SV} \qquad (9.105)$$

and the one-touch is priced higher in local volatility.

This is a purely heuristic argument. But that one-touches are priced higher in local volatility is taken as given by exotic option traders since true counter examples are rarely if ever observed. The arguments extend to more general barrier options. Contracts with a continuous knock-in barrier are usually priced higher in local volatility than stochastic volatility. If there is a knock-out barrier, as in the classic example of a no-touch option that pays 1 if the barrier is not hit, the relation ko + ki = knockless tells us it is the other way round.

9.8 Key Points

- Local volatility and stochastic volatility represent two extremes of model that can be used to explain the volatility smile.
- Local stochastic volatility allows us to mix between the two.
- The model consists of an underlying stochastic volatility model with parameters that partially explain the implied volatility smile, together with a local volatility component that exactly makes up the difference.
- The local volatility correction function is calibrated by solving a PDE forwards in time, giving an exact match to market vanilla prices and the volatility smile.
- The most important exotic contracts are continuous barrier options (also called first generation exotic options). Their value depends significantly on the mixing between local and stochastic volatility.
- Each financial institution uses its own underlying stochastic volatility model. However, all institutions can agree on the values of continuous barrier options because they are mainly sensitive to the effective vol-of-vol up to the expiry date, and not to the full details of the model dynamic. We used engineering arguments as opposed to rigorous mathematics to reach this conclusion.

9.9 Further Reading

In addition to being the work horses for exotic option trading in investment banks, local stochastic volatility models exhibit a delightful beauty to financial engineers. It is remarkable how perfectly the forward induction technique works for calculating the local volatility correction.

The earliest LSV models that are cited in the literature were developed in the investment banks JP Morgan (Jex 1999)[25] and Chase Manhattan (Blacher 2001). The JP Morgan model uses forward induction, while the Chase model calibrates a parametric form for the local volatility correction. The forward induction technique was applied to interest rate models before LSV (Jamshidian 1991).

While Jex (1999) solves the problem on a tree, the more modern approach is to use a PDE solver with implicit stepping as shown in Lipton (2002) and see Lipton and McGhee (2002) and Ren, Madan, and Qian (2007).

As long as pricing is confined to barrier options, we argued in Section 9.5.3 that it is reasonable to use a raw mixture model to underlie local stochastic volatility. Brigo and Mercurio (2000, 2002) use a mixture model as an elegant building block to construct a well-defined and analytically tractable local volatility model which does not suffer from the problems pointed out by Piterbarg (2003). Johnson and Lee (2003) have pointed out the ability of mixture models to generate a realistic smile in some cases.

Our approach in Section 9.5.3 was to note that in a stochastic volatility model without correlation a barrier option price depends mainly on the terminal volatility and then to condition on that terminal volatility. This argument was presented in Austing (2013).

A much more sophisticated approach is provided by McGhee (2008, 2011, 2012) and McGhee and Trabalzini (2013) aimed at European options. Here concrete expansions for the distribution of the terminal volatility are developed and improved on by further conditioning on the final instantaneous volatility (whose true distribution is often known). The zero correlation assumption is also relaxed. These references also provide a gold mine of insight into stochastic volatility modelling.

We have now encountered the major techniques of smile modelling, and it is timely to provide a small number of references on the subject as a whole. The books by Gatheral (2006) and Clark (2011) are each outstanding for their clarity on the subject. For readers who are hungry for more technically advanced treatments of derivatives pricing theory, the three volumes of Andersen and Piterbarg (2010a,b,c) are remarkable in providing a comprehensive and readable compendium of the state of the art. When one is faced with a difficult technical problem in derivatives pricing, an excellent place to look for solutions or inspiration is Lipton (2001), which contains a treasure trove of mathematical approaches.

---

[25] The JP Morgan LSV paper appears anonymously in Risk magazine with a foreword by the Foreign Exchange group head Klaus Said.

10 Volatility Products

10.1 Overview

In earlier chapters, we have seen that trading vanilla options allows one to take a position on volatility. However, to obtain pure volatility exposure, it is necessary to continuously delta hedge in order to eliminate the exposure to the underlying spot. This is not practical for a small investor or hedge fund wishing to follow a volatility strategy. Furthermore, when spot moves so that the vanilla option becomes strongly in- or out-of-the-money, the volatility exposure is lost.

For this reason, investment banks create contracts that provide investors with direct exposure to volatility. This may be exposure to the actual volatility realised over the trade lifetime, or to changes in market implied volatility.

10.2 Variance Swaps

We shall begin by looking at the variance swap. It is a simple contract in which one calculates the variance of a set of spot samples, and pays that amount to the client in exchange for a fixed cash payment. It is clear from everything we have learned so far that variance is a fundamental quantity in option pricing. True to form, the variance swap has a number of properties that make it special, and cast some fascinating light on the nature of the volatility smile.

10.2.1 The Variance Swap Contract

A variance swap contract includes a number of fixing dates at times $t_0, t_1, \cdots, t_N$ with the final date t_N also acting as the expiry date of the contract. At each fixing date t_i, a spot sample S_i will be taken. The contract will specify at what time in the day the sample should be taken, and it is likely to be the value provided by a third party data supplier (for example, Reuters).

The next step is to calculate the variance of the spot samples, which is known as the *realised variance*. A number of versions of the contract are traded. The formula for the realised variance is

$$V = \frac{M}{N - \delta_1} \sum_{i=1}^{N} \left(\log \frac{S_i}{S_{i-1}} - \delta_2 \mu \right)^2 \tag{10.1}$$

$$\mu = \frac{1}{N} \sum_{i=1}^{N} \log \frac{S_i}{S_{i-1}} \equiv \frac{1}{N} \log \frac{S_N}{S_0}, \tag{10.2}$$

where δ_1 and δ_2 are numbers that can be 0 or 1 depending on the contract type. If we expand out the square, the sums can be simplified to obtain

$$V = \frac{M}{N - \delta_1} \left(\sum_{i=1}^{N} \left[\log \frac{S_i}{S_{i-1}} \right]^2 - \frac{\delta_2}{N} \left[\log \frac{S_N}{S_0} \right]^2 \right). \tag{10.3}$$

Note that there are $N + 1$ spot samples $S_0, \cdots, S_N$, which give us N log-returns $\log S_i / S_{i-1}$.

The parameter M is called the annualisation factor, and a typical choice is

$$M = N/T \tag{10.4}$$

where $T = t_N - t_0$ is the time in years from first fixing to expiry of the trade. This means that, for daily sampling, M is usually chosen to be the number of business days in a year.

When δ_2 is chosen to be 1, the idea is to subtract the mean from the log returns to get a better estimate of the true variance. The idea of choosing $\delta_1 = 1$ is to get closer to an unbiased estimator of the true variance (in the case when $\delta_2 = 1$). It is a simple exercise to check that in the case of a Black–Scholes world with no term structure of rates and evenly spaced fixings, this does give an unbiased estimator $E[V] = \sigma^2_{Black-Scholes}$.

The payout of a variance swap contract is

$$P_{Var} = V - \sigma^2_K. \tag{10.5}$$

Here σ^2_K is an agreed variance strike. It is expressed as the square of σ_K so that it can be quoted like a volatility. As an example, at the trade inception one could choose σ_K so that the initial value of the trade (given by the risk-neutral expectation) is zero

$$E[V - \sigma^2_K] = 0. \tag{10.6}$$

Chosen this way, σ^2_K represents the market expectation of future variance. In this case, we will call σ_K the fair volatility for the variance swap, and denote it $\sigma^{var}_{fair} \equiv \sqrt{E[V]}$. An investor who buys a variance swap with that strike is hoping that the true variance realised will be higher.

10.2.2 Idealised Variance Swap Trade

In a typical contract, the spot samples are taken once per day. Clearly, more frequent spot samples provide a better estimate of the true variance. We will be able to make great progress in understanding the variance swap by approximating with the large N limit so that spot is sampled continuously.

The first thing to note is that the mean μ (10.2) of the log returns vanishes when $N \to \infty$. This tells us that when measuring the volatility of a stochastic path, we need not be concerned with the drift, and explains why the version of the contract with $\delta_2 = 0$ is often traded so that the mean subtraction is missing.

In the large N limit, we can represent the time intervals between fixings and the log returns by their infinitesimal counterparts

$$t_i - t_{i-1} = dt \tag{10.7}$$

and

$$\log \frac{S_i}{S_{i-1}} \equiv \log S_i - \log S_{i-1} \tag{10.8}$$

$$= d \log S_t. \tag{10.9}$$

Then, in the large N limit, the sum in the definition of variance (10.3) becomes a stochastic integral

$$V_{cts} = \frac{1}{T} \int_0^T (d \log S)^2. \tag{10.10}$$

Here we denote the realised variance by V_{cts} to indicate that it is the idealised continuous sampled variance. In the next section, we will see how to use knowledge of the stochastic process $d \log S$ to value the trade.

10.2.3   Valuing the Idealised Trade

One might think that the value of the variance swap would depend heavily on the particular dynamic causing the volatility smile. Remarkably, as long as the spot process is continuous and cannot jump, this is not the case.

The no jumps assumption means we are going to assume a continuous process of the form

$$\frac{dS}{S} = \mu dt + \sigma(t, \cdots) dW \tag{10.11}$$

$$d\sigma = \cdots . \tag{10.12}$$

Here the dots $\cdots$ indicate that we are allowing a fairly general but unspecified continuous process for the spot. The instantaneous volatility $\sigma(t, \cdots)$ is stochastic and may depend on numerous stochastic factors including the spot level itself. It must (of course) be adapted to the filtration $\mathcal{F}_t$, as we cannot see into the future. We also need the model to be 'well behaved', in that we insist the process X_t defined by

$$\frac{dX}{X} = \sigma(t, \cdots) dW \tag{10.13}$$

must be a Martingale.[26] Certainly, the local stochastic volatility models from Chapter 9 are included.

Ito's lemma tells us that

$$d\log S = (\mu - \tfrac{1}{2}\sigma^2)dt + \sigma\,dW \tag{10.14}$$

and that

$$(d\log S)^2 = \sigma^2\,dt. \tag{10.15}$$

So under the above assumptions, the realised variance (10.10) becomes

$$V_{cts} = \frac{1}{T}\int_0^T \sigma^2(t,\cdots)\,dt. \tag{10.16}$$

For example, in the Black–Scholes world in which σ is constant, we would have $V = \sigma^2 T$. This is our favourite property of Brownian motion: that the total up and down movements squared are always equal to the vol-squared, no matter what path is taken. However, more generally V is a random variable.

The trick is simply to take the risk-neutral expectation of equation (10.14),

$$E[d\log S] = E[(\mu - \tfrac{1}{2}\sigma^2)dt + \sigma\,dW]. \tag{10.17}$$

The $-\tfrac{1}{2}\sigma^2 dt$ term will give us exactly what we need. Meanwhile, by the Martingale property (which we can apply since σ is well behaved), the dW term drops out: $E[\sigma\,dW] = 0$. Then rearranging and integrating gives

$$\frac{1}{2}E\left[\int_0^T \sigma^2\,dt\right] = E\left[\int_0^T \mu\,dt - d\log S\right] \tag{10.18}$$

$$= \mu T - E[\log S_T - \log S_0] \tag{10.19}$$

where we made the crucial assumption that the drift μ is deterministic. On the left, we have exactly half the expectation of the variance, while we can simplify the right hand side by recalling that the forward level is $F_T = S_0 e^{\mu T}$,

$$E[V_{cts}] = -\frac{2}{T}E\left[\log\frac{S_T}{F_T}\right]. \tag{10.20}$$

---

[26] One would imagine that the process X_t in (10.13) is always a Martingale since σ is determined by the filtration $\mathcal{F}_t$ while dW is independent of $\mathcal{F}_t$, so $E[\sigma\,dW] = E[\sigma]\,E[dW] = 0$. However, Sin (1998) finds that not all processes are well behaved in this way. See also Lewis (2000) and Andersen and Piterbarg (2006).

Formula (10.20) is remarkable. It relates the price of a variance swap to the price of a simple European contract paying $\log S_T$ at expiry.

Since the log payout only depends on spot at expiry, it can be replicated using calls and puts as in Section 6.2

$$\log \frac{S_T}{F_T} = \log \frac{\alpha}{F_T} + \frac{S_T}{\alpha} - 1 - \int_{\alpha}^{\infty} \frac{1}{k^2}(S_T - k)_+ \, dk - \int_0^{\alpha} \frac{1}{k^2}(k - S_T)_+ \, dk \quad (10.21)$$

where α is a conveniently chosen constant. Typically, α will be chosen to be the forward level F_T measured at the time the trade is first put on.

The variance swap replication formula (10.21) shows that we can hedge a variance swap by putting on a portfolio of vanillas with strikes K in quantities $1/K^2$. In addition, we need a cash investment of $\log(\alpha/F_T) - 1$ and an investment in the asset forward contract of $1/\alpha$ (having payout at expiry S_T/α). The cash investment must be rebalanced as time goes on or spot moves so that the forward level F_T changes. However, the hedging portfolio of vanillas is fixed and, if the strikes are chosen carefully, can be put on once at the beginning of the trade and then left until the expiry.

10.2.4 Beauty in Variance Swaps

That the variance swap price can be replicated from vanilla options is already remarkable. However Gatheral (2006) provides an alternative representation of the price that is truly delightful.

We begin with the Breeden–Litzenberger style formulation of the undiscounted value of the variance

$$E[V_{cts}] = -\frac{2}{T} E\left[\log \frac{S_T}{F_T} \right] \quad (10.22)$$

$$= -\frac{2}{T} \int_0^{\infty} p_T(K) \log \frac{K}{F_T} \, dK \quad (10.23)$$

where $p_T(K)$ is the risk-neutral probability density function that can be derived from the implied volatility smile as in Section 6.2. The idea is to make a clever change of variables due to Matytsin (2000).

Looking back to the definition of the Black–Scholes delta of a vanilla call option in Table 4.1, we recall that it is

$$\Delta = e^{-r_{yield} T} N(d_1) \quad (10.24)$$

where d_1 is the usual Black–Scholes parameter defined in equation (3.56). This quantity Δ tells us how much spot we should buy to hedge a vanilla position. We could use forward contracts instead of spot to delta hedge. In that case, the formula would be $N(d_1)$, the same quantity but without the discount factor.

We are interested in a closely related quantity

$$\widetilde{\Delta} = N(-d_2) \tag{10.25}$$

where d_2 is given by equation (3.57). If one does one's accounting in the asset itself (rather than in currency) then delta hedging involves buying or selling the currency. In that case the appropriate Black–Scholes forward delta is exactly $\widetilde{\Delta}$.[27] This may seem an odd concept when one considers trading in the stock market, but it can be quite natural for currency derivatives. In any case, it justifies our use of the Greek letter $\widetilde{\Delta}$ which will be useful for the stylistic conclusion we are about to draw.

We are not in a Black–Scholes world but have a smile, and the dependence of the implied volatility on strike feeds into d_2

$$d_2 = \frac{\log(F/K) - \frac{1}{2}\sigma(K)^2 T}{\sigma(K)\sqrt{T}}, \tag{10.26}$$

so that $\widetilde{\Delta}$ is a function of the strike K including that dependence on the smile

$$\widetilde{\Delta}(K) = N(d_2(K,\sigma(K))). \tag{10.27}$$

As long as there is no arbitrage in the volatility smile, $\widetilde{\Delta}(K)$ increases from 0 when $K=0$ to 1 when $K \to \infty$. We can change variables in the Breeden–Litzenberger pricing formula (10.23) from strike K to delta $\widetilde{\Delta}$. Furthermore, the probability density is obtained by differentiating vanilla prices which are determined by the volatility smile $\sigma(K)$. We can therefore replace $p_T(K)$ with a rather complicated function of $\sigma(K)$.

When one performs the change of variables and substitution, the result simplifies to

$$E[V_{cts}] = \int_0^1 \sigma^2(\widetilde{\Delta})\,d\widetilde{\Delta}. \tag{10.28}$$

This result is truly wonderful. Remember that variance is a quantity that is calculated by summing squared log returns through time. Yet the fair value of variance can be calculated simply by integrating the square of implied volatility at the expiry date in delta space. Details of the calculation leading to the formula (10.28) can be found in Gatheral (2006).

In addition to providing a fundamental relation between variance and the volatility smile, formula (10.28) provides an easy way to see the impact of the smile on the variance swap price. If the smile is flat so that $\sigma = \sigma_{ATM} = const$, then $E[V_{cts}] = \sigma_{ATM}^2$. Usually, the at-the-money volatility is close to the bottom of the smile with $\widetilde{\Delta}_{ATM} \approx 0.5$. Therefore if we begin with flat volatility but then add convexity to give a true smile, the fair value of variance will increase to above the at-the-money variance σ_{ATM}^2.

---

[27] To see this, replace F and K with $1/F$ and $1/K$ in the definition of $N(d_1)$.

On the other hand, if we add skew to the smile (as measured in $\widetilde{\Delta}$ space) this will have no impact on the variance swap price, since the price is invariant when we replace $\widetilde{\Delta}$ with $\to 0.5 - \widetilde{\Delta}$. If we measure skew with respect to another variable, say strike K or ordinary Black–Scholes delta Δ, then there may be an impact of skew on variance swap price, but it will be small.

To summarise, formula (10.28) tells us that:

- all regions of the volatility smile in delta space are equally important in their contribution to the variance swap price;
- the fair variance strike σ_K satisfying $E[V_{cts}] = \sigma_K^2$ is usually higher than the at-the-money volatility σ_{ATM};
- the variance swap price increases when the smile gets steeper (more convex);
- the skew of the volatility smile has little impact on the variance swap price.

10.2.5 Delta and Gamma of a Variance Swap

In Section 4.6, we noted that trading a vanilla option can be thought of as taking a position in volatility. However, the difficulty with using a single vanilla contract is that one must continuously delta hedge it, and that if spot moves far in- or out-of-the-money, then the exposure to volatility goes away. In this chapter we have seen that we can set up a portfolio of vanilla contracts to give a direct exposure to volatility.

However, so far, we have only seen how to value future variance. This is only useful for quoting a price when we first put the trade on. As we risk manage the trade through its life, part of the value will come from those fixings that are now in the past. In this section we will fill in this gap, and that will allow us to examine the Greeks for the trade.

Let us first consider the delta for the variance swap in which none of the fixing dates have yet been reached so that the trade measures future variance. It is important to distinguish the true hedging delta of the variance swap that we discuss now from the Black–Scholes formula delta of a vanilla contract that we used in Section 10.2.4. The true delta is the derivative of the contract price with respect to the spot level. Its value depends on the assumptions we make for how the implied volatility smile changes when spot moves.

Referring back to Section 9.3, we recall that we might assume either a sticky strike dynamic, or a sticky delta dynamic in our implied volatility interpolation. We are going to assume a sticky delta smile so that we will treat implied volatility as a function of the ratio of strike and spot $\sigma_{imp}(K/S, T)$. In that case, our *asset accounting Black–Scholes vanilla forward delta* parameter $\widetilde{\Delta}$ defined in equation (10.25) is also a function of K/S and we can write

$$\sigma_{imp}(K/S, T) \equiv \sigma_{imp}(\widetilde{\Delta}, T). \tag{10.29}$$

In our variance swap pricing formula (10.28), we abbreviated $\sigma_{imp}(\widetilde{\Delta}, T)$ with simply $\sigma(\widetilde{\Delta})$. The important point is that the implied volatility has no further dependence on

S beyond that implicit in $\tilde{\Delta}$. If we differentiate (10.28) we obtain

$$\frac{\partial}{\partial S} E[V_{cts}] = 0. \tag{10.30}$$

Therefore, the delta of a variance swap in which none of the spot samples have yet fixed is zero. This makes sense. In a sticky delta world, we expect the value of future variance not to be impacted by a spot move now. Similarly, the gamma is also zero.

However, mid-way through a variance swap's lifetime, some of the spot samples have fixed, and others have not. Looking back at the definition of the variance contract (10.3), we will work, for simplicity, with the contract having $\delta_1 = \delta_2 = 0$ and $M = N/T$. We can split the log returns $\log S_i / S_{i-1}$ into three categories: those for which S_i and S_{i-1} have both fixed, those for which neither have fixed, and the special case in which S_{i-1} has fixed but S_i has not.

The log returns that are entirely fixed just contribute a constant to the price. We will use the continuous sampling approximation for the log returns that are entirely in the future. This leaves the special intermediate case, and as t_i is not too far in the future, we will simply approximate S_i (the next spot fixing) with current spot level S. Then the undiscounted value of the variance is approximated by

$$E[V] \approx const + \frac{1}{T}\left(\log \frac{S}{S_{i-1}}\right)^2 + \frac{(t_N - t_i)}{T}\int_0^1 \sigma(\tilde{\Delta})\, d\tilde{\Delta}, \tag{10.31}$$

where t_i is the next fixing date.

If we differentiate to obtain the delta, only the middle term contributes

$$\frac{\partial}{\partial S} E[V] \approx \frac{2}{T}\frac{1}{S}\log \frac{S}{S_{i-1}}. \tag{10.32}$$

This delta is expressed in units of the asset. If we multiply by spot to convert it into cash terms, we obtain

$$S\frac{\partial}{\partial S} E[V] \approx \frac{2}{T}\log \frac{S}{S_{i-1}}. \tag{10.33}$$

Assuming spot has not moved far since the last fixing, the delta is small. This is exactly what we wanted to achieve: a trade that has exposure to volatility but does not require (much) delta hedging. At the moment of a fixing, there is zero delta, and then we pick up a bit of delta as spot moves away from the fixing level before the next fixing date.

However, if spot does not move around in between the fixing dates, the final realised variance will be small and the trade will perform poorly. Looking back to Section 4.5, we recall this means the variance swap trade must have gamma.

It is neat to calculate a slightly unusual version of gamma that we will call the *cash gamma*, obtained by differentiating the delta expressed in cash terms and converting it back into cash terms by multiplying by spot. It can easily be related to the standard gamma using the chain rule. We obtain

$$\Gamma_{cash} = S\frac{\partial}{\partial S}S\frac{\partial}{\partial S}E[V] \tag{10.34}$$

$$\approx S\frac{\partial}{\partial S}\frac{2}{T}\log\frac{S}{S_{i-1}} \tag{10.35}$$

$$= \frac{2}{T}. \tag{10.36}$$

As soon as the first fixing has fixed, the (undiscounted) variance swap acquires a cash gamma that is approximately constant and equal to $2/T$.

10.2.6   Practical Considerations

From all that we have discussed, one might think that variance swaps are perfect contracts to trade volatility. However, there are a number of subtleties that make managing them trickier than one would like.

Typically, the cost of a variance swap is higher than historical variance over a given recent period. Therefore a classic strategy run by a hedge fund might be to sell a variance swap to an investment bank and expect to pay out less at expiry than the original premium. As always with derivatives, it is important to remember that you get what you pay for. In this case, the higher premium is allowing for the fact that a rare high volatility event may occur during the life of the trade. This would cause a high payout at expiry and losses to the hedge fund.

From an investment bank's perspective, one might naively think that the trader can perfectly hedge the variance swap with vanilla contracts and therefore have a safe position. However, there are a number of complications.

Firstly, the variance swap replication argument assumes the spot rate does not jump. Although overall the variance swap has little delta, the hedging strategy involves a fixed portfolio of vanillas plus dynamic cash and asset positions offsetting the vanillas' delta. Therefore the trader needs to continuously rebalance the position. In practice, rebalancing can only be done at discrete times. If spot jumps, or moves significantly between those times, the dynamic hedge will not work properly.

Secondly, if the variance swap is long enough dated (that is, if the expiry is far in the future) the assumption of deterministic interest rate and yield has a significant impact. If one studies models in which rates are stochastic, it turns out that the implied volatility is really the volatility of the forward level rather than of the spot level. As the variance swap contract measures the variance of the spot, the contribution of interest rate volatility to the variance swap replication price needs to be subtracted off. Depending on the volatility of the rates, it is usually considered that a variance swap with expiry at best five years, but perhaps as low as one year, will require a stochastic interest rate adjustment.

However, even for a short dated variance swap in a non-jumpy market, there remains a challenge that can be described as *wingyness.* The formula (10.28) shows us that the wings of the smile, that is the regions at far low and high strikes, contribute just as much to the contract value as the region near the at-the-money strike. In foreign exchange, for example, vanilla options are only considered liquid in the region corresponding to roughly $0.1 \leq \tilde{\Delta} \leq 0.9$. As a result, at least 20% of the price is coming from a region of the smile in which we do not have market information about vanilla prices. The particular choice of how to extrapolate the implied volatility smile into the wings can have a significant impact on the price.

The uncertainty in the wing contribution to the price of the variance swap is telling us that we do not know how to value the impact of possible very large market moves. This leads us to some helpful insight into the nature of the volatility smile and derivatives trading.

Let's consider for a moment what happens to an ordinary derivative contract like a vanilla option when there is a large market correction. The fact is that it is hard to maintain a perfect hedging strategy for a number of reasons. Even if the risk of such a market move is correctly priced into the volatility smile, and near perfect delta and vega hedges are in place beforehand, it will not be possible to rebalance them fast enough to maintain the true continuous dynamic hedging strategy. In all probability, the position will have lost money or made money once the market has settled down again.

However, a vanilla option that was roughly at-the-money before the market moved will be strongly in- or out-of-the-money afterwards. That is, it will either have turned into a forward contract, or be worthless. If it is worthless, so be it. If it has become a forward contract, then the delta hedge is effectively a perfect replication of the payout. In either case, the contract has lost its sensitivity to the implied volatility and become benign.

A trader managing a variance swap is not so blessed. Imperfect hedging will again lead to losses or perhaps gains. But after the correction, the variance swap is still there with large vega, and remains exposed to further market turbulence or aftershocks. For this reason, variance swaps have been neatly yet brutally described as the cockroaches of the derivatives world. After a nuclear explosion, when almost everything else is gone, the cockroaches survive.

10.3 Volatility Swaps

While variance swaps are popular in equity markets, they are seldom traded when the underlying is a foreign exchange rate. Instead, volatility swaps are used. Individual traders will point to the advantages of their preferred contract, but this is really a matter of market convention and not related to any fundamental difference between foreign exchange and equities.

Referring back to the variance swap contract payout in equation (10.5), the volatility swap payout is formed by applying a square root in order to measure volatility rather than variance,

$$P_{Vol} = \sqrt{V} - \sigma_K. \tag{10.37}$$

This time, σ_K is the agreed volatility strike, while V is the realised variance as defined in equation (10.3). As with the variance swap, we define the fair volatility to be the strike making the present value zero

$$\sigma_{fair}^{vol} = E[\sqrt{V}]. \tag{10.38}$$

The square root breaks the variance swap replication argument and it is not possible to perfectly hedge a volatility swap with a portfolio of vanillas. As a result, the value of a volatility swap depends not only on the smile, but on the particular dynamic that causes the volatility smile. As we recall from Chapter 9, this is the standard situation for path dependent contracts. One might hope that, by analogy with the variance swap, the impact of the dynamic on the price is small. This is not the case. When the at-the-money volatility is 10% and there is a fairly ordinary smile, the fair volatility $E[\sqrt{V}]$ (with a one-year expiry) might easily be around 10% in a stochastic volatility model versus 10.5% in local volatility.

10.3.1 Volatility Swap in Stochastic Volatility Models and LSV

One might think that the particular underlying volatility process is important when valuing a volatility swap. After all, it is precisely a contract on volatility. A counterargument would be that a similar contract, the variance swap, is entirely indifferent to the dynamic causing the smile.

Let's consider a pure stochastic volatility model in which there is no correlation between the spot and volatility processes. As usual, this will generate a smile that is not skewed. We will consider the idealised continuous sampling version of the volatility swap and try to calculate the (undiscounted) fair value. Then we can use the representation for continuous sampled variance provided by equation (10.16)

$$E\left[\sqrt{V_{cts}}\right] = E\left[\sqrt{\frac{1}{T}\int_0^T \sigma_t^2\, dt}\right]. \tag{10.39}$$

First though, it will be helpful to price a simple vanilla call option struck at-the-money, that is, with strike set equal to the forward level. We denote the corresponding implied volatility as σ_{ATM}, and plug this into the Black–Scholes formula to get the price. We recall from Section 3.11 that the value of an at-the-money option is almost linear in volatility, and is very well approximated using equation (3.64)

$$PV_{ATM} \approx \frac{1}{\sqrt{2\pi}} e^{-r_{yield}T} S_0 \sigma_{ATM}\sqrt{T}. \tag{10.40}$$

On the other hand, we can value the call option directly in the stochastic volatility model. Conditional on the instantaneous volatility path, we can use the Black–Scholes formula, and therefore reduce the value to an expectation over volatility paths,

$$PV_{ATM} = e^{-r_{dom}T} E[(S_T - K)_+] \tag{10.41}$$
$$= e^{-r_{dom}T} E[E[(S_T - K)_+|\{\sigma_t\}]] \tag{10.42}$$
$$= e^{-r_{dom}T} E[BS(K,\sigma)], \tag{10.43}$$

where the strike K is actually equal to the forward level F. This is a similar argument to that used in Section 9.5.3 for barrier options. Here $BS()$ is the Black–Scholes formula for the call option, and σ is the terminal volatility

$$\sigma = \sqrt{\frac{1}{T} \int_0^T \sigma_t^2 \, dt} \tag{10.44}$$

first introduced in Section 2.7, and is of course identical to the continuous sample realised volatility $\sqrt{V_{cts}}$.

The thing is, we can make exactly the same approximation of the Black–Scholes formula, and so obtain

$$PV_{ATM} \approx \frac{1}{\sqrt{2\pi}} e^{-r_{yield}T} S_0 E[\sigma] \sqrt{T}. \tag{10.45}$$

Then equating the two approximations (10.40) and (10.45) tells us that the fair realised volatility is well approximated by the at-the-money implied volatility

$$E\left[\sqrt{\frac{1}{T} \int_0^T \sigma_t^2 \, dt} \right] = \sigma_{ATM} + \mathcal{O}(\sigma^3). \tag{10.46}$$

We conclude that in a pure stochastic volatility model in which there is no correlation between the spot and volatility processes, the fair volatility for a volatility swap is equal to the at-the-money volatility, at least to a very good approximation.

It is important to remember that this only applies when the implied volatility smile is caused by a stochastic volatility dynamic without spot–volatility correlation. Nevertheless, it demonstrates that the volatility swap and variance swap can behave fundamentally differently. While the variance swap is always *wingy*, as it depends on the volatility smile at all strikes, here the volatility swap depends only on the at-the-money volatility.

In Section 9.5.4 we studied first generation exotic options in LSV. For those contracts, we gave a heuristic argument that the particular SV model underlying the LSV is not important. In the absence of correlation, the volatility swap price is equal to the at-the-money volatility in a pure SV model, and therefore is independent of the particular SV model used. As a result, we can apply exactly the same argument to the volatility swap.

Volatility swaps fall into the same nice category as first generation exotics. Although the mixing between stochastic and local volatility is important, the price doesn't depend heavily on the details of the underlying SV model.

10.3.2   Volatility Swap Versus Variance Swap

In order to compare the volatility swap price with the variance swap, we can look at their respective fair volatility strikes

$$\sigma_{fair}^{vol} = E[\sqrt{V}] \qquad (10.47)$$

$$\sigma_{fair}^{var} = \sqrt{E[V]}. \qquad (10.48)$$

Let's consider the variance of the random variable $\sqrt{V}$, defined by

$$\mathrm{Var}(\sqrt{V}) = E[(\sqrt{V} - E[\sqrt{V}])^2] \qquad (10.49)$$

$$= E[V] - (E[\sqrt{V}])^2. \qquad (10.50)$$

As $\mathrm{Var}(\sqrt{V})$ is positive, this tells us

$$E[\sqrt{V}] \leq \sqrt{E[V]} \qquad (10.51)$$

and therefore

$$\sigma_{fair}^{vol} \leq \sigma_{fair}^{var} \qquad (10.52)$$

is always true. As shorthand, we can say that the variance swap is an upper bound on the volatility swap. More properly, we are of course referring to the fair volatilities for the two contracts.

The upper bound of the variance swap on the volatility swap applies irrespective of the dynamic causing the volatility smile, and does not rely on any continuous sampling approximation.

We can rewrite equation (10.50) as

$$\sigma_{fair}^{var} = \sigma_{fair}^{vol} + \frac{\mathrm{Var}(\sqrt{V})}{\sigma_{fair}^{var} + \sigma_{fair}^{vol}}. \qquad (10.53)$$

The difference between the fair variance swap and the fair volatility swap strikes is roughly proportional to the variance of the realised volatility. When the volatility smile is flat, sensible models reduce to Black–Scholes and have (continuous sampled) realised volatility that is deterministic. In that case, the variance of the realised volatility is zero and the fair strikes are equal. If we add convexity to the smile, then the variance of the realised volatility increases and the fair variance strike becomes bigger than the fair volatility. This is another way of seeing that the variance swap is more wingy than the volatility swap, since its price increases more when we increase the wings

10.3.3   Valuing a Volatility Swap

As the value of a volatility swap depends on the dynamic causing the implied volatility smile, one must first choose a model in which to value the contract. If at all possible, this should be the same model used to value the other exotic contracts in one's trading book. If a particular LSV model is being used for first generation exotics, then it is best to use the same model for volatility products unless it can be demonstrated that the model misses an important risk factor, or it is simply too hard to use for some reason.

If different models are used across a trading book, there may be circumstances in which inconsistency leads to an internal arbitrage. More importantly for practical trading, contracts with offsetting risk will be missed if different models are used. For example, it may be that the trading desk have a position in the LSV mixing parameter arising from first generation exotic contracts that is offset somewhat by the position in volatility swaps.

Having chosen an LSV model, the simplest thing one can do is to value the volatility swap using Monte Carlo. One is never keen to use Monte Carlo if an alternative is available because simulation is slow and the numerical stability of Greeks is poor. Therefore we would prefer to use the PDE approach.

The volatility swap is an example of an Asian option, since the payout depends on the spot level at a set of fixing dates over the life of the trade. Then, as in Section 8.2.4, we need to use the method of planes in order to evaluate the price in PDE. However, unfortunately this cannot be achieved with a single set of planes.

We recall that, in the method of planes, we add extra dimensions to our PDE to model variables that would otherwise be undetermined having solved backwards to time t. For an average rate option, we used the part of the average that is undetermined. We solve backwards, and update the planes and the solution every time we get to a fixing date.

For a volatility swap (or other payout depending on the realised variance) we assume we have solved our PDE back as far as time t, and wish to model the part of the variance that is not yet determined

$$V' = \sum_{i:t_i<t} \left(\log \frac{S_i}{S_{i-1}} \right)^2 \qquad (10.54)$$

with a plane. Let's suppose that t_n is the latest undetermined fixing time. We solve back to $t = t_n$ and wish to perform interfacing to remove S_n (which is now determined) from V'. The problem is that S_{n-1} remains undetermined, and therefore we cannot simply drop the $(\log(S_n/S_{n-1}))^2$ term from V' to form the new plane.

The solution is to maintain another plane representing S_{n-1} (or its logarithm). Then the value from this plane can be used to fill in the missing S_{n-1} at the interfacing step for V'. In this way we see that two dimensions of planes are required to value a volatility swap in PDE.

In Section 8.2.5 we noted that three dimensions are often considered the limit for finite difference PDE schemes. If we are using an LSV model with one dimension required for the stochastic volatility and another for the spot rate, then adding two dimensions of planes takes us to four dimensions. However, the dimensions formed from planes do not have any partial derivatives to compute, and one can often get away with a relatively small number of grid points for their discretisation. For this reason, it is just feasible to use this approach.

The simplest LSV models (those based on a mixture model or regime switching model for example) only have one stochastic factor so that adding in the planes takes us to only three dimensions. We saw in Section 10.3.1 (perhaps surprisingly) that it is reasonable to use this kind of model for a volatility swap.

Even so, the approach remains numerically intensive for what we would hope is a fairly simple product. To simplify valuation further, we can approximate the realised variance with its continuous sampled counterpart

$$V_{cts} = \frac{1}{T} \int_0^T \sigma_t^2 \, dt. \tag{10.55}$$

As the instantaneous volatility σ_t is known at any point on the standard PDE grid, we can treat the volatility swap in the same way as an average rate option where the average is over the instantaneous variance at each point on the time grid. This requires only a single-dimensional plane, and the problem becomes much more tractable. If in addition a simplified single factor LSV model is used, then the PDE solution can be highly efficient and stable.

10.3.4   Stochastic versus Local Volatility

Every trader 'knows' that the price of a volatility swap is higher in local volatility than in stochastic volatility. This is purely an empirical observation that applies to 'sensible' stochastic volatility models,[28] and can be tested numerically by valuing in LSV and adjusting the mixing parameter between pure stochastic and pure local volatility to see the impact on the price. However, following Dupire (2005a), we can prove this result in the limiting case of short dated volatility swaps.

Consider a continuous sampled volatility swap for which sampling starts at a future time t and continues for short time δt. Then the undiscounted value is simply given by the expectation of the instantaneous volatility at time t

$$E[\sqrt{V_{cts}}] = E\left[\sqrt{\frac{1}{\delta t} \int_t^{t+\delta t} \sigma_t^2 \, dt}\right] \tag{10.56}$$

$$\to E[\sigma_t] \quad \text{as } \delta t \to 0. \tag{10.57}$$

We can call this contract an instantaneous volatility swap.

---

[28] Indeed, Beiglböck, Friz, and Sturm (2010) construct a counterexample using a mixture model.

The trick is to condition on the spot rate S, and then use the same convexity property of the square root function as in Section 10.3.2 to obtain a bound

$$E[\sigma_t] = E[\sqrt{\sigma_t^2}] = E\left[E[\sqrt{\sigma_t^2}|S]\right] \qquad (10.58)$$

$$\leq E\left[\sqrt{E[\sigma_t^2|S]}\right]. \qquad (10.59)$$

Now we can use the fundamental theorem of on-smile pricing (Gyöngy's theorem) in the form provided in equation (9.5),

$$E[\sigma_t^2|S] = \sigma_{local}^2(S, t) \qquad (10.60)$$

where $\sigma_{local}(S, t)$ is the Dupire local volatility function. Then the bound becomes

$$E[\sigma_t] \leq E[\sigma_{local}(S, t)] \qquad (10.61)$$

which exactly states that the price of the instantaneous volatility swap is bounded above by the local volatility price.

10.4   Forward Volatility Agreements

The variance swap and volatility swap provide exposure to actual realised volatility over the trade lifetime. A schedule of spot fixings (usually daily) is required, and this can make the trades rather fiddly and hard to manage. A forward volatility agreement (FVA) provides exposure instead to *implied* volatility.

To understand how FVAs work, we should first look at one of the simplest structured products, the straddle. A straddle is a call plus a put option, both having matching expiry T and strike K, so that the payout is

$$P_{ST} = (S_T - K)_+ + (K - S_T)_+ \qquad (10.62)$$

$$\equiv |S_T - K|. \qquad (10.63)$$

Often, the strike K will be set equal to the forward F_T at the trade inception so that the call and put are both initially struck at-the-money.

A speculator who believes that the market is underpricing volatility could buy a straddle. The contract payout is positive as long as spot ends up away from the strike. If spot moves far enough, then the payout will overcome the initial premium paid, and the overall strategy will make money. By put–call parity, the at-the-money call and put options have equal price, and we saw in Section 3.11 that this price is almost linear in implied volatility.

The strategy is likely to do well if the market underpriced volatility, for then the premium would be low, but the actual higher volatility realised will cause the spot to move far. However, there is the possibility that spot moves a lot, but happens to end up close to the strike, in which case the strategy will lose the premium paid, with no gain at payout. For this reason, an ordinary straddle is useful but not perfect for gaining exposure to volatility.

A forward volatility agreement is a forward starting straddle. The term forward starting means that the strike is determined in the future. We have two dates $T_1 < T_2$. At the first date T_1, the strike is set equal to F_{12}, the forward level measured at T_1, expiring at T_2. In this way, the contract can be thought of as an agreement to trade an at-the-money straddle at the future time T_1, and the payout is

$$P_1 = |S_2 - F_{12}| \tag{10.64}$$

where S_2 is the spot level at final expiry date T_2.

In practice, the contract is likely to be closed out on the fixing date T_1 when it becomes an ordinary straddle. The straddle is composed of two at-the-money options: a call plus a put, which have equal value by put–call parity (at least at times before T_1). Since, for all practical purposes, an at-the-money vanilla option is linear in volatility, the contract is simply a position on the future at-the-money implied volatility. To see this a little more explicitly, we can write down the value by taking the discounted expectation, and conditioning on the filtration[29] at T_1,

$$PV_1 = e^{-r_{dom} T_2} E[|S_2 - F_{12}|] \tag{10.65}$$

$$= e^{-r_{dom} T_2} E\left[E[|S_2 - F_{12}| \,|\, \mathcal{F}_{T_1}] \right] \tag{10.66}$$

$$\approx 2 \frac{1}{\sqrt{2\pi}} e^{-r_{dom} T_2} \sqrt{T_2 - T_1}\, E[F_{12}\, \sigma_{12}^{ATM}] \tag{10.67}$$

$$= 2 \frac{1}{\sqrt{2\pi}} e^{-r_{dom} T_2} \sqrt{T_2 - T_1}\, \kappa\, E[S_1\, \sigma_{12}^{ATM}]. \tag{10.68}$$

Here, we used the approximation (3.63) for the value of an at-the-money option. We introduced $\kappa = e^{(r_{dom} - r_{yield})(T_2 - T_1)}$ so that $F_{12} = \kappa S_1$, and σ_{12}^{ATM} is the at-the-money implied volatility as seen at T_1 with expiry T_2.

In equation (10.68), we see that the value of the FVA depends linearly on the risk-neutral expectation $E[S_1 \sigma_{12}^{ATM}]$. There is a factor of S_1 which is the spot at fixing time T_1. The appearance of S_1 shows that the contract is a position in the at-the-money volatility that pays in units of the asset, and S_1 is there to convert back into cash terms. We will call this the *asset FVA*.

In order to obtain direct exposure to the forward volatility in cash terms, a second version of the contract is often traded. We call this case the *cash FVA*, and the payout

---

[29] We recall from Section 2.6 that the filtration $\mathcal{F}_{T_1}$ denotes all the information available at time T_1.

formula is

$$P_2 = \frac{|S_2 - F_{12}|}{S_1}.$$ (10.69)

Dividing by spot at the fixing date T_1 converts the forward volatility exposure from asset terms into cash terms, and equation (10.68) becomes

$$PV_2 \approx 2 \frac{1}{\sqrt{2\pi}} e^{-r_{dom}T_2} \sqrt{T_2 - T_1}\, \kappa\, E[\sigma_{12}^{ATM}].$$ (10.70)

We quote valuations in volatility terms. The FVA volatility is *that volatility we would put into the Black–Scholes equation to get back the true value.* Therefore it is useful to know the (undiscounted) Black–Scholes premiums. It is a simple exercise (left to the reader)[30] to check that they are

$$P_{1,BS} = F_1 B(F_2/F_1, \kappa, \sigma, T_2 - T_1)$$ (10.71)

$$P_{2,BS} = B(F_2/F_1, \kappa, \sigma, T_2 - T_1)$$ (10.72)

where $B(F, K, \sigma, T)$ is the Black–Scholes formula for a vanilla struck at K given forward F, time to expiry T and vol σ.

For a given volatility surface, the value of a forward volatility agreement is heavily dependent on the underlying dynamic causing the smile. In order to understand how the value changes as one moves from a stochastic volatility to a local volatility dynamic, we will relate an FVA to a kind of barrier option. For simplicity, we will concentrate on the asset FVA here, but a similar though slightly more involved analysis can be performed for the cash FVA.

For simplicity, we will work with zero interest rates. Since, by put–call parity, the forward starting call and put components of the FVA have equal value, we will price only the forward starting call option. The value is

$$PV = E[(S_2 - S_1)_+]$$ (10.73)

where, as ever, the expectation is taken in the risk-neutral measure.

In order to calculate this expectation, we need to use the joint probability density function $f_{12}(S_1, S_2)$. The two marginal densities $f_1(S_1)$ and $f_2(S_2)$ are determined by the volatility smiles at T_1 and T_2, but the joint density cannot be determined from the volatility surface. This is why the value of the FVA is dependent on the dynamic that causes the smile.

---

[30] To obtain the Black–Scholes prices (10.71), (10.72), first condition on the filtration $\mathcal{F}_{T_1}$ to obtain the Black–Scholes formula, and then perform the overall expectation.

We will denote the corresponding *cumulative* distribution functions by $F_{12}(S_1, S_2)$ (for the joint distribution) and $F_1(S_1)$, $F_2(S_2)$ for the two marginal distributions. We can relate the joint density to the cumulative distributions via

$$f_{12}(S_1, S_2) = \frac{\partial^2}{\partial S_1 \partial S_2} \{F_{12}(S_1, S_2) - F_1(S_1)\}. \tag{10.74}$$

The first term on the right hand side of equation (10.74) is the standard expression of the density function as the derivative of the cumulative distribution. The second term disappears when the derivatives are applied, but will be important to get boundary terms right when we integrate by parts in a moment.

We can express the expectation in the pricing equation (10.73) using the joint density function

$$PV = \int (S_2 - S_1) + \frac{\partial^2}{\partial S_1 \partial S_2} \{F_{12}(S_1, S_2) - F_1(S_1)\} \, dS_1 \, dS_2 \tag{10.75}$$

and then integrate by parts twice, noting that all boundary terms vanish

$$PV = \int \frac{\partial^2}{\partial S_1 \partial S_2} (S_2 - S_1) + \{F_{12}(S_1, S_2) - F_1(S_1)\} \, dS_1 \, dS_2. \tag{10.76}$$

The standard trick is now available to us. Performing the second derivative of the call payout gives a delta function, and this allows us to do one of the integrations exactly,

$$PV = - \int \delta(S_2 - S_1) \{F_{12}(S_1, S_2) - F_1(S_1)\} \, dS_1 \, dS_2 \tag{10.77}$$

$$= \int \{F_1(S_1) - F_{12}(S_1, S_1)\} \, dS_1 \tag{10.78}$$

$$\equiv \int \{E[1_{S_1 < B}] - E[1_{S_1 < B, S_2 < B}]\} \, dB. \tag{10.79}$$

In the final equation (10.79), the integration variable S_1 has been renamed B, and we have recalled that cumulative distribution functions are simply expectations of digital payouts.

This result is illuminating. We have expressed the value of the FVA as the value of an infinite portfolio of digital contracts, indexed by the parameter B. There are two terms in the integral in equation (10.79) that defines the portfolio. Individually, each of those two terms would diverge, but their combination makes the integral convergent. The first term is a portfolio of simple digital options on S_1 expiring at T_1. As they are European contracts, their value is determined by the volatility smile (see Section 6.2).

It is the contracts in the second term of equation (10.79) that make the FVA value depend on the dynamic causing the smile. The contract payout is

$$1_{S_1 < B, S_2 < B} \qquad (10.80)$$

and we can think of the parameter B as a barrier level. The contract pays one dollar as long as spot does not breach the barrier at either of the two times T_1 and T_2. We can think of it as a no-touch option, but instead of a continuous barrier it has discrete barriers at the two dates.

We saw in Section 9.7 that continuous barrier no-touch options are priced higher in stochastic volatility models and lower in local volatility models (at least, for almost all practical purposes). It is but a small leap of faith to conclude that the discrete barrier no-touch should behave in the same way. After all, if the continuous barrier is significantly breached, then the chances are that the barrier will also be breached at one or both of T_1 and T_2. Then, taking account of the minus sign that appears in front of the discrete barrier payout in the FVA replication formula (10.79), the FVA is priced higher in local volatility and lower in stochastic volatility models.

As with barrier options, what an exotic options trader really cares about is experience based on pricing up contracts on a daily basis in his or her local stochastic volatility model. Based on such empirical evidence, it is treated as a well-known fact by derivatives traders that FVAs are priced higher in local volatility than stochastic volatility models. As a quant, one should keep in mind that the argument we have presented here is heuristic. Therefore, in the absence of a proof with carefully laid out assumptions, we must treat it as a rule of thumb that works in practical circumstances.

10.4.1   Practicalities

If a good local stochastic volatility model is available for valuation, an FVA has some advantages over variance and volatility swaps. It can be rather fiddly to manage the schedule of daily fixings required for the variance and volatility swaps while, assuming it is closed out at the start date T_1, only one fixing is necessary for an FVA. In order to value correctly using a numerical PDE solver, two-dimensional planes are required for volatility and variance swaps while the FVA fixing S_1 can be modelled with just one extra dimension.

However, there is one major disadvantage when it comes to actually trading an FVA. To understand why, we can go back to the Black–Scholes formulae (10.71) and (10.72). There we provided the Black–Scholes value for the forward starting vanilla option given a constant volatility σ. In reality, the trade is exposed only to the implied volatility that acts between T_1 and T_2. Therefore this is a case in which it is sensible to provide a pricing formula taking account of the term structure of volatility.

Section 2.7 provides the hint of how to proceed. If we introduce a time-dependent volatility σ_t, then the same Black–Scholes formulae will work, but we should use equation (2.53) and replace the constant volatility with

$$\sigma_{12} = \sqrt{\frac{1}{T_2 - T_1} \int_{T_1}^{T_2} \sigma_t^2 \, dt}. \qquad (10.81)$$

We can simplify this formula by using the implied volatilities that apply respectively at T_1 and T_2,

$$\sigma_1 = \sqrt{\frac{1}{T_1} \int_0^{T_1} \sigma_t^2 \, dt} \tag{10.82}$$

$$\sigma_2 = \sqrt{\frac{1}{T_2} \int_0^{T_2} \sigma_t^2 \, dt}, \tag{10.83}$$

giving

$$\sigma_{12} = \sqrt{\frac{1}{T_2 - T_1}(T_2\sigma_2^2 - T_1\sigma_1^2)}. \tag{10.84}$$

This quantity is known as the forward–forward volatility. Then the Black–Scholes formula for the asset FVA becomes

$$P_{1,\text{BS}} = F_1 \, B(F_2/F_1, \kappa, \sigma_{12}, T_2 - T_1), \tag{10.85}$$

which we will now abbreviate with $P_{1,\text{BS}}(\sigma_{12})$.

In order to properly hedge the vega of the FVA, we will need to buy (or sell) vanilla options to neutralise the sensitivity to both σ_1 and σ_2. That is, we have a vega exposure at the two expiries T_1 and T_2. We can use the chain rule to compute the vegas

$$\frac{\partial}{\partial \sigma_1} P_{1,\text{BS}} = \left(\frac{-T_1\sigma_1}{(T_2 - T_1)\sigma_{12}}\right) \frac{\partial}{\partial \sigma_{12}} P_{1,\text{BS}} \tag{10.86}$$

$$\frac{\partial}{\partial \sigma_2} P_{1,\text{BS}} = \left(\frac{T_2\sigma_2}{(T_2 - T_1)\sigma_{12}}\right) \frac{\partial}{\partial \sigma_{12}} P_{1,\text{BS}}. \tag{10.87}$$

To illustrate the problem, let's think of a contract in which T_1 is mid-way between now and T_2 so that $T_2 = 2T_1$, and the term structure is currently flat so that $\sigma_1 = \sigma_2$. Then the vegas break down as

$$\frac{\partial}{\partial \sigma_1} P_{1,\text{BS}} = -\frac{\partial}{\partial \sigma_{12}} P_{1,\text{BS}} \tag{10.88}$$

$$\frac{\partial}{\partial \sigma_2} P_{1,\text{BS}} = 2\frac{\partial}{\partial \sigma_{12}} P_{1,\text{BS}}. \tag{10.89}$$

The problem for the exotic options trader is that the client may be buying one unit of vega exposure and therefore expects to pay only one unit of spread on the cost of volatility. But the trader must buy two units of vega at T_2 and sell one unit at T_1 and this costs three units of spread. In this way, it is expensive to hedge FVAs and it is often hard to price them at a level that clients find acceptable.

Setting aside practical trading issues, modelling is also more complex for an FVA than for other products we have encountered so far. We have seen that because the vega of a continuous barrier option or volatility swap is concentrated at the expiry, the details of how a stochastic volatility model achieves the final spot distribution (characterised by the volatility smile) does not have a great impact on the price.

This is not true for FVAs since they have significant vega at the two dates T_1 and T_2. The play off between mean reversion and vol-of-vol in a stochastic volatility model may impact the price. Traders often think of this effect in terms of two distinct behaviours of the implied volatility surface. Imagine there is a market event causing an increase in the instantaneous spot volatility now. Then implied volatilities with short expiries will increase. If the volatility surface has *parallel shift* behaviour, then the longer dated implied volatilities will also increase. On the other hand, if the behaviour is *mean reverting*, they will not (at least, not to the same extent).

For those who believe that the volatility smile is partly caused by a stochastic volatility dynamic, these two behaviours are clearly related to the strength of the mean reversion versus the vol-of-vol. Since the FVA measures forward implied volatility, its value will depend on this interplay. As we commented in Section 9.5.4, it may be that in an LSV model, the necessity of matching barrier prices and vanilla smiles at both dates T_1 and T_2 imposes sufficient constraints to pin down a forward starting option price fairly tightly. Whether or not this is the case is simply not well known.

10.5 Key Points

- We have studied three contracts that provide exposure to volatility. The variance swap and volatility swap measure the actual volatility that is realised over the trade lifetime, while the forward volatility agreement measures future implied volatility.
- Under some fairly reasonable assumptions, the value of a variance swap can be replicated from the values of vanilla options at its expiry date and is therefore independent of the particular model causing the implied volatility smile.
- By contrast, the value of a volatility swap depends on the mixing between local and stochastic volatility, but is relatively insensitive to the details of the underlying stochastic volatility model.
- Forward volatility agreements measure future implied volatility and are therefore dependent on the mean reversion as well as the vol-of-vol.
- Each contract is initially alluring but presents its own challenges, and trading in volatility products is quite a specialised business.

10.6 Further Reading

The main result that the price of the idealised variance swap is determined by the value of a log contract was discovered by Neuberger (1990) and Dupire (1992, 2004). Two particularly well known and useful treatments of volatility products are Demeterfi et al. (1999a,b) and Gatheral (2002), while Carr and Lee (2009) provide a fascinating history of volatility trading in addition to useful technical results.

Further references include Chriss and Morokoff (1999), Gatheral (2005) and Windcliff, Forsyth, and Vetzal (2006). The replication argument for variance swaps was extended to the *corridor variance swap* in Carr and Lewis (2004). This trade only includes contributions to the realised variance when the spot level is between two fixed levels (the corridor) and can avoid the wingyness problem of variance swaps.

A particularly illuminating illustration of the dependence of forward volatility agreements on the dynamic causing the volatility smile is provided by Johnson (2008), and further insights can be found in Wilmott (2002) and Nauta, Zilber, and Backer (2008). For further interesting reading on smile dynamics, see Rebonato and Joshi (2002), Lucic (2003), Ayache et al. (2004) and Baker, Beneder, and Zilber (2004).

The replication of FVAs from discrete barrier options can be found in McGhee (2008).

11 Multi-Asset

11.1 Overview

This chapter is about valuing derivative contracts on more than one asset. That is, the payout depends on several different spot rates. Often the underlying assets will be from one asset class, say foreign exchange or equities, but the methods of this chapter can also be used to combine assets from different classes.

We will refer to such contracts as *multi-asset products*. Clearly, when valuing a contract depending on more than one asset, the correlation between the assets is important. Therefore, we shall interchangeably refer to them as *correlation products* since they provide exposure to correlation.

A classic example is a basket option, paying the average of the spot rates at expiry. For example, an investor may be exposed to euro–dollar and sterling–dollar exchange rates, and so buy a call option on a basket containing euros and dollars. If the two exchange rates are S_1 dollars per euro and S_2 dollars per pound sterling, then the payout at expiry could be

$$N(0.5S_1 + 0.5S_2 - K)_+ \tag{11.1}$$

where N is the notional in dollars, K is the strike, and the weights of the two assets in the basket are both 0.5.

It may be that during the life of the option S_1 goes up but S_2 goes down so that the change in the value of the basket is smaller than those of the individual currencies. Because of this averaging effect, the volatility of the basket is smaller than the largest volatility of the individual spot rates, and the basket option is cheaper than buying two individual options.

11.2 Local Volatility with Constant Correlation

Our first thought for modelling multi-asset options is to write down stochastic processes for the underlying assets that are correlated. In the above example, we may choose to model both S_1 and S_2 with Dupire local volatility, with instantaneous correlation ρ_t between the two processes at time t

$$\frac{dS_1}{S_1} = \mu_1 dt + \sigma_1(S_1, t) dW_1 \tag{11.2}$$

$$\frac{dS_2}{S_2} = \mu_2 dt + \sigma_2(S_2, t)dW_2 \tag{11.3}$$

$$dW_1\, dW_2 = \rho_t dt. \tag{11.4}$$

The notation $dW_1\, dW_2 = \rho_t dt$ means that the two Brownian increments dW_1 and dW_2 at time t are correlated by ρ_t. It is however more than just notation. It is a literally correct formula in the same sense as equation (2.10) in Chapter 2. We can write dW_1 and dW_2 in terms of independent Brownian motions $d\tilde{W}_1$ and $d\tilde{W}_2$ (satisfying $d\tilde{W}_1\, d\tilde{W}_2 = 0$) as follows:

$$dW_1 = d\tilde{W}_1 \tag{11.5}$$

$$dW_2 = \rho_t d\tilde{W}_1 + \sqrt{1 - \rho_t^2}\, d\tilde{W}_2. \tag{11.6}$$

This relation follows from the similar relation for normal variables. After all a Brownian increment is just a normal variable with variance dt. It is easy to check that $dW_1\, dW_2 = \rho_t dt$ if dW_1 and dW_2 are defined this way.

Now that we have written down a stochastic process, we can go ahead and use Monte Carlo simulation (as in Section 8.1.2) to price options. Alternatively, we could derive the PDE (which will be two dimensional in this case) and solve it numerically.

If we consider the process followed by the first asset S_1, it is standard Dupire local volatility, and the same applies to the second asset S_2. Therefore if we use the two-dimensional model to value vanilla options on either of the two assets, they will be priced correctly. We say that the model correctly reprices the implied volatility smiles.

We will call this model *local volatility with constant correlation* (LVCC). This name may be a little confusing since we do allow the instantaneous correlation to be time dependent. It emphasises the fact that there is no stochastic or local component to the correlation.

The LVCC model is popular because of its simplicity. Often, the correlation is chosen by calculating the correlation for a time series of observed spot values over, say, the last half year. If there is a two-asset product that is quite liquid, then the correlation may be tuned to hit its market value. If possible, the latter approach is strongly preferred. An *implied correlation* (implied from the value of liquid instruments) can in principle be hedged by buying or selling those instruments.

11.3 Copulas

The basket option outlined in Section 11.1 is a European contract. The payout only depends on the spot rates at the expiry time T. It seems a shame to have to solve a PDE, or run a Monte Carlo simulation, to value such a simple payout. If only we knew the joint probability distribution of S_1 and S_2, we could simply integrate against the distribution.

We are provided with the smiles for the two assets at the expiry T, and the correlation between the spot rates. The smile for each asset allows us to construct its implied probability distribution, as in Section 6.2. We call these the two marginal distributions. Our model must correctly reprice the smiles for the two assets. That is, it must get the two marginal probability distributions right. Therefore, our task is to construct a joint probability distribution with the property that the marginal distributions are correct. The copula construction allows us to do this.

We will work with cumulative distribution functions. Let's suppose that $F_1(S_1)$ and $F_2(S_2)$ are the cumulative probability distribution functions implied by the volatility smiles for the two assets. We now pick any convenient joint probability distribution. The simplest choice is the Gaussian, and we will denote its joint cumulative distribution by

$$P(X_1 < x_1, X_2 < x_2) \equiv N_2(x_1, x_2; \rho) \qquad (11.7)$$

where ρ is the correlation, and X_1, X_2 are the correlated normal random variables. The marginals of the joint Gaussian distribution are simply standard normal distributions, and we denote the univariate cumulative normal distribution by $N_1(x)$.

Using these building blocks, we can construct the copula. Consider the *Gaussian copula* function defined by

$$C(S_1, S_2) = N_2(N_1^{-1}(F_1(S_1)), N_1^{-1}(F_2(S_2)); \rho), \qquad (11.8)$$

where $N_1^{-1}()$ is the inverse cumulative normal function.

This is a cumulative distribution function. One can easily check by differentiating twice that the corresponding density function is positive, and the limits are correct when S_1 and S_2 go to zero and infinity.

It remains to check that the marginal distributions match the asset smiles. If we take $S_2 \to \infty$, then $F_2(S_2) \to 1$ and $N_1^{-1}(F_2(S_2)) \to \infty$. As its second argument goes to ∞, the bivariate cumulative normal function $N_2()$ reduces to its own marginal, which is simply the univariate normal function, and we have

$$C(S_1, S_2) \to N_2(N_1^{-1}(F_1(S_1)), \infty; \rho) \qquad (11.9)$$

$$= N_1(N_1^{-1}(F_1(S_1))) \qquad (11.10)$$

$$= F_1(S_1), \qquad (11.11)$$

which is indeed the true marginal obtained from the smile of the first asset.

We have chosen to present the copula in its cumulative distribution form, because that makes it easy to write down, and easy to check the marginals are correct. However, it is straightforward to differentiate and work with the copula density function for the purpose of numerical calculations.

One can form a copula from any multivariate distribution, and many efforts have been made to choose the copula to provide desirable properties for the joint distribution (a correlation smile, for example). Ultimately though, copulas are quite limited. To match an arbitrary correlation smile would require a copula with an infinite number of parameters to tweak, and efforts to match a given property of the joint distribution tend to become prohibitively complicated.

If one uses the LVCC model and the Gaussian copula to value a given European contract, the prices tend to match quite closely. This is purely an empirical observation, not backed up with any mathematical evidence. It is perhaps not so surprising though. The LVCC model also uses an underlying joint Gaussian based process (correlated Brownian motion) to join up the two marginal distributions into a joint distribution.

11.4   Correlation Smile

So far we have looked at two constant correlation models: the local volatility constant correlation (LVCC) model, and the Gaussian copula. In reality, it is easy to see that there has to be an implied correlation smile in the same way that there is an implied volatility smile.

Let's think about the basket option contract from Section 11.1, but consider the case in which the two assets are equities rather than foreign exchange. The two spot rates S_1 and S_2 might, for example, be the prices of IBM shares and of shares in a large house building company.

When everything is going well in the economy, S_1 and S_2 will appear fairly uncorrelated. Therefore the appropriate correlation to use for a basket contract struck at-the-money is likely to be rather small. But let's think about a basket struck strongly in-the-money. If something horrible happens to the economy, the chances are that both assets will fall in value, and they will suddenly appear strongly correlated, and the basket option may actually move out-of-the-money. Therefore the appropriate correlation to use will be larger.

When there are big market moves, assets become more correlated. If we were to plot the appropriate correlation for pricing against the basket strike, we would see a smile or skew shape much like an implied volatility smile.

11.5   Marking Correlation Smile

In order to understand the meaning of a correlation smile, we can think back to the meaning of the volatility smile. We recall that implied volatility is *that volatility we would plug into the Black–Scholes equation for a vanilla option in order to get the true market price*. The implied volatility depends on the vanilla option strike, and tends to take on a smile shape if we plot it.

Then, the definition for implied correlation should be *that correlation we plug into the Black–Scholes formula to get the true market price*. The question is, with respect to which contract should we define the implied correlation? In other words, for which contract are we trying to match the market price?

In a sense, there is no right or wrong answer to this question. How one thinks of the correlation smile may depend on the products one is trading, or on the products that are most liquid. We will examine the possibilities and then settle on a preferred choice. Later, when we come to modelling, this choice will allow us to extend the smile models from previous chapters to the multi-asset case in a way that is quite compelling. However, we will provide a tool to convert to and from other choices.

11.5.1   Common Correlation Products

In order to decide with respect to which product we should mark our implied correlation smile, let's look at the common two-asset correlation products.

Basket Option

We have already seen a basket payout. It represents the (weighted) average of the asset spot rates

$$(w_1 S_1 + w_2 S_2 - K)_+, \tag{11.12}$$

where S_i are the spot rates at the expiry date T years from now.

This payout can be a cash settled contract simply paying out according to the formula. But it is also the value at expiry of a physical settled contract in which one has the option to receive w_i units of each of the assets i in exchange for payment K. That is, it is literally an option to buy a basket of assets at the strike price.

The weights w_1 and w_2 are important. It may be that the current spot rate for S_1 is around 100, while for S_2 it is around 0.1. Clearly the weights should be chosen to bring the contributions from the two assets into line. The obvious choice is $w_i = 0.5 / F_i$ where F_i is the forward level to time T.

This necessity to scale the spots is unsatisfactory, though not a deal breaker for defining implied correlation. It would be a shame to have the contract defining implied correlation depending on market data, but a similar situation exists (in foreign exchange for example) when brokers and dealers agree the implied volatility of at-the-money options. However, we will see later that this scale issue is important when it comes to building correlation smile aware models. The need to have non-matching weights for contracts with differing expiries is problematic.

There are further difficulties. The Black–Scholes value of a basket depends on the implied volatilities of the two assets as well as the correlation, and so there is the question of which volatilities to use. One might perhaps choose the volatilities at strikes KF_i. But there is no knowing if these make sense. They might lead to an implied correlation outside ± 1.

Finally, there is no simple analytic formula for the Black–Scholes value of a basket option. One must either make an approximation, or perform numerical integration against the Black–Scholes probability density. This is rather unsatisfactory since one would wish to make fast transformations between the implied correlation and the basket value.

Quanto

A *quanto* (short for quantity adjusted) option pays in the 'wrong' currency. Imagine a vanilla call option on IBM shares. It has payout $(S_1 - K)_+$ where S_1 is the IBM spot rate measured in dollars. This is the value at expiry of a physical trade which is the option to buy shares at strike price K. However, we could take that payout formula, calculate it as a number, and then pay it in pounds sterling instead of dollars.

This is a quanto. The trade has lost its meaning as a contract that can be physically settled by the exchange of cash and shares at the expiry, but it is still a well-defined contract with a cash settled payout. We can write down the payout formula in dollars by using the sterling–dollar exchange rate, having spot rate S_2 (dollars per pound) at expiry,

$$(S_1 - K)_+ S_2. \tag{11.13}$$

When we write the payout this way, it is clearly a two-asset contract, and depends on the correlation between S_1 and S_2.

Although the payout 'does not make sense', quanto contracts are popular. To understand why, imagine a sterling investor who watches the value of IBM shares, or perhaps gold, both of which are reported in dollars. The investor wishes to make money in pounds following the spot price fluctuations, without worrying about the exchange rate. This can be achieved with a quanto contract.

However, the lack of symmetry between the two assets in the payout formula makes the quanto a very poor choice of contract for defining implied correlation. We would like the implied correlation to mean the same thing for S_1 as it does for S_2, but this could not be the case.

Spread Option

A spread option has a payout formula that is similar to a basket option, but depending on the difference between the two spot rates rather than their average

$$(w_1 S_1 - w_2 S_2 - K)_+. \tag{11.14}$$

While the averaging effect in a basket option tends to reduce risk compared to contracts on the individual assets, this is not so of the spread option, and they can be quite tricky to trade and risk manage. Nevertheless, they are popular with investors who may have a strong view on the relative performance of two related assets.

The spread option is not usually an appropriate instrument for use to define implied correlation for all the same reasons as the basket contract. Like the basket payout, the scaling issue in which one needs to choose the weights based on market data is problematic when it comes to modelling.

There is one major market, the constant maturity swap (CMS) interest rate market, in which spread options are traded so frequently that they can often be considered liquid. In this particular case, the appropriate weights are $w_1 = w_2 = 1$ because the two CMS rates S_1 and S_2 are interest rates for the same currency and therefore measured on the same scale. In this case, the spread option is an appropriate instrument to define implied correlation.

Best-of and Worst-of Options

Best-of and worst-of options will be important to us shortly. For now we simply explain the contract (and their unsuitability for use as the instrument defining implied correlation).

We have two assets in mind. They might be, say, IBM shares and Apple shares, and we consider a vanilla contract on each. At expiry, we check the value of the two vanilla contracts and pay the one with the greater value if it is a best-of, or the smaller value for a worst-of. Alternatively, one can think of providing a choice of which contract is delivered either to the buyer or seller of the option. Then a rational buyer will choose the maximum payout, while a rational seller would choose the minimum.

Then the payout formulas are

$$\max\{(S_1 - K_1)_+/K_1, (S_2 - K_2)_+/K_2\} \quad \text{(best-of)} \tag{11.15}$$

$$\min\{(S_1 - K_1)_+/K_1, (S_2 - K_2)_+/K_2\} \quad \text{(worst-of).} \tag{11.16}$$

Here we note that the individual vanilla payouts include a division by the appropriate strike K_1 or K_2. This allows us to provide the notional for both contracts in dollar terms rather than in units of the asset, with the conversion rate being the strike.

Best-ofs and worst-ofs are popular two-asset contracts. A best-of allows an investor to select the return of the best performing asset. On the other hand, a worst-of is cheaper than either of the two underlying options, and therefore provides a useful tool for investors or hedgers who are agnostic to the asset they receive for some reason.

However, as there are two strike parameters in the contract, defining implied correlation with respect to these instruments would lead to a two-dimensional implied correlation surface rather than a one-dimensional smile. This would be much too complicated. We would lose the nice interpretation of a correlation smile with higher correlation away from the money. Therefore we will not use best-of or worst-of options to define our implied correlation smile.

Geometric Basket Option

The geometric basket option has payout

$$(\{S_1 S_2\}^{\frac{1}{2}} - K)_+. \tag{11.17}$$

It is much like a standard basket option, except that it uses the geometric rather than arithmetic average.

The nice thing about geometric baskets is that the weighting issue present for standard arithmetic baskets has gone away. For this reason, geometric baskets are sometimes used to define indices representing a set of assets, and then options may be written on these indices.

However, unlike the standard basket payout, there is no physically settled trade whose value at expiry can be represented by this payout, and the trade must always be cash settled. For this reason perhaps, geometric baskets are rather rare. Although they are mathematically appealing for defining implied correlation, they are less so financially, and we will not use them to define our correlation smile.

Composite Option

The composite option is the contract we are going to use to define the implied correlation smile. The payout is

$$(S_1 - K S_2)_+. \tag{11.18}$$

It is similar to a spread option except that the strike parameter is multiplicative rather than additive.

The weighting issue present for basket and spread options has gone away. Any weights introduced for S_1 and S_2 can be absorbed into the strike K by rescaling the payout. Using put–call parity, we could equally well consider the contract

$$(KS_2 - S_1)_+ \tag{11.19}$$

and therefore the two assets S_1 and S_2 are treated perfectly symmetrically.

What makes composite options particularly appealing is the following interpretation. Let's suppose the two assets are IBM and Apple shares. In the payout formula (11.18), we have chosen to value the payout in dollars. But we can write down the payout in units of any asset we choose, and if we use Apple shares, the payout becomes

$$(S_1/S_2 - K)_+. \tag{11.20}$$

Here we could replace S_1/S_2 with S_3, the spot rate representing the value of IBM shares measured in Apple shares.

The contract is really just a vanilla option on IBM shares denominated in Apple shares. Its value is determined by the implied volatility smile for the asset S_3. We will call this the *cross asset*.

The composite option is particularly familiar to foreign exchange traders. If we replace S_1 with the euro–dollar exchange rate, and S_2 with the yen–dollar exchange rate, then S_3 becomes the euro–yen rate. Options on euro–yen are traded in huge volumes, and so foreign exchange practitioners have the luxury of instruments defining the correlation smile that are very liquid.

While their most familiar setting certainly is foreign exchange, composite options are used and are even sometimes fairly liquid in other asset classes. These include equities, in which some at-the-money composite volatilities are liquid, and precious metals, in which the entire composite smile may be marked (as in a smile for gold denominated in sterling rather than dollars).

11.5.2 The Triangle Rule

Derivatives trading desks in investment banks usually act as market makers. The implied volatility smile is really just a construction telling us the value of vanilla options at all strikes. Therefore vanilla option traders are making a market in implied volatility. Where vanilla contracts are liquidly traded, the trader must use those prices. Where there are no prices visible in the market, it is up to the trader to decide at what price to buy and sell. Effectively the trader is *marking* the volatility smile by using his or her skill and knowledge of the market.

In the same way, multi-asset traders are making markets in implied correlation. One of the advantages of using composite options to define the meaning of implied correlation is that they are simply vanilla options on the cross asset, and therefore can be defined with an implied volatility smile. Traders can use all of their skills at marking vanilla smiles to help mark the cross smiles, or equivalently, the correlation smiles.

There is a simple rule for converting between the volatility of the cross asset and the correlation. The rule only works in Black–Scholes, but that's fine because implied correlation is *that value we plug into the Black–Scholes pricing formula to get the true market price.*

If we suppose that S_1 and S_2 follow two correlated Black–Scholes processes with volatilities σ_1 and σ_2 and correlation ρ

$$d\log S_1 = (\mu_1 - \tfrac{1}{2}\sigma_1^2)dt + \sigma_1 dW_1 \tag{11.21}$$

$$d\log S_2 = (\mu_2 - \tfrac{1}{2}\sigma_2^2)dt + \sigma_2 dW_2 \tag{11.22}$$

$$dW_1\, dW_2 = \rho\, dt, \tag{11.23}$$

then we can find the process followed by $S_3 = S_1/S_2$ simply by subtracting the log processes

$$d\log S_3 = d\log S_1 - d\log S_2 \tag{11.24}$$

$$= (\mu_1 - \mu_2 - \tfrac{1}{2}\sigma_1^2 + \tfrac{1}{2}\sigma_2^2)dt + \sigma_1 dW_1 - \sigma_2 dW_2 \tag{11.25}$$

$$= (\mu_3 - \tfrac{1}{2}\sigma_1^2 + \tfrac{1}{2}\sigma_2^2)dt + \sqrt{\sigma_1^2 - 2\rho\sigma_1\sigma_2 + \sigma_2^2}\, dW_3. \tag{11.26}$$

Here we have introduced $\mu_3 = \mu_1 - \mu_2$ and combined the two correlated Brownian increments dW_1 and dW_2 into one dW_3 using the standard property of correlated normal variables.

The drift term in equation (11.26) looks a little unfamiliar, but that is simply because the process we have written down is risk-neutral with respect to the dollar bond numeraire, while S_3 is denominated in units of asset 2. If we had the energy, we could rectify this by changing the measure to use asset 2 as the numeraire.

What is important is that we now have a formula relating the volatility σ_3 of the cross asset with the other two volatilities and the correlation. Reading off from (11.26) gives us

$$\sigma_3 = \sqrt{\sigma_1^2 - 2\rho\sigma_1\sigma_2 + \sigma_2^2} \tag{11.27}$$

which can be rearranged to

$$\rho = \frac{\sigma_1^2 + \sigma_2^2 - \sigma_3^2}{2\sigma_1\sigma_2}. \tag{11.28}$$

This formula is known as the triangle rule, and we can use it to convert between the implied correlation ρ and the composite option (cross asset) implied volatility σ_3.

Many people prefer to work with an implied correlation smile rather than directly with the cross asset smile. If we wish to go ahead and use the triangle rule to convert between the two, we have the difficulty of choosing what values of σ_1 and σ_2 to use

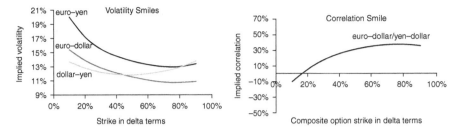

Figure 11.1   Composite option implied correlation smile.

for the implied volatilities of the two assets. In a sense it doesn't matter what we use. It is the market values of the correlation instruments (the composite options) that are important. These are fully defined by the cross asset volatility smile, and a translation of this into implied correlation terms is merely to aid human interpretation. However, a poor choice may lead to implied correlations outside the range $[-1, +1]$.

A choice that seems to work well is to use the *matching delta* prescription. We choose strikes K_1 and K_2 for the two assets, and the implied volatilities will be taken from the volatility smiles at those strikes. We insist that K_1/K_2 be equal to the cross strike K, but this still leaves one degree of freedom. If we calculate the call option Black–Scholes delta $\Delta_1(K_1)$ for the first asset, and (the absolute value of) the put option delta $\Delta_2(K_2)$ for the second, then a good choice is to adjust the strikes until the two deltas match. This ensures that the two asset strikes have matching 'moneyness' as measured in delta space.

Figure 11.1 shows volatility smiles for the foreign exchange assets euro–dollar and yen–dollar, together with the smile for the cross asset euro–yen. They are true market smiles as they were in December 2011 for contracts of one-year expiry. We can think of the two assets as being euros and Japanese yen, each denominated in dollars, and the composite option smile corresponds to euros denominated in yen. The correlation smile is plotted using the matching delta prescription to determine the two asset volatilities. The most noticeable feature of the composite implied correlation smile is, rather, that it is frown shaped. A moment's thought shows why this is so. If a composite option is initially struck at-the-money and the correlation is close to 100%, then the option is unlikely to end up strongly in- or out-of-the-money because the assets move together. For this reason, large market moves as seen by a composite option are associated with low or negative correlation. As the purpose of the correlation smile is to encode higher probabilities for large market moves, we see a frown shape.

In Section 11.9 we will convert the composite implied correlation smile into a basket implied correlation smile. There, as we would expect, we will see a traditional smile shape.

11.6   Modelling

So far, we have defined our implied correlation smile at a fixed expiry date. The implied correlation at strike K is that correlation we would plug into the Black–Scholes formula to get the true market price of the composite option with that strike. We can use the triangle formula to convert between the implied correlation and the cross volatility. As we have seen, the choice of asset volatilities to use in the Black–Scholes formula is somewhat arbitrary, and therefore it is often easier to work directly with the cross volatility smile, which determines the values of the composite options.

Naturally, we may wish to value products that are not European, and we can extend the cross volatility smile (or implied correlation smile) into surface with values at all expiry dates.

Our task then is to construct models that correctly reprice the asset volatility surfaces and the cross volatility surface. That is, if we use the model to value vanillas on either of the two assets, we must get the true market price. Furthermore, if we value the correlation instruments, which are composite options, we must get the true market price as defined by the cross volatility surface.

11.6.1 Local Correlation

Local correlation is a remarkably simple extension of Dupire's local volatility model into the multi-asset world. If we allow the two assets to follow local volatility dynamics, then asset vanillas will be correctly priced by construction. The trick is to allow the correlation to depend on the spot levels (and time) in just such a way that the correlation instruments are repriced correctly.

Then our model takes the form

$$d\log S_1 = (\mu_1 - \tfrac{1}{2}\sigma_1(S_1,t)^2)dt + \sigma_1(S_1,t)dW_1 \tag{11.29}$$

$$d\log S_2 = (\mu_2 - \tfrac{1}{2}\sigma_2(S_2,t)^2)dt + \sigma_2(S_2,t)dW_2 \tag{11.30}$$

$$dW_1\,dW_2 = \rho(S_1,S_2,t)dt, \tag{11.31}$$

where $\sigma_1(S_1,t)$ and $\sigma_2(S_2,t)$ are the asset local volatility functions obtained from their implied volatility surfaces using equation (6.35), and $\rho(S_1,S_2,t)$ is the local correlation function.

Our task is to choose $\rho(S_1,S_2,t)$ in just such a way that when we use the model to value composite options, we get the values correct. A composite option is really just a vanilla option on $S_3 = S_1/S_2$, and we can find the process followed by $\log S_3$ by subtracting

$$d\log S_3 = d\log S_1 - d\log S_2 \tag{11.32}$$

$$= (\mu_1 - \mu_2 - \tfrac{1}{2}\sigma_1(S_1,t)^2 + \tfrac{1}{2}\sigma_2(S_2,t)^2)dt$$

$$+ \sigma_1(S_1,t)dW_1 - \sigma_2(S_2,t)dW_2. \tag{11.33}$$

If we look at the Brownian terms $\sigma_1(S_1,t)dW_1 - \sigma_2(S_2,t)dW_2$ in (11.33), they can be rewritten using a single Brownian motion dW_3

$$\sqrt{\sigma_1(S_1,t)^2 - 2\rho(S_1,S_2,t)\sigma_1(S_1,t)\sigma_2(S_2,t) + \sigma_2(S_2,t)^2}\,dW_3. \tag{11.34}$$

We can take the cross volatility surface and compute its local volatility function $\sigma_3(S_3,t)$, again using equation (6.35), and then set it equal to the volatility factor in equation (11.34). Then rearranging gives us the local volatility version of the triangle rule

$$\rho(S_1,S_2,t) = \frac{\sigma_1(S_1,t)^2 + \sigma_2(S_2,t)^2 - \sigma_3(S_3,t)^2}{2\sigma_1(S_1,t)^2\sigma_2(S_2,t)^2},$$

(11.35)

and the process for S_3 becomes

$$d\log S_3 = (\mu_1 - \mu_2 - \tfrac{1}{2}\sigma_1(S_1,t)^2 + \tfrac{1}{2}\sigma_2(S_2,t)^2)dt$$
$$+\sigma_3(S_3,t)\,dW_3.$$

(11.36)

The drift term looks a little strange because the SDE is risk-neutral with respect to the dollar numeraire rather than the asset 2 numeraire. We could go through the formal process of changing the measure, but it is easier simply to note that the process (11.36) must value forward contracts on the cross asset S_3 correctly. In either case, the risk-neutral process with respect to the asset 2 bond numeraire is

$$d\log S_3 = (\mu_3 - \tfrac{1}{2}\sigma_3(S_3,t)^2)dt + \sigma_3(S_3,t)dW_3,$$

(11.37)

where $\mu_3 = \mu_1 - \mu_2$. As this is the Dupire local volatility process for the cross asset, the composite options are priced correctly at all strikes and all expiries by construction.

A simple application of the triangle rule in local volatility space has provided us with a powerful model that is fully correlation smile aware. Local correlation is only one of a series of models that can be constructed this way. We start to see that there is something quite special about the choice of using composite options as the fundamental implied correlation instruments.

11.6.2 Practicalities

Having written down the SDEs (11.29)–(11.31) of our local correlation model, we can go ahead and value, either with a PDE solver, or in Monte Carlo as usual. The partial differential pricing equation can be derived quite straightforwardly as in Section 3.12,

$$\frac{\partial C}{\partial t} + \mu_1 S_1 \frac{\partial C}{\partial S_1} + \mu_2 S_2 \frac{\partial C}{\partial S_2}$$

(11.38)

$$+\frac{1}{2}\left(S_1^2\sigma_1^2\frac{\partial^2 C}{\partial S_1^2} + 2\rho S_1 S_2\sigma_1\sigma_2\frac{\partial^2 C}{\partial S_1\partial S_2} + S_2^2\sigma_2^2\frac{\partial^2 C}{\partial S_2^2}\right) - r_{dom}C = 0.$$

Here we have dropped the spot and time dependence of the local volatility and local correlation functions in order to express the PDE more compactly.

The model extends naturally to more than two assets. We simply use the triangle rule to calculate the local correlation function for each entry in the matrix of local correlations, and then simulate in Monte Carlo in order to calculate derivative prices.

One practical difficulty is that it can be hard for traders to mark a set of cross volatility surfaces that are perfectly arbitrage free. This becomes apparent when the local correlation is calculated and comes outside the range $[-1, 1]$ for some values of S_1, S_2 and t. If the correlation smile is liquid, or has been carefully marked by a market maker, the regions in which the local correlation goes bad will typically be restricted to spots that are far in- or out-of-the-money.

We recall from Section 8.1.2 that, in the multi-asset case, we require the correlation matrix to be positive definite (that is, have positive eigenvalues). As more assets are added to the model, it becomes harder and harder to keep the full local correlation matrix positive definite everywhere.

In an ideal world, when one finds market data making the local correlation matrix go bad, this would indicate either a true arbitrage opportunity, or poorly marked market data. In reality though, setting up a trade to take advantage of a theoretical arbitrage is often infeasible, even in the two-asset case (if for example it occurs far away from the money). The problem may be attributed to inconsistently marked market data, but it is not necessarily easy for a market maker to alter their correlation surfaces in a way that would fix all possible local correlation matrices.

A more pragmatic approach is to regularise any bad local correlations that are encountered during the valuation algorithm. If it is a two-asset problem, any local correlation outside $[-1, 1]$ can simply be capped or floored. In a multi-asset Monte Carlo simulation, one can floor the eigenvalues of any bad local correlation matrix encountered, and then rescale the entries to ensure it remains a true correlation matrix.

The result of regularisation is that the correlation instruments will not be correctly repriced. However, if the correlation surfaces (also known as cross volatility surfaces) are reasonably consistent, then the impact should be minimal.

What is delightful about the local correlation model is that it appears remarkably robust to correlation regularisation. One can do, say, a four-asset Monte Carlo simulation, and value composite options (cross vanillas) at various different strikes and expiries. The foreign exchange market provides an excellent laboratory to do this experiment since the cross assets are often liquid. One might worry that correlation regularisation would spoil the repricing of the cross smiles in an unpredictable way. But one tends to see that the cross smiles are incorrectly priced only in certain localised regions of strike space. These provide an indication of where the cross smiles may be badly marked, or where the market is pricing inconsistently and there may be a theoretical arbitrage opportunity.

11.6.3   Local Stochastic Correlation

In Chapter 9 we learned that pure local volatility is often not suitable for single asset path dependent contracts. The classic examples are continuous barrier options. In many markets they trade liquidly enough to distinguish between the value in local volatility and the value in stochastic volatility models, the true price being some way in between. Investment banks use local stochastic volatility models in order to capture this effect.

Path dependent contracts involving more than one asset are subject to the same effects. If we are unable to take account of the stochastic versus local volatility dynamic, we will get prices wrong. Naturally, if we use our multi-asset model to value a single asset contract, we would wish it to give the same price as the single asset model. If we fail to achieve this, we expose ourselves to potential arbitrage.

For example, imagine we wish to value a dual no-touch option on gold and silver. The contract pays 1 dollar at expiry as long as neither a continuous barrier on the gold spot rate nor a continuous barrier on the silver spot rate is breached. It may be that during the life of the trade the silver spot rate moves far enough from the barrier so that the contract effectively becomes a single asset no-touch on gold. If we were to use the local correlation model to value the contract, we would get the price wrong.

We were able to take the local volatility model and extend it to a multi-asset local correlation model simply by applying the triangle rule. The beauty is that we can use exactly the same trick to create a local stochastic correlation model from the underlying local stochastic volatility models applying to each of the assets and the cross.

We are provided with an implied volatility surface for the two assets (in this case, gold and silver) and a calibrated local stochastic volatility model for each. In addition, we have an implied correlation surface, which is provided to us as the volatility surface for the cross asset, gold denominated in silver. We can calibrate an additional local stochastic volatility model to the cross surface.

In order to provide a specific example, we can use the λ-SABR style stochastic volatility process to underlie our LSV models, as in equations (9.34)–(9.36). In Section 9.5.1, we argued that it is not necessary to include spot–volatility correlation in an LSV. It will simplify things now to work with zero correlation between the spot and volatility processes. Then our local stochastic correlation model will be

$$\frac{dS_1}{S_1} = \mu_1\,dt + A_1(S_1,t)\sigma_1\,dW_1 \tag{11.39}$$

$$\frac{dS_2}{S_2} = \mu_2\,dt + A_2(S_2,t)\sigma_2\,dW_2 \tag{11.40}$$

$$d\sigma_1 = -\lambda_1(\sigma_1 - \overline{\sigma_1})dt + v_1\sigma_1\,dZ_1 \tag{11.41}$$

$$d\sigma_2 = -\lambda_2(\sigma_2 - \overline{\sigma_2})dt + v_2\sigma_2\,dZ_2 \tag{11.42}$$

$$d\sigma_3 = -\lambda_3(\sigma_3 - \overline{\sigma_3})dt + v_3\sigma_3\,dZ_3 \tag{11.43}$$

$$dW_i\,dZ_j = 0 \tag{11.44}$$

$$dZ_i\,dZ_j = c_{ij}dt \tag{11.45}$$

$$dW_1\,dW_2 = \rho(S_1,S_2,\sigma_1,\sigma_2,\sigma_3,t)dt. \tag{11.46}$$

Here we have two asset spot processes with local stochastic volatilities, and three volatility processes, one each for the assets and one for the cross. The spot–volatility correlations are zero, but we allow correlations c_{ij} between the three volatility processes.

The most important thing is that the local stochastic correlation $\rho(S_1, S_2, \sigma_1, \sigma_2, \sigma_3)$ must be chosen so that the cross asset follows its LSV process

$$\frac{dS_3}{S_3} = \mu_3 dt + A_3(S_3, t)\sigma_3 dW_3 \qquad (11.47)$$

(when expressed in the measure that is risk-neutral with respect to the asset 2 numeraire). Just as in the local correlation model, this is achieved with the triangle rule

$$\rho(S_1, S_2, \sigma_1, \sigma_2, \sigma_3, t) = \frac{(A_1(S_1, t)\sigma_1)^2 + (A_2(S_2, t)\sigma_2)^2 - (A_3(S_3, t)\sigma_3)^2}{2(A_1(S_1, t)\sigma_1)(A_2(S_2, t)\sigma_2)}. \qquad (11.48)$$

The choice of zero for the spot–volatility correlations means that the measure change from the dollar numeraire to the asset 2 numeraire has no impact on the process for the instantaneous cross volatility σ_3. This is a welcome simplification, because it allows us to use the stochastic volatility process calibrated to the cross volatility surface without a measure change.

By using the instantaneous correlation defined in equation (11.48), we have constructed a model in which the asset smiles and correlation smile are correctly repriced, and furthermore the assets and the cross asset all follow local stochastic volatility processes. As the instantaneous correlation depends on the stochastic volatilities as well as the spot levels, it is a *local stochastic correlation.*

Local stochastic correlation models are much trickier to use than local correlation. If a poor choice of the volatility–volatility correlations c_{ij} is used, the instantaneous correlation may go outside $[-1, 1]$ too much of the time, or be too rapidly varying, and lead to poor repricing of the cross smile.

To work well, the instantaneous volatility processes must be strongly correlated so that the c_{ij} are close to 1. This is understandable when looking at equation (11.48) defining the instantaneous correlation, as this choice will make the terms in the numerator and denominator move together and therefore limit its range. It also makes sense financially. The chances are that if one of the assets becomes more volatile for some reason, then so will the other asset and the cross.

Our aim is always to find the simplest model that reprices our hedging instruments and does not have any unreasonable properties. Then, given that they must be strongly correlated and we have no other relevant market information, we may as well choose the instantaneous volatility processes to be perfectly correlated and share a single Brownian motion dZ for each. In that case, what was a five-factor model reduces to three factors, and the PDE approach to pricing becomes feasible.

We have seen in Section 9.5.4 that simple mixture or regime switching style LSV models are appropriate for certain contracts like barrier options. If such models are used to replace the stochastic volatility processes in our LSC model, then we have reduced the complexity further, to only two true stochastic factors, and fast pricing can be achieved with a PDE solver.

11.7 Valuing European Contracts

So far, we have seen how to mark a correlation smile as a composite option (or cross option) volatility surface, and how to extend the true dynamic smile models (local volatility and local stochastic volatility) into multiple dimensions.

This is great: we can now go ahead and use a PDE solver or Monte Carlo to value many instruments. However, looking back to Section 11.5.1, there are a large number of simple European correlation products that we would like to value, and it seems a shame to have to use such heavy numerical techniques to achieve that.

To value a European contract we do not need a full dynamic model matching the smiles at all expiries. All we need is a joint PDF for the spot rates at the expiry date. In this section we will see how to construct such a density.

11.7.1 Special Properties of Best-of Options

In order to construct the PDF, we are going to study best-of options. A best-of has the property that, depending on spot movements, its value can converge to that of a vanilla option on either of the two assets, or on the cross asset. The idea is to postulate a valuation formula for best-ofs that respects the known vanilla prices in its limits, and use this to construct our PDF.

We recall from equation (11.15) that the payout of a best-of option is

$$P = \max\left\{\frac{(S_1 - K_1)_+}{K_1}, \frac{(S_2 - K_2)_+}{K_2}\right\}. \tag{11.49}$$

At expiry, we check which asset performed best, and pay a vanilla contract on it.

If at any time S_1 becomes strongly out-of-the-money while S_2 does not, then the contract reduces to a vanilla on S_2 with strike K_2. Likewise, in opposite circumstances, it can become a vanilla on S_1 with strike K_1.

What, though, if both S_1 and S_2 become strongly in-the-money? Then the optionality becomes a choice between S_1 and S_2. In that case, the payout can be expressed as

$$\max\left\{\frac{(S_1 - K_1)_+}{K_1}, \frac{(S_2 - K_2)_+}{K_2}\right\} = \max\left\{\frac{(S_1 - K_1)}{K_1}, \frac{(S_2 - K_2)}{K_2}\right\} \tag{11.50}$$

$$= \frac{S_2}{K_1}\max\left\{\frac{S_1}{S_2}, \frac{K_1}{K_2}\right\} - 1 \tag{11.51}$$

$$= \frac{S_2}{K_1}\left(\frac{S_1}{S_2} - \frac{K_1}{K_2}\right)_+ + \frac{S_2}{K_2} - 1, \tag{11.52}$$

which is a call option on the cross with strike $K_3 = K_1/K_2$ together with a forward contract.

Then, depending on spot movements, a best-of option can become arbitrarily close in value to a vanilla on either asset or on the cross. Then any model used to value a best-of option must correctly reprice vanillas on the drivers and the cross, otherwise the valuation will be directly arbitrageable with a vanilla contract.

Suppose we know the value of best-of options for all possible strikes K_1 and K_2. We will now see that this implies complete knowledge of the risk-neutral joint PDF.

By differentiating the best-of payout P from equation (11.49), we obtain the dual digital payout

$$\left(1 + K_1 \frac{\partial}{\partial K_1} + K_2 \frac{\partial}{\partial K_2}\right) P + 1 = 1_{\{S_1 < K_1, S_2 < K_2\}}, \tag{11.53}$$

whose undiscounted value is the bivariate cumulative distribution. Two more differentiations give us the probability density. Then, if we denote the undiscounted value of the best-of with strikes K_1, K_2 by $B(K_1, K_2)$, and the joint PDF by f, they are related by

$$\frac{\partial^2}{\partial K_1 \partial K_2} \left(K_1 \frac{\partial}{\partial K_1} + K_2 \frac{\partial}{\partial K_2} + 1\right) B(K_1, K_2) = f(K_1, K_2). \tag{11.54}$$

This formula tells us that if we know the value of best-of options at all strikes K_1, K_2, then this is equivalent to knowing the joint probability density.

In summary, there are two properties making best-of options special:

1 a best-of with strikes K_1, K_2 can reduce into a vanilla on either of the drivers, or on the cross with strike $K_3 = K_1/K_2$;
2 the set of all possible best-of options completely defines the market for European options.

11.7.2   Valuing a Best-of Option in Black–Scholes

Best-of options can be valued analytically in Black–Scholes. The Black–Scholes pricing formula is going to be an important component of our PDF construction, and therefore we will take a moment or two to work out the formula here. Those who are happy to take it as read may skip to the next section, but will miss a treat as this derivation is truly delightful.

The (undiscounted) value is[31]

$$B(K_1, K_2; \sigma_1, \sigma_2, \sigma_3) = \frac{F_1}{K_1} N(d_1^+, d_3^+; \rho_{13})$$

$$+ \frac{F_2}{K_2} N(d_2^+, -d_3^-; \rho_{23})$$

$$+ N(-d_1^-, -d_2^-; \rho_{12}) - 1 \tag{11.55}$$

---

[31] This formula was originally worked out by Margrabe (1978) and Stulz (1982), while the compact derivation provided here was provided by Johnson (1987) and Ouwehand and West (2006).

where N is the bivariate cumulative normal function, and the correlations are given by

$$\rho_{12} = \frac{\sigma_1^2 + \sigma_2^2 - \sigma_3^2}{2\sigma_1\sigma_2} \tag{11.56}$$

and cyclic permutations. The parameters d_i are defined by

$$d_i^{\pm} = \frac{\log(F_i/K_i) \pm \sigma_i^2 T/2}{\sigma_i\sqrt{T}}, \quad i = 1,2,3, \tag{11.57}$$

where $K_3 = K_1/K_2$ is the cross strike. To evaluate the pricing function (11.55) requires the ability to call a bivariate cumulative normal function. Genz (2004) provides an approximation of the necessary high quality that can easily be implemented on a computer.

In order to derive equation (11.55), we are going to use the same approach of using measure changes that was used in Section 3.13 to obtain the standard Black–Scholes formula for a vanilla option. We first note that the payout (11.49) can be rewritten

$$\max\left\{\frac{(S_1 - K_1)_+}{K_1}, \frac{(S_2 - K_2)_+}{K_2}\right\} \equiv \frac{S_1}{K_1}1_{\{S_1 > K_1, S_3 > K_3\}}$$

$$+ \frac{S_2}{K_2}1_{\{S_2 > K_2, S_3 < K_3\}}$$

$$+ 1 - 1_{\{S_1 > K_1, S_2 > K_2\}}. \tag{11.58}$$

For the first term, we use asset 1 as numeraire, so that the risk-neutral processes are

$$S_1 = F_1 e^{\sigma_1^2 T + \sigma_1\sqrt{T}X_1}, \quad X_1 = N(0,1) \tag{11.59}$$

$$S_3 = F_3 e^{\sigma_3^2 T + \sigma_3\sqrt{T}X_3}, \quad X_3 = N(0,1) \tag{11.60}$$

$$E[X_1 X_3] = \rho_{13}. \tag{11.61}$$

Then, using the Martingale pricing equation (3.30), the value of the first term, with domestic currency discount factor removed, is

$$V_1 = \frac{F_1}{K_1}E[1_{\{S_1 > K_1, S_3 > K_3\}}], \tag{11.62}$$

with the expectation taken under the measure given by equations (11.59)–(11.61), giving the joint cumulative probability

$$V_1 = \frac{F_1}{K_1}N(d_1^+, d_3^+; \rho_{13}). \tag{11.63}$$

The second term works identically by using asset 2 as the numeraire. Finally, the third term is a simple cumulative probability in the standard (dollar bond) measure.

By using a thoughtful measure for each term in the payout, we have practically been able to write down the Black–Scholes formula for a best-of option. To have done the calculation all in the standard measure would have required a great deal of tedious algebra.

11.7.3   Construction of a Joint PDF

Let us now return to our task of constructing a joint PDF. If we could find a smooth function $B(K_1, K_2)$ reproducing the market values of the vanillas in the appropriate limits, then equation (11.54) tells us this is equivalent to finding a candidate joint PDF $f(K_1, K_2)$. As long as f satisfies all the usual necessities of a PDF, we will have a mechanism for valuing multi-asset European contracts.

In order to write down an appropriate function B, we make use of the Black–Scholes formula for a best-of (11.55). To set up our function $B(K_1, K_2)$ that matches all three smiles in the limits, we simply plug into equation (11.55) volatilities taken from the smile curve of each asset

$$\sigma_i = \sigma_i(K_i). \tag{11.64}$$

By choosing

$$B(K_1, K_2) = B(K_1, K_2; \sigma_1(K_1), \sigma_2(K_2), \sigma_3(K_3)), \tag{11.65}$$

Black–Scholes ensures for us that $B(K_1, K_2)$ correctly reprices vanillas on all three assets. To understand why this is so, we can look back to Section 11.7.1 and take one of the limits that make the best-of become a vanilla. For example, we can take $K_2 \to \infty$ so that it becomes a vanilla option on S_1. In that case, as the payout only depends on S_1, the Black–Scholes pricing formula only depends on σ_1. As we used the smile volatility $\sigma_1(K_1)$ we get the correct smile price for the vanilla.

We can check this more formally by taking the appropriate limit of equation (11.55). If you try this you will see that it is also necessary to assume that the implied volatilities do not grow too fast at large and small strikes. As long as the asymptotic condition

$$\sigma_i(K_i)^2 = o(|\log K_i/F_i|) \text{ as } K_i \to 0, \infty \tag{11.66}$$

is true, the $d_i^\pm$ stay under control when we take limits and everything works as expected. The condition (11.66) is the Lee (2004) no-arbitrage condition for individual smiles. A volatility smile that is arbitrage free must satisfy this condition, otherwise the values of vanilla options will not behave correctly at small and large strikes.

Then our PDF is given by

$$f(K_1, K_2) = \frac{\partial^2}{\partial K_1 \partial K_2} \left(K_1 \frac{\partial}{\partial K_1} + K_2 \frac{\partial}{\partial K_2} + 1 \right) B(K_1, K_2) \tag{11.67}$$

and, by construction, it correctly reprices vanillas at all strikes on all three assets.

This construction can be extended to N dimensions, though in practice it is most useful in two dimensions.

Although we have referred to the density function $f(K_1, K_2)$ as a PDF throughout this section, it is important to recognise that it may not be a true *probability* density. Since it gives correct prices for vanilla options, the density is guaranteed to integrate to 1. However it is not guaranteed to be real and positive for all configurations of input smiles. This is not surprising as the functional form of the two asset smiles will impose some constraints on the smile possible for the cross. For example, if the two assets each have a low constant volatility of 1% say, the cross asset must also have a low volatility, since it is formed by dividing the two assets. In fact, the triangle rule (11.28) tells us that we need $\sigma_3 \leq \sigma_1 + \sigma_2$ to keep the correlation in $[-1, 1]$. If a bad configuration of asset and cross smiles is provided, then the density is bound to go wrong.

The situation is similar to the local correlation model in which we may need to cut off the local correlations if they go outside the range $[-1, 1]$. In our PDF construction, we may need to cut off the correlations ρ_{ij}. In practice, like local correlation, the density appears very robust. Although we have no proof that it is a true PDF even when the triangle of asset and cross smiles are arbitrage free, it gives good prices (as compared against the local correlation model, for example).

The density we have constructed can be compared with a copula, since it joins two probability distributions, defined by the two driver smiles. Unlike standard copulas, rather than having a number of parameters that define the underlying distribution, it can fit to an entire additional dimension, in our case the cross smile.

It is interesting to compare our results with the Breeden–Litzenberger formula from Section 6.2. There, in the single asset case, knowledge of the implied volatility smile was enough to give us the unique PDF. When there are two or more assets, this is no longer true. If we are provided only with asset smiles and cross smiles, this is not enough information to make the joint density function unique. The function we have constructed is just one possibility.

11.7.4   Using the Density Function for Pricing

The formula (11.67) is an analytic representation of our joint density function, but it is not an explicit formula since it involves third order differentiations. If one tries to perform all the differentiations, a huge number of terms are generated, and are practically unmanageable. It is much easier to work with the cumulative probability distribution

$$F(K_1, K_2) = \left(K_1 \frac{\partial}{\partial K_1} + K_2 \frac{\partial}{\partial K_2} + 1 \right) B(K_1, K_2) + 1 \tag{11.68}$$

which simplifies to

$$F(K_1, K_2) = N(-d_1^-, -d_2^-; \rho_{12})$$
$$+ \left(K_1 \sigma_1' \frac{\partial}{\partial \sigma_1} + K_2 \sigma_2' \frac{\partial}{\partial \sigma_2} \right) B(K_1, K_2; \sigma_1, \sigma_2, \sigma_3) \tag{11.69}$$

and can be evaluated explicitly fairly easily. Here we note that, if the volatility smiles are flat, so that the first derivatives $\sigma_1'(K_1)$ and $\sigma_2'(K_2)$ are zero, the formula reduces to the Black–Scholes cumulative distribution, which is just a bivariate cumulative normal function.

Then, to value an arbitrary European payout, one can create an integration grid and use the cumulative distribution to calculate the probability of each square on the grid, and sum over all the squares to get the expectation.

Some simple contracts can be valued analytically. The value of a two-asset best-of option in the model is given simply by equation (11.65). Similarly, the worst-of option can be valued by plugging smile volatilities into its Black–Scholes formula. Alternatively, the worst-of can be replicated from the best-of since their sum is equal to the sum of the two underlying vanillas.

One common two-asset product that we did not meet in Section 11.5.1 is the dual asset digital. It has payout

$$1_{\{S_1<K_1,\,S_2<K_2\}} \tag{11.70}$$

representing a fixed cash payment if both spots are smaller than their strikes. The (undiscounted) value of a dual asset digital is given simply by the joint cumulative distribution $F(K_1, K_2)$.

A product that we will be interested in is the two asset basket option. There is no analytic formula for it, but we can value it much more efficiently than a standard two asset payout. It is easier to consider a put option on the basket. The call option value can then be recovered using put–call parity. Then the payout is

$$(K - w_1 S_1 - w_2 S_2)_+ \tag{11.71}$$

and the undiscounted value is obtained by integrating the payout against the density function

$$V_{Basket} = \int f(S_1, S_2)\,(K - w_1 S_1 - w_2 S_2)_+\, dS_1\, dS_2. \tag{11.72}$$

As the density function is the second derivative of the cumulative distribution function, we can rewrite this, and then integrate by parts twice

$$V_{Basket} = \int \frac{\partial^2 F(S_1, S_2)}{\partial S_1 \partial S_2}\,(K - w_1 S_1 - w_2 S_2)_+\, dS_1\, dS_2 \tag{11.73}$$

$$= \int F(S_1, S_2)\frac{\partial^2}{\partial S_1 \partial S_2}(K - w_1 S_1 - w_2 S_2)_+\, dS_1\, dS_2 \tag{11.74}$$

$$= \int F(S_1, S_2) w_1 w_2 \delta(K - w_1 S_1 - w_2 S_2)\, dS_1\, dS_2 \tag{11.75}$$

$$= \int_0^K F\left(\frac{U}{w_1}, \frac{K - U}{w_2}\right) dU. \tag{11.76}$$

The second derivative acting on the basket payout gave us a delta function that we could then use to perform one of the integrals analytically.

The formula (11.76) gives us the value of the basket option as a single-dimensional integral that can be evaluated on a computer very fast. A similar approach can be used to value the spread option.

11.8 Numeraire Symmetry

We have seen a number of indications that composite options (also known as cross vanillas) are the 'right' instruments to use to define our fundamental correlation smile:

- they are heavily correlation dependent;
- they have a simple asset-symmetric definition involving only one parameter, the strike;
- they are equivalent to simple vanilla contracts on asset 1 denominated in asset 2;
- as a result, their values can be obtained from an implied volatility surface for the cross asset;
- they are sometimes liquid;
- single asset local and stochastic volatility models can be extend by using the triangle rule to create local correlation and stochastic correlation models.

The fact that we can actually construct models like local correlation and local stochastic correlation is, of course, already quite a tempting argument. However, there is also a strong moral reason for using this approach, which we can call *numeraire symmetry*.

When valuing a derivative contract using the Martingale approach, a quant must first choose the numeraire. This, we recall, is a tradeable asset in units of which we measure the value of all other assets in the problem. The important point is that the choice of numeraire has no impact on the final value obtained. A quant is indifferent to the choice of numeraire (other than that a thoughtful choice often gives a simpler calculation).

Now let's think about a two-asset contract, depending on (say) the gold and silver spot rates. Let's suppose we want to use local volatility for the two assets. Although we have some criticisms of the local volatility model, it's really not a bad model. If spot moves far from the current level, then it's true that the instantaneous volatility is likely to increase, just as local volatility predicts.

Now, if we wish to, we can choose to use gold as the numeraire and measure our assets (now silver and dollars) in units of gold. What kind of a smile model should we use for silver denominated in gold? Well, it would be very odd indeed if we did not feel that local volatility is again appropriate for the same reason.

To emphasise the point, let's look at what happens if we choose to use a constant (or perhaps time-dependent) correlation between the two assets gold and silver. The SDEs are provided in equations (11.2)–(11.4). Using the same approach as in all our triangle rule arguments, we can write down the process followed by the cross asset $S_3 = S_1/S_2$

$$\frac{dS_3}{S_3} = (\cdots)dt + \sqrt{\sigma_1^2(S_1,t)^2 - 2\rho\sigma_1(S_1,t)\sigma_2(S_2,t) + \sigma_2(S_2,t)^2}\, dW_3. \qquad (11.77)$$

The drift term is not important and so we have left it unwritten. We are interested in the volatility term. It is like a local volatility except that it depends on the two asset spot rates S_1 and S_2 rather than directly on S_3. The resulting process for S_3 is complex and makes no financial sense.

This logic leads us to the conclusion that we should use local volatility for each of our assets and crosses. We have arrived at the local correlation model, and therefore we need to be provided with a cross smile.

11.9 Baskets as Correlation Instruments

We have developed an approach to correlation smile modelling based on using composite options (also known as cross vanillas) as the instruments used to define the correlation smile. By using the triangle rule, we have constructed models that calibrate to the cross smile.

Some traders may wish to mark their correlation smile with respect to other instruments, the most likely being two asset basket options. This may be because the trader finds them more intuitive, or simply because they are more liquid.

Fortunately, the semi-analytic basket pricing formula (11.76) provides a fast way to convert between a basket implied correlation smile and a cross smile.

Let's suppose we wish to mark a correlation smile with respect to two asset baskets. We may have one or two liquid basket prices around the at-the-money basket strike, and may have strong views on how the implied correlation should be marked in the limit of large and small basket strikes. For simplicity, we assume that the two asset spot rates have similar scale so that we do not need to include weights. Then the basket payout we use is

$$(0.5S_1 + 0.5S_2 - K)_+. \tag{11.78}$$

Our first task is to decide on the asset volatilities we will use in the Black–Scholes formula for the basket. There are many ways of doing this and the choice is not very important as long as we remain consistent. One choice that seems to work well (in the sense that implied correlations mostly stay in the range $[-1, 1]$) is to use a matching delta approach. That is, we choose strikes K_1 and K_2 satisfying $0.5K_1 + 0.5K_2 = K$ and having deltas that match (see Hakala and Wystup (2008) for more details).

Once we have decided on the asset volatilities, we can choose the correlation smile $\rho(K)$ so that any known basket prices are matched, and the implied correlation behaves according to our strong views at small and large strikes.

At this stage, we have a basket implied correlation smile. Our aim is to find a cross smile that correctly reprices the correlation smile when we use our models. Since we can value baskets very fast using the semi-analytic basket pricing formula (11.76), we can iteratively try and improve candidate cross smiles until we get the basket prices right to a given tolerance.

In this way, we have allowed the trader to mark a correlation smile with respect to the two-asset basket, but can still use all of the correlation smile models we have developed in this chapter.

It is important to note that strictly speaking this is a financial engineering solution rather than an exact mathematical solution. As we noted in Section 11.7.3, the asset and cross smiles do not fully determine the joint density function. Therefore, local correlation and local stochastic correlation may give slightly different values for basket options than the joint density model, even though they all price the cross smiles correctly that were calibrated using the joint density. In practice though, all three models tend to agree closely on European option prices (see Austing 2012).

In Section 11.5.2, we considered some foreign exchange market data from December 2011 for contracts expiring one year later, and the composite implied correlation smile is plotted in Figure 11.1. The corresponding basket implied correlation smile is shown in Figure 11.2. The assets are the euro–dollar and yen–dollar exchange rates, and the weights of the two assets in the basket are chosen to be the inverse of their forward levels so that they are measured on equivalent scales. For the purpose of extracting the correlation smile the asset volatilities are chosen using the matching delta method.

The correlation smile is plotted against Black–Scholes delta rather than directly against the strike. As usual, this provides a nice scale between 0 and 1 on which to plot the smile. We have chosen the weights of our basket so that the basket forward level is equal to 1. In order to obtain the delta, we first find the *basket volatility* which gives the basket value in the standard Black–Scholes vanilla formula, and then use the Black–Scholes delta $N(d_1)$ calculated from this volatility.

The plot in Figure 11.2 is indeed smile shaped, appropriately reflecting the higher correlations associated with large market moves. This is as it should be. Yet, we can marvel at the efficiency of the market that has allowed it to be so. After all, this correlation smile has been caused by vanilla traders, not multi-asset traders. They simply make markets in vanilla options in the three currency pairs that are the assets

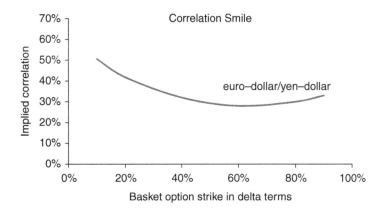

Figure 11.2   Basket implied correlation smile.

and cross, with little explicit regard for the shape of basket implied correlation smile they should produce. Yet a multi-asset trader who troubles to check the basket implied correlation smile sees that it behaves as expected purely as a result of the underlying vanilla trading.

11.10 Summary

In this chapter we have seen how to extend the smile models from previous chapters in order to value contracts depending on more than one asset. Models must take correlation between the assets into account. Assets become more strongly correlated when there are big market moves, and this causes the implied correlation to take on a smile shape (in close analogy with the implied volatility smile). Failure to include correlation smile in models causes significant undervaluation of the risk from large market moves.

Implied correlation must be defined with respect to a two-asset instrument, and there is a choice of possible instruments. The most appropriate instruments for modelling are composite options, which are also known as cross vanillas. In this case, the triangle rule can be used to extend dynamic models like local volatility and local stochastic volatility to multi-asset problems, correctly valuing the correlation smile.

Some traders prefer to visualise and mark their correlation smile with respect to alternative instruments. A popular choice is the two-asset basket. This does not present any problem since fast conversion between basket correlation smile and composite option correlation smile is available using equation (11.76).

There is some flexibility in choosing the asset volatilities to plug into a Black–Scholes pricing formula in order to determine an implied correlation smile. This applies irrespective of the correlation instrument used to define implied correlation. What we really care about are the values of the correlation instruments. Correlation smile is just an alternative representation of those values. For this reason it can make more sense to define the correlation smile more directly as a cross smile (in the case of composite options) or perhaps as the basket implied volatility smile (for baskets). A sophisticated trading operation can have tools to display the correlation smile in various representations.

In practice, liquid quotes are not always available for correlation instruments. In this case, it is a market making trader's *responsibility* to mark an appropriate correlation smile. Any liquid quotes can be used, and then all the trader's skill and intuition is available to mark the illiquid parts of the curve. For example, if marking correlation smile with respect to cross vanillas, all knowledge of how to mark asset vanilla smiles can be applied. On the other hand, if marking with respect to two-asset baskets, one might wish to ensure the implied correlation gets close to 100% in the wings in order to provide conservative hedging in case of major market moves.

Although a correlation smile marked in the absence of liquid quotes may not be perfect, it allows us to calculate risk. This is crucial. As soon as we can value with the correlation smile, we can calculate Greeks by bumping the smile and revaluing. This allows traders and risk managers to understand their true exposure to (say) the wings of the correlation smile.

11.11 Key Points

- When valuing multi-asset derivatives, we must take account of the implied correlation smile as well as implied volatility smiles.
- The most appropriate instruments for marking correlation smiles are composite options, and the correlation smile can be alternatively represented as a cross volatility smile.
- The local correlation model is the extension of local volatility to multi-asset problems, and local stochastic volatility can similarly be extended to local stochastic correlation.
- European contracts can be valued using a joint probability density constructed using best-of options.
- Some traders prefer using basket options over composite options to mark correlation smile. The joint probability density can be used to convert between them.
- Models with constant correlation like copulas and multi-asset local volatility should be avoided. They cannot match the correlation smile, and they provide rather strange dynamics to the cross asset.

11.12 Further Reading

The construction of the joint probability density for valuing European options described in Section 11.7 can be found in Austing (2011b), and it can also be applied when the correlation instruments are spread options (Austing and Piterbarg 2011). The technique can be extended to value N-asset basket options with asset smile and correlation smiles (Austing 2011a).

We commented in Section 11.7.3 that certain configurations of asset smiles and cross smile may not be compatible with a well-defined joint probability density. In that case, there is arbitrage in the market. Piterbarg (2011) provides necessary and sufficient conditions for the existence of a joint probability distribution, and gives a concrete numerical approach to check for arbitrage and find payouts that realise it.

Alternative approaches to local correlation are provided in Langnau (2010) and Reghai (2010). The correlation smile is particularly important in credit default option modelling, where local and stochastic style techniques for the correlation have also been applied. References include Burtschell, Gregory, and Laurent (2007) and Ferrarese (2006).

Afterword

Let us now take stock of some of the most important things we have learned. To begin with, there is no denying that derivative pricing is an exciting subject. The quality that can make any quantitative subject thrilling is the pure power of mathematics leading to simple conclusions that otherwise seem impossible or counterintuitive. Famous examples come from physics: quantum theory and relativity lead to remarkable unexpected conclusions about the true nature of our world. Quantitative finance, in its own small way, contains one of these thrilling insights. Whoever would have thought that, in a Black–Scholes world, we can provide a trading strategy to exactly replicate any derivative payout?

It is this remarkable insight that elevates the mathematics of derivative pricing beyond mere probabilistic accounting of cash flows into a subject worthy of study almost for its own sake. The future responsibility of becoming custodians of the huge financial transactions that take place in investment banks, and the importance that managing them well has to our economy, certainly add to the sense of excitement for students of the subject.

It is rather surprising (to a mathematician at least) that numerical techniques can be delightful in their own right. There is something quite wonderful about the forward induction procedure that forms the basis of the local stochastic volatility model. That the procedure exists is already remarkable, but that it is a stable algorithm and in production across numerous financial institutions makes it the triumph of modern smile pricing theory.

The partial differential equation approach also is a numerical procedure that is fascinating of itself. The possibility of instabilities appearing and causing the solution to explode turn an otherwise dull process of problem solving on a grid into a major intellectual challenge. It seems remarkable that the problem can be solved with thoughtful choice of the finite difference scheme, and one wonders how it is that nature always finds the stable solution.

As for our core business of valuing derivative contracts when there is a volatility smile: well, we must return to earth from the high ideals of Black–Scholes theory and be practical. The fact that we have a volatility smile at all tells us that we are not in a Black–Scholes world. Volatility is not a constant but can change. Indeed, all the market parameters we use in derivative pricing change all the time according to market conditions. Even if we have a perfect smile model, it is no good simply delta hedging and hoping to replicate the payout.

Instead, we must calculate Greeks to all our market input parameters, and put on hedges to neutralise them all (or as many as possible). For the smile risk, we can calculate Greeks to all the volatility inputs (at a range of strikes and expiries) that we used to interpolate our volatility surface. Then we can use vanilla contracts to eliminate these risks. In this way, we are dynamically vega hedging and smile hedging in the same way that we delta hedge. Where we have risk that we cannot hedge, perhaps because the market instruments are not liquid enough, we must monitor the position, and our risk managers will impose limits on the size of that position we are allowed to take.

Once we have put in place our hedging instruments, we will have a portfolio of contracts offsetting the risk of the original derivative we sold. The hedging portfolio will have its own effective total payout, and with luck this will be 'close' to the original contract payout. If so, then we are in particularly good shape because we have come close to a static replication of the payout.

Numerous smile models have been introduced in this book, and we need to choose which one to use. Crucially, our model must correctly value all the instruments that may be useful for hedging. These are the instruments that are relatively liquid, and whose value can reasonably be thought to be related to or have an impact on our contract value. If we fail in this step, we are in trouble. Our aim when hedging is to get something as closely approaching a replicating portfolio as possible. If our model values the instruments in the hedging portfolio wrongly then we are certainly misvaluing our contract.

Once we have narrowed down the possible models, we can try out two or three, and experiment with varying their parameters. If the value of the contract varies significantly between the models, then this is a dangerous trade and we should think very carefully before executing it. In practice this means we would not want to execute it unless the client is prepared to pay a high enough premium to amply cover the model uncertainty.

Some models may have clearly unreasonable features. Such models should be rejected unless we are very sure that the undesirable feature has no impact on the valuation of the contract.

Having taken all these points into consideration, one should choose the simplest model that captures all of the risk of the trade. Here is the point at which we must be most stoical. That the model captures the risk of the trade means it correctly values all appropriate hedging instruments, and leaves little remaining degree of freedom in the price. There is not necessarily a requirement for the model to be particularly close to reality. In a sense, smile models are merely sophisticated interpolators or extrapolators of market prices to give the value of more exotic contracts.

A / **Appendix**

Measure Theory and Girsanov's Theorem

In Section 3.7 we offered a proper treatment of measure theory and Girsanov's theorem to interested readers, and here we fulfil that promise.

The purpose of Girsanov's theorem is to establish a method of performing measure changes, and to show that one can perform a measure change that has the effect of changing the drift of an Ito process.[32]

It is helpful to introduce the notation of formal probability theory, but this should not be a source of anguish. Readers new to this formalism should keep in mind that the concepts described are of everyday probabilities and nothing more complex.

We are studying random processes. For example, we might be interested in the random path S_t followed by a stock price. If we do an experiment, and let the process run, there are a continuum of possible outcomes. In our example, the outcomes are the set of possible paths followed by the stock. Each possible outcome could be represented graphically as a classic jagged financial graph following the progress of the stock price over time. We'll use Ω to represent the set of all possible outcomes. For us, Ω is the set of all possible paths. We call Ω the sample space.

Individually, each possible outcome has zero probability. However, if we were to group them into a number of sets of outcomes, then some of those sets would have non-zero probability. For example, we could look at all the paths that have $S_T > K$ for some fixed $t = T$ and K. Clearly the outcome $S_T > K$ is likely to have finite probability, even though all of the individual paths have infinitesimal probability.

For this reason, we consider a collection of subsets of Ω and call this collection $\mathcal{F}$. For $\mathcal{F}$ to make sense for defining probabilities, we must insist on three properties:

1 the empty set $\emptyset$ is in $\mathcal{F}$;
2 if A is in $\mathcal{F}$ then so is its complement $\bar{A}$ (the events that are in Ω but not A);
3 if a (possibly infinite) sequence of sets A_1, A_2, $\cdots$ are in $\mathcal{F}$, then so is their union $\cup_i A_i$.

These conditions will allow us to sensibly assign probabilities to the sets in $\mathcal{F}$. For example, 1. and 2. together tell us that Ω is itself in $\mathcal{F}$. We will certainly want to assign a probability of 1 to Ω, since there must be *some* outcome. Together 2. and 3. also tell us that the intersection of sets is also in $\mathcal{F}$, since $A_1 \cap A_2 = \overline{\bar{A_1} \cup \bar{A_2}}$. The space $\mathcal{F}$ is called a *σ-algebra*.

---

[32] Recall that we model stock price evolution with Ito processes, see equation (2.29).

Now we can define a probability measure $\mathbb{P}$. It is a function that assigns a probability (between 0 and 1) to each set A in $\mathcal{F}$. It must satisfy:

1 $\mathbb{P}(\Omega) = 1$;
2 given $A_1, A_2, \cdots$, a sequence of disjoint sets, $\mathbb{P}(\cup_i A_i) = \sum_i \mathbb{P}(A_i)$.

A sample space together with a σ-algebra and probability measure, $(\Omega, \mathcal{F}, \mathbb{P})$ are called a *probability space.*

The two conditions defining a probability measure are enough to ensure that it behaves as we would expect. For example, since $\mathbb{P}(A) + \mathbb{P}(\overline{A}) = \mathbb{P}(A \cup \overline{A}) = \mathbb{P}(\Omega) = 1$, we have $\mathbb{P}(\overline{A}) = 1 - \mathbb{P}(A)$. Similarly, if A and B are not disjoint, one can check that $\mathbb{P}(A \cup B) = \mathbb{P}(A) + \mathbb{P}(B) - \mathbb{P}(A \cap B)$.

Now that we know more formally what a probability measure is, we can turn our attention to *changing* the measure. Let's remind ourselves what we are trying to achieve. We are interested in arbitrage. That is, we care about portfolios that make money with probability 1. Since avoiding arbitrage is all that matters, we may change the probabilities as long as we preserve the sets of outcomes that have probability 1. This is equivalent to preserving the sets that have probability zero.

The probability space notation we have introduced is helpful, because it reminds us that the sample space of events remains the same when we change measure. We simply assign different probabilities, so that we move from one probability space $(\Omega, \mathcal{F}, \mathbb{P})$ to another $(\Omega, \mathcal{F}, \tilde{\mathbb{P}})$. The two probability measures $\mathbb{P}$ and $\tilde{\mathbb{P}}$ are called *equivalent* if they agree on the sets of events having zero probability.

Next, we need to understand what a random variable is, and how to calculate its probability distribution and expectation. For our purpose, a random variable Y has a value that depends on the outcome of an experiment, and therefore it is a function acting on the sample space Ω.[33] In our running example, Ω is the set of possible paths followed by a stock price. Then S_T, the stock price at time T, is a random variable. If we pick a particular value α, then clearly $\mathbb{P}(S_T = \alpha) = 0$. That is, the set of paths for which the final stock price is exactly α has probability measure zero. On the other hand, the probability that S_T is greater than α ought to be positive. This should be equal to the sum of the probabilities of all paths for which S_T is greater than that level: $\mathbb{P}(S_T > \alpha) \equiv \sum_{\omega \in \Omega : S_T(\omega) > \alpha} \mathbb{P}(\omega)$. The problem is, this sum is meaningless because each individual term $\mathbb{P}(\omega)$ is zero.

The expectation of a random variable Y ought to be the sum of its possible values multiplied by the probabilities of taking those values. Our difficulty is that each of those probabilities is zero. Therefore really we want to define an integral

$$E[X] = \int_\Omega Y(\omega) d\mathbb{P}(\omega), \tag{A.1}$$

representing the sum over all the infinitesimal probabilities. Ordinarily, we define an integral by splitting the x-axis into a mesh of widths dx, and adding up all the

[33] Strictly speaking, we also need to assume that for any interval $[a, b] \subset \mathbb{R}$, the subset of Ω defined by $Y(\omega) \in [a, b]$ is in the σ-algebra $\mathcal{F}$. This will allow us to define the concept of integration over the probability space and then define the expected value of the random variable.

rectangles that touch the curve we are integrating. Here though, we are integrating over the sample space Ω rather than the real line. Therefore instead we split the possible values of the variable Y into a mesh, of width dy say. Then, for a given y, the meaning of $d\mathbb{P}(\omega)$ is the probability that the random variable Y is in the interval $[y, y + dy]$.

By defining the infinitesimal probability measure $d\mathbb{P}$ in this way, we have given precise meaning to the integral in equation (A.1). While the traditional high school technique of integrating by splitting the x-axis into infinitesimal slices is the Riemann integral, the integral that we have defined in equation (A.1), in which we instead discretised the y-axis, is called the Lebesgue integral. It is easy to check that this definition of expectation agrees with the standard definitions when the probability space is discrete, or has a simple PDF.

We needn't restrict ourselves to integrating over the entire sample space Ω, but can consider sets of possible outcomes. That is, we can also integrate over sets in the σ-algebra. With this in mind, we now have the following meaningful formula expressing a probability as an infinite sum over the sample space

$$P(S_T > \alpha) = \int_A d\mathbb{P}(\omega) \tag{A.2}$$

$$A = \{\omega \in \Omega : S_T(\omega) > \alpha\}.$$

This formula acts as a sense check rather than adding any new information. The Lebesgue method tells us to evaluate the integral by dividing the values of the integrand into a mesh, and adding up their probabilities. As the integrand can only take two values (1 if $\omega \in A$ and 0 if $\omega \notin A$) the value is simply $1 \times P(A)$.

Our aim is to change the probability measure. That is, we want to find a new probability measure with the property that the set of outcomes having zero probability is preserved. Two probability measures $\mathbb{P}$ and $\mathbb{Q}$ are called *equivalent* if the sets in the σ-algebra $\mathcal{F}$ having zero probability are identical under the two measures.

There is a simple trick for generating a new probability measure from an existing one. Given the measure $\mathbb{P}$, take a random variable Y that is non-negative and has expected value 1. That is, it satisfies $Y(\omega) \geq 0$ for $\omega \in \Omega$, and $E[Y] = 1$. Then, for any set of outcomes A in the σ-algebra $\mathcal{F}$, define its probability in the new measure by

$$\mathbb{Q}(A) = \int_A Y(\omega)\, d\mathbb{P}(\omega). \tag{A.3}$$

It is easy to see that $\mathbb{Q}(A)$ is between 0 and 1 and that the total probability is 1 since

$$\mathbb{Q}(\Omega) = \int_\Omega Y(\omega)\, d\mathbb{P}(\omega) = E[Y] = 1. \tag{A.4}$$

For $\mathbb{Q}$ to be a probability measure, we also need to check that probabilities over disjoint sets add up. This is clear because integration is additive

$$\mathbb{Q}(A_1 \cup A_2) = \int_{A_1 \cup A_2} Y(\omega)\, d\mathbb{P}(\omega) \tag{A.5}$$

$$= \int_{A_1} Y(\omega)\, d\mathbb{P}(\omega) + \int_{A_2} Y(\omega)\, d\mathbb{P}(\omega), \quad A_1 \cap A_2 = \emptyset. \tag{A.6}$$

The new probability measure $\mathbb{Q}$ that we have just generated may not be equivalent to $\mathbb{P}$. That is, $\mathbb{P}$ and $\mathbb{Q}$ may not agree on the zero probability outcomes. However, if we make sure we use a random variable Y that is almost surely positive, then we are guaranteed that the new measure will be equivalent. By saying *almost surely* positive, we simply mean that we insist $\mathbb{P}(Y > 0) = 1$, but acknowledge the fact there may be outcomes with zero probability measure for which $Y = 0$.

To see that this is true, start with A having $\mathbb{P}(A) = 0$, assume $\mathbb{P}(Y > 0) = 1$, and calculate $\mathbb{Q}(A)$:

$$\mathbb{Q}(A) = \int_A Y(\omega) d\mathbb{P}(\omega). \tag{A.7}$$

Intuitively, this is clearly zero. Formally, we should think about the definition of the Lebesgue integral and split the y-axis into segments. As the probability of an outcome being in A is zero, then so is the probability of being in A and having Y within any segment. No matter how fine we choose the mesh of segments, we always get zero, and therefore the integral converges to zero. Conversely, if $\mathbb{Q}(A)$ is zero, then so must be $\mathbb{P}(A)$.

When we want to calculate the expected value of a random variable X under the $\mathbb{Q}$ probability measure, we can do so using the formula

$$E_{\mathbb{Q}}[X] = \int_\Omega X(\omega)\, d\mathbb{Q}(\omega) \tag{A.8}$$

$$= \int_\Omega X(\omega)\, Y(\omega) d\mathbb{P}(\omega) \tag{A.9}$$

$$= E_{\mathbb{P}}[XY], \tag{A.10}$$

which follows from the definition of the Lebesgue integral. Similarly, we can change from the $\mathbb{Q}$ to the $\mathbb{P}$ measure via

$$E_{\mathbb{P}}[X] = E_{\mathbb{Q}}[X/Y]. \tag{A.11}$$

This leads to some particularly helpful notation for the random variable (in this case Y) that generates the change of measure. It is called the *Radon–Nikodým derivative,* and denoted $\frac{dQ}{dP}$. With this notation, our formula for calculating expectation under the new measure becomes

$$E_Q[X] = \int_\Omega X(\omega)\,dQ \tag{A.12}$$

$$= \int_\Omega X(\omega)\,\frac{dQ}{dP}\,dP. \tag{A.13}$$

The Radon–Nikodým derivative $\frac{dQ}{dP}$ tells us where in the probability space we need to boost up probabilities ($\frac{dQ}{dP} > 1$) and where we need to reduce probabilities ($\frac{dQ}{dP} < 1$) in order to change the measure.

So far, we have come to understand what a probability measure is, how to integrate over a probability space to calculate expectations, and how to change the probability measure. We are interested in stochastic processes so that our probability spaces need the concept of time. Therefore we can look at the set of events whose outcome is known at time t. These form a σ-algebra, which we denote $\mathcal{F}_t$. As time progresses, more information becomes available, and so the $\mathcal{F}_t$ must satisfy

$$\mathcal{F}_s \subset \mathcal{F}_t, \quad \text{when } s \le t. \tag{A.14}$$

The set of σ-algebras $\{\mathcal{F}_t\}$ is called the *filtration*. More formally, one would work the other way and define a filtration as a set of σ-algebras with the property (A.14), and use this to associate a concept of time with a probability space. Quantitative analysts and financial mathematicians regularly use notation $E[X|\mathcal{F}_t]$ which simply means the expected value of the random variable X conditional on all the events in the σ-algebra whose outcome is known at time t (that is, conditional on all information at t). Given a filtration, an *adapted process* Z_t is a process for which the information at time t, $\mathcal{F}_t$, determines Z_t. That is, it respects the concept of time provided by the filtration, and does not need to 'see into the future'.

So far, we have considered a general probability space. Now, at last, we can reintroduce Brownian motion, and give Girsanov's theorem. The idea is to show how to change the measure in a probability space generated by a Brownian motion, and what the impact of the measure change is on a Brownian motion. We state the theorem as provided in the excellent Shreve (2004), to which readers are referred for more rigorous treatment and proof.

Let W_t be a Brownian motion on a probability space $(\Omega, \mathcal{F}, \mathbb{P})$ with filtration $\mathcal{F}_t$. Let $g_t(\omega)$ be an adapted process. Define

$$Z(t) = \exp\left\{-\int_0^t g_u\,dW_u - \frac{1}{2}\int_0^t g_u^2\,du\right\} \tag{A.15}$$

$$\widetilde{W}_t = W_t + \int_0^t g_u\,du \tag{A.16}$$

and assume that the expectation

$$E\left[\int_0^T g_u^2 Z(u)^2 du\right] \tag{A.17}$$

is finite. Then, for a fixed T, $Z(T)$ satisfies $E[Z(T)] = 1$ and so defines a Radon–Nikodým derivative and measure change from $\mathbb{P}$ to a new measure $\mathbb{Q}$. In the new measure $\mathbb{Q}$, the process $\widetilde{W}_t$ for $0 \leq t \leq T$ is a Brownian motion, $Z(T)$ is almost surely positive, and so the two measures are equivalent.

In quantitative finance, we almost always write our stochastic processes in terms of Brownian motions. For example, our classic Black–Scholes process for a spot rate S_t is

$$\frac{dS_t}{S_t} = \mu dt + \sigma dW_t. \tag{A.18}$$

Therefore, what we need to know is the impact a measure change will have on a Brownian motion. Girsanov's theorem answers this beautifully. Let's suppose equation (A.18) applies to the real world probability measure $\mathbb{P}$. We can choose the process $g_t(\omega)$ in equation (A.15) to be a constant g. Then equation (A.16) tells us that, under the new measure $\mathbb{Q}$, $\widetilde{W}_t$ is a Brownian motion, satisfying $d\widetilde{W}_t = dW_t + gdt$. Then our process for S_t becomes

$$\frac{dS_t}{S_t} = (\mu - g\sigma)dt + \sigma d\widetilde{W}_t. \tag{A.19}$$

In practice, to a financial engineer, changing the measure has the impact of giving drift to a Brownian motion, and allows us to change the drift in stochastic processes. This is exactly what allowed us to change to the risk-neutral measure in Section 3.6 in order to derive an arbitrage-free price for derivative contracts.

We will not give a complete proof of Girsanov's theorem. It is a matter of calculation, and if we had enough energy we could do so. Instead we will satisfy ourselves with understanding why it is true.

Ito's lemma tells us that

$$dZ_t = -g_t Z_t dW_t \tag{A.20}$$

and, as it has no drift, it is a Martingale. In particular, $E[Z_T] = Z_0 = 1$. Next we need to check that $\widetilde{W}_t$ is a Martingale under $\mathbb{Q}$. Since $E_{\mathbb{Q}}[\widetilde{W}_t] = E_{\mathbb{P}}[Z_t\widetilde{W}_t] = E_{\mathbb{P}}[Z_t(W_t + \int_0^t g_u du)]$, this means we need to check that $Y_t = Z_t(W_t + \int_0^t g_u du)]$ is a Martingale under $\mathbb{P}$. Another application of Ito's lemma and the product rule gives

$$d\left(Z_t\left[W_t + \int_0^t g_u du\right]\right) = \left(-g_t Z_t\left[W_t + \int_0^t g_u du\right] + Z_t\right) dW_t \tag{A.21}$$

which has no drift, and therefore Y_t is a Martingale. Finally, using the familiar property of Brownian motions, we note that $(d\widetilde{W}_t)^2 = (dW_t + g_t dt)^2 = (dW_t)^2 = dt$. Therefore $\widetilde{W}_t$ satisfies three properties:

1   $\widetilde{W}_0 = 0$;
2   $(d\widetilde{W}_t)^2 = dt$;
3   $\widetilde{W}_t$ is a Martingale under $\mathbb{Q}$.

We noted informally in Section 3.7 that there can only be one possibility for such a process. This is made rigorous in *Lévy's theorem*, which states that a process satisfying 1–3 must be a Brownian motion.

References

Ahmad, Riaz and Paul Wilmott. "Which free lunch would you like today, sir? Delta hedging, volatility arbitrage and optimal portfolios". *Wilmott* (2005) pp. 64–79.

Albrecher, Hansjörg, Philipp Mayer, Wim Schoutens, and Jurgen Tistaert. "The little Heston trap". *Wilmott Magazine* January (2007) pp. 83–92.

Andersen, Leif B. G. "Simple and efficient simulation of the Heston stochastic volatility model". *Journal of Computational Finance* 11.3 (2008) p. 1.

Andersen, Leif B. G. and Jesper Andreasen. "Volatility skews and extensions of the Libor market model". *Working paper* (1998)

Andersen, Leif B. G., Jesper Andreasen, and David Eliezer. "Static replication of barrier options: some general results". *Journal of Computational Finance* 5.4 (2002) pp. 1–26.

Andersen, Leif B. G. and Vladimir V. Piterbarg. "Moment explosions in stochastic volatility models". *Finance and Stochastics* (2006)

– *Interest rate modeling, Volume I: Foundations and vanilla models.* Atlantic Financial Press London, 2010.

– *Interest rate modeling, Volume II: Term structure models.* Atlantic Financial Press London, 2010.

– *Interest rate modeling, Volume III: Products and risk management.* Atlantic Financial Press London, 2010.

Andreasen, Jesper and Brian Huge. "Volatility interpolation". *Risk* March (2011)

Austing, Peter. "Valuing basket options: On smile and correlation skew". *Talk at ICBI global derivatives* (2011)

– "Repricing the cross smile: An analytic joint density". *Risk* July (2011)

– "Valuing with correlation smile". *Talk at ICBI global derivatives* (2012)

– "The (local) stochastic volatility puzzle or how to relieve a hangover". *Talk at ICBI global derivatives* (2013)

Austing, Peter and Vladimir V. Piterbarg. "Repricing spread option smiles with methods from foreign exchange". *Talk at WBS advanced interest rate modelling workshop* (2011)

Ayache, Elie, Philippe Henrotte, Sonia Nassar, and Xuewen Wang. "Can anyone solve the smile problem?" *Wilmott Magazine* January (2004)

Bachelier, Louis. *Théorie de la spéculation.* Gauthier-Villars, 1900.

Baker, Glyn, Reimer Beneder, and Alex Zilber. "FX barriers with smile dynamics". *Working paper* (2004)

Baxter, Martin and Andrew Rennie. *Financial calculus: An introduction to derivative pricing.* Cambridge University Press, 1996.

Beiglböck, Mathias, Peter Friz, and Stephan Sturm. "Overprized options on variance swaps in local vol models". *Universität Wien talk* (2010)

Benhamou, Eric and Alexandre Duguet. "Small dimension PDE for discrete Asian options". *Journal of Economic Dynamics and Control* 27.11 (2003) pp. 2095–2114.

Blacher, Guillaume. "A new approach for designing and calibrating stochastic volatility models for optimal delta-vega hedging of exotic options". *Presentation at ICBI global derivatives* (2001)

Black, Fischer and Myron Scholes. "The pricing of options and corporate liabilities". *The Journal of Political Economy* 81.3 (1973)

Breeden, Douglas T. and Robert H. Litzenberger. "Prices of state-contingent claims implicit in option prices". *The Journal of Business* 51 (1978)

Brigo, Damiano and Fabio Mercurio. "A mixed-up smile". *Risk* September (2000)

– "Lognormal-mixture dynamics and calibration to market volatility smiles". *International Journal of Theoretical and Applied Finance* 5.4 (2002) pp. 427–446.

Broadie, Mark, Paul Glasserman, and Steven Kou. "A continuity correction for discrete barrier options". *Mathematical Finance* 7.4 (1997) pp. 325–349.

Burtschell, X., J. Gregory, and J-P. Laurent. "Beyond the Gaussian copula: Stochastic and local correlation". *Journal of Credit Risk* 3.1 (2007) pp. 31–62.

Carr, Peter and Andrew Chou. "Hedging complex barrier options". *Working paper* (1997)

– "Breaking barriers". *Risk* September (1997) pp. 139–145.

Carr, Peter and Roger Lee. "Volatility derivatives". *Annual Review of Financial Economics* 1 (2009) pp. 319–339.

Carr, Peter and Keith Lewis. "Corridor variance swaps". *Risk* February (2004) pp. 67–72.

Carr, Peter and Dilip Madan. "Towards a theory of volatility trading". In: *Volatility: New estimation techniques for pricing derivatives.* Ed. by Robert A. Jarrow. London: Risk Books, 1998. Chap. 29, pp. 417–427.

– "A note on sufficient conditions for no arbitrage". *Finance Research Letters* 2.3 (2005) pp. 125–130.

Chesney, Marc and Louis Scott. "Pricing European currency options: A comparison of the modified Black-Scholes model and a random variance model". *Journal of Financial and Quantitative Analysis* 24 (1989) pp. 267–284.

Chriss, Neil and William Morokoff. "Market risk for volatility and variance swaps". *Risk* October (1999) pp. 55–59.

Clark, Iain. *Foreign exchange option pricing: A practitioners guide.* Wiley, 2011.

Cont, Rama and Yu Gu. "Local vs non-local forward equations for option pricing". *Working paper* (2012)

Cox, John C., Jonathan E. Ingersoll, and Stephen A. Ross. "A theory of the term structure of interest rates". *Econometrica* 53.2 (1985)

Craig, I. and A. Sneyd. "An alternating direction implicit scheme for parabolic equations with mixed derivatives". *Comput. Math. Applic* (1988)

Crank, John and Phyllis Nicolson. "A practical method for numerical evaluation of solutions of partial differential equations of the heat-conduction type". In: *Mathematical proceedings of the Cambridge Philosophical Society.* Vol. 43. 01. Cambridge Univ Press. 1947, pp. 50–67.

Demeterfi, Kresimir, Emanuel Derman, Michael Kamal, and Joseph Zou. "More than you ever wanted to know about volatility swaps". *Goldman Sachs Quantitative Strategies Research Notes* (1999)

– "A guide to volatility and variance swaps". *The Journal of Derivatives* 6-4 (1999) pp. 9–32.

Dempster, Michael Alan Howarth and Akilesh Eswaran. "Wavelet based PDE valuation of derivatives". In: *European congress of mathematics*. Springer. 2001, pp. 347–365.

Derman, Emanuel and Iraj Kani. "The volatility smile and its implied tree". *Goldman Sachs Quantitative Strategies Research Notes* (1994)

– "Riding on a smile". *Risk* February (1994) pp. 32–39.

– "Stochastic implied trees: Arbitrage pricing with stochastic term and strike structure of volatility". *International Journal of Theoretical and Applied Finance* 1.1 (1998) pp. 61–110.

Dupire, Bruno. "Arbitrage pricing with stochastic volatility". In: *Proceedings of AFFI conference*. Paris, 1992.

– "Pricing with a smile". *Risk* January (1994)

– "Arbitrage pricing with stochastic volatility". In: *Derivatives pricing: The classic collection*. Ed. by Peter Carr. London: Risk Books, 2004. Chap. 7, pp. 197–216.

– "Exploring volatility derivatives: New advances in modelling". *Talk at ICBI global derivatives and risk management* (2005)

Feller, William. "Two singular diffusion problems". *Annals of Mathematics* 54.1 (1951) pp. 173–182.

Ferrarese, Claudio. "A comparative analysis of correlation skew modeling techniques for CDO index tranches". *MSc thesis, Kings College, London* (2006)

Fouque, Jean-Pierre, George Papanicolaou, and K. Ronnie Sircar. "Financial modeling in a fast mean-reverting stochastic volatility environment". *Asia-Pacific Financial Markets* 6.1 (1999) pp. 37–48.

– "Mean-reverting stochastic volatility". *International Journal of Theoretical and Applied Finance* 3.1 (2000) pp. 101–142.

Gatheral, Jim. "Lecture 6: Volatility and variance swaps". In: *Case studies in financial modelling course notes*. Courant Institute of Mathematical Sciences, New York University, 2002.

– "Valuation of volatility derivatives". *Talk at ICBI global derivatives and risk management* (2005)

– *The volatility surface: A practitioner's guide*. Wiley, 2006.

Genz, Alan. "Numerical computation of rectangular bivariate and trivariate normal and t probabilities". *Statistics and Computing* 14 (2004)

Giles, Michael B. and Rebecca Carter. "Convergence analysis of Crank-Nicolson and Rannacher time-marching". *Journal of Computational Finance* 9 (2006) pp. 89–112.

Glasserman, Paul. *Monte Carlo methods in financial engineering*. Springer, 2003.

Gyöngy, I "Mimicking the one-dimensional marginal distributions of processes having an Itô differential". *Probability Theory and Related Fields* 71.4 (1986)

Hagan, Patrick S., Deep Kumar, Andrew S. Lesniewski, and Diana E. Woodward. "Managing smile risk". *Wilmott Magazine* (2002)

Hakala, Jurgen and Uwe Wystup. "FX basket options". *Frankfurt School of Finance and Management* (2008)

Haug, Espen Gaarder. *The complete guide to option pricing formulas*. McGraw-Hill, 1997.

Henry-Labordère, Pierre. "A general asymptotic implied volatility for stochastic volatility models". *Working paper* (2005)

Heston, Steven L. "A closed form solution for options with stochastic volatility with applications to bond and currency options". *Review of Financial Studies* 6 (1993)

Hull, John. *Options, futures, and other derivatives*. Pearson, 2010.

Hull, John and Alan White. "The pricing of options on assets with stochastic volatilities". *The Journal of Finance* 42.2 (1987) pp. 281–300.

Jäckel, Peter. *Monte Carlo methods in finance*. Wiley, 2002.

– "Stochastic volatility models: Past, present and future". In: *The best of Wilmott 1: Incorporating the quantitative finance review*. Ed. by Paul Wilmott. 2004, pp. 379–390.

Jamshidian, Farshid. "Forward induction and construction of yield curve diffusion models". *The journal of fixed income* 1 (1991)

Jex, Mark. "Pricing exotics under the smile". *Risk* November (1999)

Johnson, Herb. "Options on the maximum or the minimum of several assets". *Journal of Financial and Quantitative Analysis* 22.3 (1987) pp. 277–283.

Johnson, Simon. "Forward volatility and linear programming". *Talk at ICBI global derivatives* (2008)

Johnson, Simon and Han Lee. "Capturing the smile". *Risk* March (2003)

Joshi, Mark S. *The concepts and practice of mathematical finance*. Cambridge University Press, 2003.

Kahl, Christian and Peter Jäckel. "Not-so-complex logarithms in the Heston model". *Wilmott Magazine* September (2005) pp. 94–103.

– "Fast strong approximation Monte Carlo schemes for stochastic volatility models". *Quantitative Finance* 6.6 (2006) pp. 513–536.

Karatzas, Ioannis Autor and Steven Eugene Shreve. *Brownian motion and stochastic calculus*. Springer, 1991.

Langnau, Alex. "A dynamic model for correlation". *Risk* April (2010)

Lee, Roger W. "Implied and local volatilities under stochastic volatility". *International Journal of Theoretical and Applied Finance* 4.1 (2001) pp. 45–89.

– "The moment formula for implied volatility at extreme strikes". *Mathematical Finance* 14.3 (2004)

Lewis, Alan L. *Option valuation under stochastic volatility*. Finance Press, 2000.

Lipton, Alexander. *Mathematical methods for foreign exchange*. World Scientific, 2001.

– "The vol smile problem". *Risk* February (2002)

Lipton, Alexander and William McGhee. "Universal barriers". *Risk* May (2002)

Longstaff, Francis A. and Eduardo S. Schwartz. "Valuing American options by simulation: A simple least-squares approach". *Rev. Financial Stud.* 14 (2001)

Lucic, Vladimir. "Forward start options in stochastic volatility models". *Wilmott Magazine* September (2003)

– "Boundary conditions for computing densities in hybrid models via PDE methods". *Stochastics an International Journal of Probability and Stochastic Processes* 84.5-6 (2012) pp. 705–718.

Margrabe, William. "The value of an option to exchange one asset for another". *The Journal of Finance* 33.1 (1978)

Matsumoto, Makoto and Takuji Nishimura. "Mersenne twister: A 623-dimensionally equidistributed uniform pseudo-random number generator". *ACM Transactions on Modeling and Computer Simulation* 8.1 (1998) pp. 3–30.

Matytsin, Andrew. "Perturbative analysis of volatility smiles". *JP Morgan* (2000)

McGhee, William. "Local-stochastic volatility: The dynamics of the forward smile". *Risk Training Course* December (2008)

– "An efficient implementation of stochastic volatility by the method of conditional integration". *Talk at ICBI global derivatives* (2011)

– "The conditional integration approach to stochastic volatility modeling". *Talk at WBS 8th fixed income conference* (2012)

McGhee, William and Romano Trabalzini. "Decoding the volatility smile". *Talk at ICBI global derivatives* (2013)

Merton, Robert C "Theory of rational option pricing". *The Bell Journal of Economics and Management Science* (1973) pp. 141–183.

Metropolis, Nicholas and Stanislaw Ulam. "The Monte Carlo method". *Journal of the American Statistical Association* 44.247 (1949) pp. 335–341.

Mikhailov, Sergei and Ulrich Nögel. "Heston's stochastic volatility model: Implementation, calibration and some extensions". *Wilmott Magazine* (2004)

Naik, Vasanttilak. "Option valuation and hedging strategies with jumps in the volatility of asset returns". *The Journal of Finance* 48.5 (1993) pp. 1969–1984.

Nauta, Bert Jan, Alex Zilber, and Berber de Backer. "Direct parameterization of transition densities and pricing of forward start options". *Wilmott Magazine* May (2008)

Neuberger, Anthony. "Volatility trading". *London Business School working paper* (1990)

Obłój, Jan. "Fine-tune your smile: Correction to Hagan et al". *Wilmott Magazine* 35 (2008) pp. 102–104.

Ouwehand, Peter and Graeme West. "Pricing rainbow options". *Wilmott Magazine* May (2006)

Piterbarg, Vladimir V. "Mixture of models: A simple recipe for a hangover". *Wilmott Magazine* (2003)

– "Time to smile". *Risk* May (2005)

– "Markovian projection method for volatility calibration". *Risk* April (2007)

– "Spread options, Farkas's lemma and linear programming". *Risk* September (2011)

Press, William H., Brian P. Flannery, Saul A. Teukolsky, and William T. Vetterling. *Numerical recipes in C* Cambridge University Press, 1992.

Rannacher, Rolf. "Finite element solution of diffusion problems with irregular data". *Numerische Mathematik* 43.2 (1984) pp. 309–327.

Rebonato, Riccardo and Mark Joshi. "Draft: Assigning future smile surfaces: conditions for uniqueness and absence of arbitrage". *Working paper* (2002)

Rebonato, Riccardo, Kenneth Mckay, and Richard White. *The SABR/LIBOR market model.* Wiley, 2009.

Reghai, Adil. "Breaking correlation breaks". *Risk* October (2010)

Ren, Yong, Dilip Madan, and Michael Qian. "Calibrating and pricing with embedded local volatility models". *Risk* September (2007)

Rogers, L. C. G. and Z. Shi. "The value of an Asian option". *Journal of Applied Probability* (1995) pp. 1077–1088.

Rubinstein, Mark. "Implied binomial trees". *The Journal of Finance* 49.3 (1994) pp. 771–818.

Rubinstein, Mark and Eric Reiner. "Breaking down the barriers". *Risk* August (1991) pp. 28–35.

Scott, Louis. "Option pricing when the variance changes randomly: theory, estimation and an application". *Journal of Financial and Quantitative Analysis* 22 (1987) pp. 419–438.

Shreve, Steven E. *Stochastic calculus for finance II: continuous-time models.* Springer, 2004.

Sin, Carlos A. "Complications with stochastic volatility models". *Advances in Applied Probability* 30 (1998) pp. 258–268.

Stein, Elias M. and Jeremy C. Stein. "Stock price distributions with stochastic volatility: An analytic approach". *Review of financial studies* 4.4 (1991) pp. 727–752.

Stulz, René M. "Options on the minimum or maximum of two assets". *Journal of Financial Economics* 10 (1982)

Taleb, Nassim. *Dynamic hedging: Managing vanilla and exotic options.* Vol. 64. Wiley, 1997.

Tavella, Domingo and Curt Randall. *Pricing financial instruments: The finite difference method.* Wiley, 2000.

West, Graeme. "Better approximations to cumulative normal functions". *Wilmott Magazine* July (2009)

Wilmott, Paul. "Cliquet options and volatility models". *Wilmott Magazine* December (2002)

– *Paul Wilmott on quantitative finance, 3 volume set.* Wiley, 2006.

– *Paul Wilmott introduces quantitative finance.* Wiley, 2007.

Wilmott, Paul, Jeff Dewynne, and Sam Howison. *Option pricing: mathematical models and computation.* Oxford Financial Press Oxford, 1993.

Windcliff, H., P. A. Forsyth, and K. R. Vetzal. "Pricing methods and hedging strategies for volatility derivatives". *Journal of Banking and Finance* 30 (2006) pp. 409–431.

Further Reading

In addition to the references cited in the text, there now follows a list of further resources. These are a selection of additional references that have been important in shaping the field of quantitative finance and smile pricing, together with further reading relevant to the chapters in this book.

Alexander, Carol. "Normal mixture diffusion with uncertain volatility: modelling short- and long-term smile effects". *Journal of Banking & Finance* 28.12 (2004)

Andreasen, Jesper. "The pricing of discretely sampled Asian and lookback options: a change of numeraire approach". *Journal of Computational Finance* 2.1 (1998) pp. 5–30.

Antonov, Alexandre and Timur Misirpashaev. "Markovian projection onto a displaced diffusion: Generic formulas with applications". *International Journal of Theoretical and Applied Finance* 12.4 (2009) pp. 507–522.

Antonov, Alexandre, Timur Misirpashaev, and Vladimir V. Piterbarg. "Markovian projection onto a Heston model". *Journal of Computational Finance* (2007)

Bakshi, Gurdip, Charles Cao, and Zhiwu Chen. "Empirical performance of alternative option pricing models". *The Journal of Finance* 52.5 (1997) pp. 2003–2049.

Balland, Philippe. "Forward smile". *Talk at ICBI global derivatives* (2006)

Benaim, Shalom and Peter Friz. "Regular variation and smile asymptotics". *Mathematical Finance* 19.1 (2009) pp. 1–12.

Benaim, Shalom, Peter Friz, and Roger Lee. "On Black-Scholes implied volatility at extreme strikes". In: *Frontiers in quantitative finance: Volatility and credit risk Modeling*. Wiley, 2008, pp. 19–45.

Brigo, Damiano and Fabio Mercurio. *Interest rate models: Theory and practice*. Springer, 2006.

Britten-Jones, Mark and Anthony Neuberger. "Option prices, implied price processes, and stochastic volatility". *The Journal of Finance* 55.2 (2000)

Broadie, Mark and Özgür Kaya. "Exact simulation of stochastic volatility and other affine jump diffusion processes". *Operations Research* 54.2 (2006) pp. 217–231.

Carr, Peter, Hélyette Geman, Dilip Madan, and Marc Yor. "Pricing options on realized variance". *Finance and Stochastics* 9-4 (2005) pp. 453–475.

Carr, Peter and Peter Laurence. "Multi-asset stochastic local variance contracts". *Mathematical Finance* 21.1 (2011) pp. 21–52.

Carr, Peter and Dilip Madan. "Option valuation using the fast Fourier transform". *Journal of Computational Finance* 2.4 (1999) pp. 61–73.

Chourdakis, Kyriakos. "Stochastic volatility and jumps driven by continuous time Markov chains". *University of London Queen Mary economics working paper* 430 (2000)

Cox, John C. "The constant elasticity of variance option pricing model". *Journal of Portfolio Management* 23 (1996) pp. 15–17.

De Col, Alvise, Alessandro Gnoatto, and Martino Grasselli. "Smiles all around: FX joint calibration in a multi-Heston model". *Journal of Banking and Finance* 37.10 (2013) pp. 3799–3818.

Doffou, Ako and Jimmy E. Hilliard. "Testing a three-state model in currency derivative markets". *Journal of Risk* 4.3 (2002)

Duffy, Daniel J *Finite difference methods in financial engineering: A partial differential equation approach.* Wiley, 2006.

Dupire, Bruno. "A unified theory of volatility". *Paribas working paper* (1996) Reprinted in Derivatives Pricing: The Classic Collection.

– "Skew modeling". *Talk at Columbia University* (2005)

Friz, Peter and Jim Gatheral. "Valuation of volatility derivatives as an inverse problem". *Quantitative Finance* 5.6 (2005) pp. 531–542.

Fuh, Cheng-Der, Ren-Her Wang, and Jui-Chi Cheng. "Option pricing in a Black-Scholes model with Markov switching". *Institute of Statistical Science working paper, Taipei* (2002)

Gatheral, Jim, Elton P Hsu, Peter Laurence, Cheng Ouyang, and Tai-Ho Wang. "Asymptotics of implied volatility in local volatility models". *Mathematical Finance* 22.4 (2012) pp. 591–620.

Geisselmeyer, Andreas K.H. "Consistent pricing of CMS and CMS spread options with SABR-like distributions and power-t copulas". *Working paper* (2012)

Gnoatto, Alessandro. "Coherent foreign exchange market models". *Working paper* (2013)

Gnoatto, Alessandro and Martino Grasselli. "An analytic multi-currency model with stochastic volatility and stochastic interest rates". *Working paper* (2013)

Henry-Labordère, Pierre. "Gaussian estimates for LSV models". *Talk at ICBI global derivatives* (2007)

Hui, Cho H "One-touch double barrier binary option values". *Applied Financial Economics* 6.4 (1996) pp. 343–346.

Jäckel, Peter. "Quanto skew". *Working paper* (2010)

– "Quanto skew with stochastic volatility". *Working paper* (2010)

Jäckel, Peter and Christian Kahl. "Positive semi-definite correlation matrix completion". *Working paper* (2009)

Jex, Mark, Robert Henderson, and David Wang. "Pricing exotics under the smile". *J.P. Morgan Securities Inc.* (1999)

Krekel, Martin, Johan de Kock, Ralf Korn, and Tin-Kwai Man. "An analysis of pricing methods for baskets options". *Wilmott Magazine* (2003)

Lipton, Alexander. "Pricing and risk-managing exotics on assets with stochastic volatility". *Deutsche Bank working paper* (2000)

Lipton, Alexander, Andrey Gal, and Andris Lasis. "Pricing of vanilla and first generation exotic options in the local stochastic volatility framework: Survey and new results". *Working paper* (2013)

Lipton, Alexander and William McGhee. "Volatility and correlation swaps". *Deutsche Bank working paper* (1999)

Lucic, Vladimir. "On singularities in the Heston model". *Working paper* (2007)

McGhee, William. "An efficient implementation of stochastic volatility by the method of conditional integration with application to exponential Ornstein-Uhlenbeck stochastic volatility and SABR models". *RBS working paper* (2010)

Piterbarg, Vladimir V. "Stochastic volatility model with time dependent skew". *Applied Mathematical Finance* 12 (2005)

Risken, Hannes. *The Fokker-Planck equation: methods of solution and applications.* Lecture Notes in Mathematics. Springer Berlin Heidelberg, 1996.

Scherer, Matthias and Jan-Frederik Mai. *Financial engineering with copulas explained.* Palgrave Macmillan, 2014.

Tan, Chia. *Demystifying exotic products: Interest rates, equities and foreign exchange.* Wiley, 2010.

Willard, Gregory A "Calculating prices and sensitivities for path-independent derivatives securities in multifactor models". *The Journal of Derivatives* 5.1 (1997) pp. 45–61.

Wilmott, Paul. *Derivatives: The theory and practice of financial engineering.* Wiley, 1998.

Wystup, Uwe. "The market price of one-touch options in foreign exchange markets". *Derivatives Week* 12.13 (2003) pp. 8–9.

– *FX options and structured products.* Wiley, 2007.

Index

adapted process, 122, 151, 204
ADI, *see* alternating direction implicit
alternating direction implicit, 118, 130
analytic solution, 34, 50, 96, 97
antithetic variates, 102
Apple, 179
arbitrage, 2, 3, 8, 21–23, 38, 60, 67, 68, 97, 123, 124, 139, 154, 184, 190, 201
arbitrage-free price, 27, 40
at-the-money, 32, 58

barrier
    continuous, 104, 114, 131, 141, 143
    discretely monitored, 56, 105, 114, 168
    knock-in, 50, 51, 67, 115, 121, 147
    knock-out, 50, 67, 121, 147
    lower, 55
    single, 55
    upper, 55
    window, 138
barrier option, *see* option, barrier
bisection search, 94
Black–Scholes, 5, 28, 46, 47, 49, 58, 59, 61, 67, 83, 134, 137, 152, 180, 198
Black–Scholes equation, 32–34, 41, 43, 66, 68
Black–Scholes formula, 28–32, 34, 38, 50, 58, 60, 69, 97, 126, 127, 145, 159, 166, 168, 190
Black–Scholes process, 54, 88
bond, 68
boundary condition, 34, 42, 43, 66, 76, 77, 84
    Feller, 80–82
    zero gamma, 108
    zero price, 107
Box–Muller transform, 99
Breeden–Litzenberger, 63, 130, 153, 154, 191
broker, 58, 123, 176

Brownian motion, 10–13, 36, 50, 51, 74, 87, 98, 103, 122, 132, 135, 173, 182, 204, 205
    correlated, 19, 180
bump function, 65, 66

calendar spread, 125
calibration, 71, 72, 80, 140–141
call, 4
call spread, 63, 103
callable trade, 105, 114, 119
cash settlement, 2, 176
cell averaging, 114
central bank, 5
central difference, 107, 116, 118
CEV, *see* constant elasticity of variance
Chase Manhattan, 148
Cholesky decomposition, 101, 102
CIR, *see* Cox–Ingersoll–Ross model
close out, 2, 165
CMS, *see* constant maturity swap
cockroach, 158
commodities, 2, 8
constant elasticity of variance, 84
constant maturity swap, 177
continuous barrier option, *see* option, barrier
copula, 173–175, 191
correlation, 19, 61, 71, 100
    asset–asset, 172
    asset-asset, 173
    implied, 175, 176, 179, 181, 196
    instantaneous, 172, 186
    local stochastic, 186
    spot–volatility, 73, 74, 83, 95, 128, 131, 132, 138, 143, 146, 159, 185
correlation matrix, 184
correlation product, 172
correlation smile, 174–182, 194–196
cost of carry, 9
Cox–Ingersoll–Ross process, 75, 80, 82

Craig–Sneyd scheme, 118, 119
Crank–Nicolson scheme, 110, 112, 118
credit rating, 5
cross asset, 179
cross smile, 179, 182–184, 191, 194
cross volatility surface, *see* cross smile
cumulative normal function, 31, 52
    bivariate, 174, 189
    inverse, 97

delta, 44, 96, 155, 156, 158
    Black–Scholes, 59, 127, 153, 181
    forward, 59, 154
delta function, *see* Dirac delta function
delta hedging, *see* hedging, delta
derivative, 1, 3
derivatives trading, 46
digital payout, *see* option, digital
Dirac delta function, 64, 78, 79, 124, 130, 193
discount factor, 30, 35, 36, 62, 63, 75, 97
discounted expectation, 30, 38
dividend, 8, 21, 22, 68
domestic currency, 7
drift, 14, 18, 23, 53, 68, 136, 151, 180, 183, 205, 206
    terminal, 18
Dupire local volatility model, *see* local volatility model
dynamic trading strategy, 42

efficient market, 2
eigenvalue, 111
energy, 2
equities, 2, 8, 58, 61, 158, 172
equivalent probability measure, *see* measure, equivalent
euro–dollar, 58, 60, 172
European payout, *see* option, European
exchange, 2
expectation, 201
expiry date, 3, 58, 93, 94
expiry time, *see* expiry date
explanatory variables, 105
explicit scheme, 108
exponential Ornstein–Uhlenbeck model, *see* Ornstein–Uhlenbeck process

factorisation method, 118
federal funds rate, 5
Feller boundary condition, *see* boundary condition, Feller

filtration, 17, 65, 122, 151, 165, 204
financial engineer, 205
financial mathematician, 204
finite difference method, 97, 105, 117, 120, 130, 163
first generation exotic option, *see* option, first generation exotic
fixed income, 6
floating smile, 127
Fokker–Planck equation, *see* forward Kolmogorov equation
foreign exchange, 2, 8, 37, 58, 60, 71, 93, 127, 141, 158, 172, 176, 179
forward contract, 1, 6–9, 21, 30, 46, 59, 60, 64, 121
forward induction, 128, 131, 140, 141, 148, 198
forward Kolmogorov equation, 65–66, 68, 69, 80, 95, 129
forward level, 1, 9, 30, 32, 36, 40, 48, 49, 136, 157, 164, 165
forward start, *see* option, forward starting
forward volatility agreement, 164–170
    asset, 165
    cash, 165
Fourier transform, 77–79
FTSE, 61, 71
fundamental theorem of on-smile pricing, 122–124, 129, 164
FVA, *see* forward volatility agreement
FX, *see* foreign exchange

gamma, 44, 45, 96, 156
Gauss–Hermite integration, 138
Gaussian, *see* normal variable
Girsanov's theorem, 24–27, 38, 50, 53, 200–206
going short, *see* short position
gold, 8, 21, 121, 177, 179, 185, 193
government bond, 22
Greeks, 43–46, 96, 119, 139, 155, 198
Gyöngy's theorem, *see* fundamental theorem of on-smile pricing

heat kernel, 85
hedge fund, 46, 157
hedging, 1, 96, 139, 158, 199
    delta, 43, 45, 46, 71, 149, 153, 198
    dynamic, 40–43, 157
hedging portfolio, 42
hedging strategy, 43

Heston model, 73–82, 85, 88, 94, 95, 99, 120

IBM, 32, 176, 179
implicit scheme, 109, 117, 120, 130, 148
implied volatility, *see* volatility, implied
implied volatility dynamic, 126, 127
implied volatility smile, *see* smile
implied volatility surface
    see volatility surface, 58
in-the-money, 32, 40, 58, 158
inflation, 22
insurance company, 40
integral
    Lebesgue, 202, 203
    Riemann, 202
integration by parts, 167
interest rate, 5–6, 21, 58, 68, 136, 142, 157
    continuously compounding, 5, 21
    stochastic, 98
interfacing, 116, 162
investment bank, 40, 46, 47, 138, 149, 157, 179, 184
Ito calculus, 14
Ito process, 15, 38, 200
Ito's lemma, 14–16, 19–20, 41, 65, 75, 76, 83, 84, 123, 129, 133, 152, 205
    product rule, 15, 29, 205

Jacobian, 99
joint probability distribution, *see*
    probability distribution, joint, 104
JP Morgan, 148
jumps, 124, 151, 157

knock-in barrier, *see* barrier, knock-in
knock-out barrier, *see* barrier, knock-out

lambda-SABR model, 85, 95, 129, 133, 140, 142, 143, 185
Laplace transform, 80, 81
law of large numbers, 98, 99
Lehman bankruptcy, 71
Lévy's theorem, 206
linear congruential generator, 99
liquid asset, 3
local correlation model, 182–184, 191, 193
local stochastic correlation model, 184–186, 193
local stochastic volatility model, 61, 95, 128–131, 137, 138, 141, 143, 147, 148, 152, 160, 162, 163, 168, 184, 185, 198

local volatility correction, 128–133, 137, 138, 140, 141, 146–148
local volatility model, 61, 65–69, 93, 95, 97, 105, 121, 123, 126, 133, 139–143, 146, 147, 168, 193
    multi-asset, 172, 175
log contract, 153, 171
log return, 150, 154, 156
log-normal, 16–17, 29, 30, 49, 50, 53, 75, 85, 98, 106, 129, 134, 136
long expiry date, 95, 157
Longstaff–Schwarz, 105
low discrepancy random numbers, *see*
    random numbers, low discrepancy
LSV, *see* local stochastic volatility model
LVCC, *see* local volatility, multi-asset

market data bump, 96
market maker, 46, 123, 179
Markov chain, 89
Markov property, 17
Martingale, 27–29, 33, 38, 68, 75, 152, 205, 206
    continuous, 28
Martingale pricing, 21
Martingale pricing equation, 28, 29, 36, 98, 119, 189
matching delta, 194, 195
mean reversion, 71, 72, 74, 82, 85–87, 95, 132, 133, 137, 139–141, 143, 170
mean reversion level, 72
measure, 23, 29, 38, 201
    equivalent, 25, 202, 205
    real world, 205
    risk-neutral, 72, 74, 166, 186
measure change, 23–27, 135, 180, 186, 189, 200–206
measure theory, 200
Mersenne twister algorithm, 99
method of characteristics, 81
method of planes, 115–116, 120, 162, 168
mixing parameter, 128, 140–147, 162, 163, 170
mixture model, 88–89, 138, 139, 143, 148, 163, 186
model uncertainty, 199
moment matching, 49, 56
money market account, *see* rolling money
    market account
Monte Carlo, 34, 97–105, 119, 120, 162, 173, 184, 187

error, 102
Greeks, 102
multiple dimensions, 100
standard deviation, 99
variance reduction, 102
multiple assets, 19, 172

Newton–Raphson method, 97
no-arbitrage principle, *see* arbitrage
normal process, 86, 134, 143
normal variable, 10, 17, 98, 99, 138, 173, 174
notional, 2, 40
numeraire, 23, 27, 29, 33, 34, 37, 38, 54, 55, 68, 77, 97, 180, 183, 186, 190, 193
numeraire symmetry, 193–194
numerical integration, 73, 97, 103, 138
numerical stability, 88, 94, 96

ODE, *see* ordinary differential equation
off-smile, 142
oil, 2
OIS, *see* overnight indexed swap
one-sided differencing, 108
optimisation problem, 93
option
    American, 105
    Asian, 48–50, 56, 115, 120, 162
    at-the-money, 32, 45, 46, 60, 71, 146, 159, 164, 165
    barrier, 50–56, 67, 128, 131, 134, 137, 138, 140, 141, 147, 148, 160, 170
    basket, 172, 176, 192, 194–196
    best-of, 38, 177, 187–190, 192
    call, 21, 28, 34, 44, 54, 60, 67, 71, 77, 124, 172
    composite, 178, 181, 183, 193, 194, 196
    digital, 35, 48, 62–64, 77, 103, 131, 144, 145, 167
    dual asset digital, 192
    European, 47–48, 56, 62, 64, 69, 97, 123, 138, 148, 173, 187
    exercise, 3
    exotic, 3, 5, 67, 72, 121, 128, 139, 140, 142, 147
    first generation exotic, 131, 138, 139, 147, 160–162
    forward starting, 139, 165
    geometric basket, 178
    in-the-money, 46, 60

no-touch, 147, 168, 185
one-touch, 140–143, 145, 146
out-of-the-money, 46, 60, 71
put, 60, 61, 71
quanto, 176
short dated, 45, 59
spread, 177
vanilla, 3, 4, 32, 44, 48, 61–63, 65–68, 72, 73, 75, 92, 97, 121, 131, 149, 153, 158
worst-of, 177, 192
ordinary differential equation, 78
Ornstein–Uhlenbeck process, 86–88, 95, 141
OU process, *see* Ornstein–Uhlenbeck process
out-of-the-money, 32, 58, 158
overnight, 45
overnight indexed swap, 5

parallel shift, 170
parameter averaging, 95
partial differential equation, 33, 34, 38, 65–69, 72, 75, 76, 78, 92, 129, 130, 140, 142, 147, 173
    multiple dimensions, 116–119
    numerical solution, 34, 94, 97, 105–120, 162, 186, 198
    parabolic, 107
    stability, 108–113
payout, 4
PDE, *see* partial differential equation
PDE approach, *see* partial differential equation, numerical solution; *see also* finite difference method
PDE solver, 115, 117, 120, 130, 131, 148, 168, 186, 187
PDF, *see* probability density function
percentage notional, 32
physical settlement, 176, 178
positive definite matrix, 184
pounds sterling, 22
precious metals, 2
predictor–corrector method, 118
present value, 30, 137
probability, 202
    risk-neutral, 77
probability density function, 62, 65, 66, 80, 81, 187
probability distribution, 65, 66, 122
    cumulative, 62

probability distribution – *continued*
    implied, 62, 97
    joint, 51, 166, 173, 190–193
    marginal, 166, 167, 173, 174
probability measure, *see* measure
probability space, 201, 204
product rule, *see* Ito's lemma, product rule
pseudo-random numbers, *see* random
    numbers, pseudo-random
put, 4
put–call parity, 60, 164, 166, 179, 192
PV, *see* present value

quant, *see* quantitative analyst
quantitative analyst, 3, 30, 37, 168, 204
quasi-random numbers, *see* random
    numbers, low discrepancy

Radon–Nikodým derivative, 24, 53, 54,
    135, 203, 205
random numbers
    low discrepancy, 103, 104
    pseudo-random, 98, 104
random variable, 201
Rannacher stepping, 114
real world probability measure, *see*
    measure, real world
real world process, 21, 23, 24, 29, 40, 43
realised variance, 149, 152, 159, 162
reflection principle, 50–54, 56, 134, 135
regime switching model, 89–92, 163,
    186
regularisation, 184
replicating portfolio, 8
replication, 7, 40, 46, 63, 64, 97, 145, 157,
    159, 168, 170, 198
    static, 199
Reuters, 149
rho, 44
risk, 96
risk free rate, 5, 22
risk management, 138
risk manager, 96, 196, 199
risk reversal, 93
risk-neutral expectation, 152, 165
risk-neutral measure, 30, *see* measure,
    risk-neutral
risk-neutral probability, 59, 63, 67, 69, 153
risk-neutral process, 29, 34, 47
rolling money market account, 22, 27, 29,
    30, 33, 34, 47, 75

SABR formula, 84, 85, 93
SABR model, 82–85, 88, 93–95, 128, 133,
    141
sample space, 200, 202
SDE, *see* stochastic differential equation
seed, 103
self-financing portfolio, 41, 42
short expiry date, 95
short position, 41
shorting, *see* short position
sigma algebra, 200–202, 204
silver, 185, 193
skew, 58, 61, 71, 93, 94, 141, 145–147, 155,
    159
smile, 50, 58–62, 67, 69, 71, 73, 83, 87, 89,
    94, 95, 121, 126, 127, 140, 142,
    145–147, 149, 154, 155, 159–161, 166,
    167, 170, 179, 191, 199
    convexity, 71, 73, 74, 83, 87, 89,
        93–95, 133, 140, 141, 154
    interpolation, 59
Sobol sequence, 104
speculation, 2
spot, 2
spot dynamic, 61, 67
spot price, *see* spot
spread, 46
standard deviation, 106
step function, 35, 62
sterling–dollar, 172, 177
sticky delta, 127–128, 140, 141,
    155
sticky strike, 126–127, 140, 141,
    155
stochastic differential equation, 13, 14, 65,
    69, 74, 83, 84, 133, 183, 193
stochastic integral, 11, 24
stochastic process, 10
stochastic variance, 80
stochastic volatility model, 61, 71–73, 83,
    88, 94, 121, 126, 128, 131, 133,
    138–140, 143, 146, 147, 159, 161, 168,
    170
    calibration, 92–95
straddle, 164, 165
strangle, 93
strike, 2, 40, 58, 62, 67, 93, 126
    at-the-money, 58
supply and demand, 60, 61
SV model, *see* stochastic volatility model
swap rate, 5

Taylor expansion, 32
term structure, 6, 18, 31, 47, 72, 134, 136,
      137, 139, 142
terminal volatility, 134
theoretical value, 142, 143
theta, 44, 45
theta scheme, 110
Thomas algorithm, 110, 118
time decay, 44, 45
time value of money, 125
tradeable asset, 22, 27, 29, 35
trader, 30, 43, 47, 96, 103, 140–142, 147,
      158, 168–170, 195, 196
trading strategy, 40
triangle rule, 179–181, 183, 185, 186, 193
TV, *see* theoretical value

unconditional stability, 113, 118, 119
US dollar, 2, 22

vanilla, *see* option, vanilla
vanilla market, 66, 67, 121–123, 128, 140
vanilla payout, *see* option, vanilla
variance reduction, *see* Monte Carlo,
      variance reduction
variance swap, 65, 149–159, 161, 170
vega, 44–46, 96, 134, 137, 146, 158, 169,
      170, 199
vol-of-vol, *see* volatility of volatility
volatility, 4, 14, 18, 23, 43, 45, 53, 71, 149
      at-the-money, 58, 94, 142, 145, 154,
            160, 165
      fair, 150, 159–161

implied, 50, 58, 60, 61, 63, 66, 69, 71,
      84, 126, 129, 146, 149, 154, 159,
      164, 165, 168, 179
instantaneous, 71, 94, 95, 128, 129,
      132, 136, 163
interpolation, 120, 155
local, 65–69, 123, 124, 126, 129, 132,
      147, 164, 182
realised, 72, 73, 139, 149, 165
stochastic, 71, 140
terminal, 18, 137, 138, 148
volatility frown, 61
volatility of variance, 74, 82
volatility of volatility, 71, 83, 87, 94, 132,
      133, 137–141, 147, 170
volatility process, 72
volatility smile, *see* smile
volatility surface, 58, 59, 61, 96, 123, 124,
      130, 142, 146, 166, 185, 199
      arbitrage, 123
volatility swap, 158–164, 170
      instantaneous, 163
volatility trading, 45

wavelets, 120
wheat, 1, 9
winding number, 80
wingyness, 157, 160, 162

yield, 7, 21, 32
yield curve, 6, 8, 9, 96

zero coupon bond, 22, 75, 77

Printed and bound by CPI Group (UK) Ltd, Croydon, CR0 4YY